# Instead of Medicating and Punishing

*Healing the causes of our children's acting-out behavior by parenting and educating the way nature intended*

## Laurie A. Couture

*Wyatt-MacKenzie Publishing, Inc.*

DEADWOOD, OREGON

Cover Logo designed by Laurie A. Couture and Brenden Sanborn, brenden@studio805.com

Contact the Author: **www.childadvocate.org**

*Wyatt-MacKenzie Publishing, Inc.*
DEADWOOD, OREGON

www.WyMacPublishing.com (541) 964-3314

Requests for permission or further information should be addressed to:
Wyatt-MacKenzie Publishing, 15115 Highway 36, Deadwood, Oregon 97430

# Dedication

**Brycen (center), Liam and Aiden**
For my son Brycen and my nephews Liam and Aiden, the three
most precious lights in my life.

**Wanda S. (Waleryszak) Sanborn**
*March 21, 1927 - March 29, 2007*

This book is also dedicated in loving memory to my grandmother,
Wanda S. Sanborn, who passed away four months after heart
surgery due to severe complications. Nana was a vibrant and
youthful woman with a deeply social, infectious, whirlwind
personality. Her playful, mischievous smile and her distinctive
"carnival" laugh drew people from every generation to her. She
was ceaselessly generous and had an undying devotion and love
for her family. She was proud of her Polish heritage and was
very dedicated to her town and community. She loved to dance
at Polka concerts, tend to her flowers, collect memorabilia, take
day trips and eat at restaurants. Nana invested in this book and
made its existence possible. I only wish she could have lived to
hold it in her hands.

# Table of Contents

Friendships should *not* be the priority for newly adoptive
	children for the first year
Safety boundary issues for your child's emotional age
When our children cannot live safely at home
Healing on a society-wide level

# Acknowledgements

To Nancy Cleary, my publisher: Thank you so much for believing in my book from the beginning, for encouraging me with your abundant positive energy and for giving me the dream-fulfilling opportunity to share my message with the world...

To Kali Wendorf: Thank you for taking time out of your deadline-laden schedule while publishing one of the world's most important magazines to support my book with your generous foreword.

To my medical teams at Boston Children's Hospital and Massachusetts General Hospital, especially Dr. Miles Keroack, Dr. Harland Winter, Dr. May Wakamatsu and Dr. Daniel Doody: Thank you for your tenacity in searching until you found the answers that saved my life.

To those that have guided me on my healing path, thank you, especially D.D., K.F. and L.P.

To those "gem" professors and teachers who inspired me by their dissidence and humanity, thank you.

To my colleagues in the mental health field who have supported my work, thank you.

To the children, adolescents and families who I have worked with over the years, thank you for all that you have taught me, for your trust in me and for the sobering truth that you tell about the way life is for children and families in our culture. It has been an honor to work with each of you.

Thank you to all of the supporters of ChildAdvocate.org. Thank you to Brenden Sanborn for your past web design work.

To those in the child advocacy world who have supported my work or offered me opportunities for my message to reach the public, I thank you, especially: Jordan Riak, Norm Lee, Mady Gomez, Mitch Hall, Lee Newman, Murray Straus, Kali Wendorf,

Wendy Priesnitz, Jane Bluestein, Naomi Aldort, Cevin Soling, Bob Bruebaker, Roland Legiardi-Laura and W. Douglas Maurer.

To my friends and colleagues at PTAVE: Jordan Riak, Mady Gomez, Mitch Hall, Norm Lee, Viviane Oglevie, Peggy Dean, Paula LeDoux-Christison, Isabelle Neal, Al Crowell, Tom Johnson and Sue Lawrence: Thank you for your support of my work and for your friendship. Thank you for your unwavering resolve to be on the frontlines of combating violence and child abuse by working tirelessly to abolish violence where and when it begins, with corporal punishment of children. To our new Board members, I look forward to working with you!

Thank you to the important people who cared for my son before I was in his life and to those who helped us come together, especially Sue R.K, Manny L., Liz H., Deb A., Wayne M. and Steve C. Thank you to my son's Birthmother for her heart-warming support of our adoption and of Brycen's healing.

To my mentor, D.E. Dale, who's vivacious, undiluted and spine-shaking philosophizing with me about life, human rights and the human spirit has inspired me to the core—Thank you for your support and your doubt-crushing faith in me.

To Isaac, who I mentor, you are a kind, caring young person who amazes me with your ability to weather challenges by standing tall. Thank you for all of the ways that you've shown your appreciation.

To the fellow Moms in the Fresh Air Friends and Bionicle Club homeschool groups, thank you for your support and encouragement for this writing project.

Thank you to Kirsten W., Colleen M., Lee S., Ryan T., Lisa and Kevin V., and Suzanne H. for your support, help and friendship.

To my dearest childhood friend, Brenden Sanborn, thank you for the legendary memories, for The Whole Shabang and the eccentric world that we created together; for the sardonic culture-jamming pranks we orchestrated, for the companionship, laughing, scheming, dreaming and musing that we've shared.

To my grandfather, Raoul Couture who passed away in September 1999, thank you for that smiling, knowing look that you graced me with the last time I saw you conscious—the look that conveyed to me a lifetime of unspoken words and a sense that you knew who I'd become.

To my uncle, Ronald Couture, thank you for your support after Papa's death and during my medical instability.

To my grandmother, Llyr Couture, thank you for your laughter, especially when you would do or say something out of charac-ter. Thank you for meals at Newick's; for the outfits; for time spent together; and of course, thank you for your intoxicating cookies.

To my grandfather, Paul Sanborn, thank you for the years of being silly with us, transporting us, rushing me to the hospital in the middle of the night, and for staying by Nana's side every day during her four-months in the hospital. I appreciate your pride in my accomplishments, your hard-work ethic and all you have done for Brycen and me.

To my great-aunt, Loretta Brown, thank you for being a grand-mother to me; for our long conversations about your life and for the fun times I had exploring at your house and field when I was a child.

To my sister, Caroline Westcott, thank you for the floor-rolling laughs and the adventures we shared together.

To Nana, my grandmother, Wanda Sanborn, who passed away March 29, 2007, thank you to the depths of my heart for every-thing you did to help me through the first 33 years of my life. You are my second mother and my kindred spirit. Despite times of pain, you were always there for me. Thank you for the walks, the fireworks, blueberry picking and singing along to polkas together. Thank you for taking us every Friday evening, for bringing us to myriads of restaurants, for letting us be children, for watching Friday-night sitcoms with us and enduring the giggling and pranks late at night. Thank you for hosting our famous yard sales, for helping me learn my "3X table" and for helping me to collect Garbage Pail Kids, et al. Thank you for your wonderful laugh and playfulness. Most of all, thank you for your love and your undying pride and faith in me. You are in my heart always and forever.

To my Dad, Brian Couture, thank you for being my stronghold when I was a young child; your scientific genius and your relentless comedy mixed with your affectionate, playful, human-jungle-gym warmth when I was little shaped the type of parent I am and the way I build rapport with the children I work with. Thank you for the intellectual conversations, the nature hikes and day trips, for playing with us, for fixing our toys and for helping me to develop a deep love and respect for nature. I thank you so much for those treasured early years with you.

To my Mom, Linda Wade, thank you for your passionate, convicted faith in me and your unwavering support of every dream, talent and endeavor that I have pursued. Your creativity and unique, excited way of learning influences how I experience life. Thank you for teaching me the sanctity of life and for our intense spiritual talks in which we never find a final answer. Thank you for your fierce medical advocacy on my behalf; I am alive today because of your tenacity. I thank you so much for your deep unconditional love and commitment to your children and grandchildren.

To my nephew, Aiden, thank you for lighting up my heart with your precious little smile and your sweet little voice.

To my nephew, Liam, thank you for the special honor of taking care of you through out your first three years of life. I cherish our closeness, the special connection that we have always shared and being able to watch you grow. Your intensity, your intelligence, your deep insight, your goodness, your sensitivity and your creativity inspire me. It is my deepest hope for you that you will always realize those beautiful qualities in your heart and that you will share them passionately with the world.

To my son, Brycen, thank you for being such a wonderfully loving son. Thank you for accepting me and my nurturing into your heart, for trusting my lifetime commitment to you and for working hard to heal despite all of the pain and losses in your life. You have a sense of spiritual wisdom, depth and unconditional understanding and compassion for all living things that is well beyond your years. You inspire me with your capacity for such compassion, justice and empathy. I know that these qualities, combined with your intellect, creative genius and brilliance with words and song will continue to sing forth from you into wonderful things for this world to behold!

Lastly, I want to acknowledge the paradigm-shifting authors, theorists, educators and activists whose diverse works influenced me and inspired me, including, Naomi Aldort, Maya Angelou, Charles Appelstein, John Bowlby, Peter Breggin, Freda Briggs, David Burns, Pema Chödrön, Noam Chomsky, Lloyd deMause, James DeMeo, John Taylor Gatto, Sue Gerhardt, Philip Greven, Mary Griffith, Steven Harrison, Daniel Hughes, Jan Hunt, Mic Hunter, Irwin Hyman, Pam Leo, Jean Liedloff, Grace Llewellyn, Alice Miller, Jane Nelsen, Peggy O'Mara, Bruce Perry, James Prescott, Wendy Priesnitz, Daniel Quinn, Marshall Rosenberg, Francine Shapiro, Murray Straus, Derek Tasker, Henry David Thoreau, Nancy Newton Verrier, Kali Wendorf, Howard Zinn and the late greats, Mahatma Gandhi, John Holt, Martin Luther King Jr., John Lennon, Abraham Maslow, A.S. Niell, Carl Rogers, Fred Rogers, Mother Teresa and the originator of "The Golden Rule"...

## By Kali Wendorf
Editor and publisher of *Kindred* magazine

There's a quiet but bold revolution afoot. You won't see it on the news, or heralded by dramatic marches upon Washington. It's not represented by lobby groups or debated in Senate. But it's gradually weaving its way into the daily lives of families all over the world. In small, ordinary, but heroic ways, mothers and fathers are rejecting the culturally-endorsed style of parenting that denies children their basic need for bonding and non-violence. Instead, they're choosing to be responsive to those needs and by doing so, are forging a new, more peaceful society.

Laurie A. Couture gives a clear voice to this new movement and her book gives us straightforward guidance. By questioning the cultural assumptions made around children and their needs— from birth, to discipline, to education—she shed's light on a kind of "insanity" that modern society has taken on. This insanity results in symptoms of collective childhood distress expressed in such phenomena as ADHD, Oppositional Defiant Disorder, Bipolar Disorder, depression and anxiety. And in response, Laurie very systematically gives us a cure for this insanity: Bonding and attachment. Drawing on the time-tested ancient wisdom of peaceful Indigenous cultures and combining that with respected neurobiological research, Laurie gives us a blue-

print for raising children through connection instead of discon-
nection, using love instead of fear.

In my work with *Kindred* magazine, I am increasingly awed by
the power we have as parents and educators to not only shape
the minds and hearts of our children, but of culture itself. A
society which supports mothers to birth naturally, breastfeed,
educate holistically and discipline gently, raises children who in
turn grow up to create a peaceful culture. And it's all done
through love. Love is a brain gestalt, created, nurtured, developed and supported by close intimate physical and emotional
contact, especially in the baby and toddler stages of life.
Children's earliest experiences of birth, affection, touch, movement, breastfeeding and physical closeness all profoundly
influence their ability throughout life to manage emotion, experience pleasure and empathy and to appreciate beauty. How we
are cared for and loved affects the early "wiring" of our brain in
infancy because it translates into neurological patterns that set
the patterns of our behaviour and how we relate to others and
ourselves—for the rest of our lives.

At a time when humanity must invent radically new strategies
for its own survival, the understanding behind children's real
needs for closeness and connection is crucial for innovative
social change. Adult issues such as domestic violence,
consumerism, alcoholism, substance abuse, depression, suicide,
divorce, crime, war, human rights abuses and environmental
destruction must be investigated through their source, not their
symptoms. That source is childhood.

We cannot, after all, expect children fed on junk food, educated
by corporations and raised by television to grow up wanting to
protect the planet and all who live there. We were all once

children and we must all learn to take care of each other and this planet. Laurie A. Couture is not just a child rights advocate; she's a human rights advocate and an earth-survival advocate. Her book is a welcome respite away from the "parenting manuals" that fill bookstore shelves and the "me-first" industrialised culture. It's an invitation into the discovery of what it means to be human, and what it requires to become humane as a society.

—Kali Wendorf

Editor and publisher, *Kindred* magazine, New South Wales, Australia
www.kindredmagazine.com.au

# Introduction
# Our Culture is Toxic to Parents and Children

*"Too often we send... young people to psychiatrists and other specialists, or into the juvenile or criminal justice systems, where they are treated as if the problem lies in them instead of us and our society."*
*-Peter R. Breggin, M.D.*

*"Insanity: Doing the same thing over and over again and expecting different results." -Albert Einstein*

## Why doesn't anything seem to really help?

Have you ever wondered why, no matter how many parenting books and philosophies come out on the market, things don't really improve much for families? Why is it that despite all of the parenting education programs, child abuse prevention programs and social services we have, things don't get significantly better for children and parents? Have you asked yourself why no amount of therapy or psychiatric medication seems to really make children feel or act significantly better? How come, despite the early intervention programs in schools, IEP (Individualized Education Plan) accommodations, special help or tutoring services your children are receiving, your child seems to dislike or rebel against school? Have you ever wondered why, when you see small gains in your child, the gains seem to erode after awhile? Do you wonder why all of the programs in the community to help troubled youth don't seem to rehabilitate them into happy, compassionate people? Is there something that all of these well intentioned approaches are missing?

I believe that it is our culture itself that is making families sick.

## Reacting in a NATURAL way to UNNATURAL circumstances

Most parenting philosophies, school curriculums and social programs operate under the assumption that there is something wrong with individual children or parents that must be fixed. No where is it suggested that our culture itself, our "civilized" way of life, has taken parents so far away from the natural way of raising and living with children, that it isn't possible for children and families to act much differently than they do. These institutions believe that children and families must be "fixed" or molded to fit into an unnatural way of life. What the books, schools, programs and services fail to tell us is that children and their families are reacting in a NATURAL way to UNNATURAL circumstances.

Isn't it "natural" for people to move away from their parents, work long hours at a job and raise their children to be obedient, independent, career-minded people? Isn't it "natural" to give your infant a bottle, put her in a crib, ignore his cries, place her in daycare, send him to school, get her involved in organized sports, discourage him from clinging, cut down on childish playing, spank him for disobedience and expect her to listen to what you demand? Isn't it natural to expect that children delay their needs, do homework and get into the working world? Isn't it "natural" to expect responsibility, respect, good study habits and cooperation from children raised in this way?

What if the institutions revealed to us that the way our society trains people to live and raise children is the OPPOSITE of what is natural and best for human happiness and fulfillment? Would we believe that another book, parenting class, therapist or medication would be the answer? Or would we try to find out what *is* natural?

This book, and many wonderful others that I will recommend, are opportunities for you to step outside of the reactive, faddish child rearing, education and mental health philosophies of our culture and consider the most important parenting, education and therapeutic "tools" that our culture overlooks: Secure parent-child attachment and natural child development.

This book will explore the healthy alarm signals our children are giving us to alert us that our "civilized", industrialized cultural practices are harming them. We will learn that a secure parent-child attachment is a necessity for optimal human development and we will learn the recipes for happy children and a secure parent-child attachment. We will discover the ways children need to learn if they are to keep their natural passion for learning. *We will explore how our everyday life and cultural practices create the very behavioral and mental health problems in children that we seek to control.* We will gain the knowledge of what it is about our culture that is traumatic for children and how that trauma permanently rewires the young brain for behavioral and mental health problems. We will compare the symptoms of commonly diagnosed mental health problems with the natural symptoms of trauma and  insecure parent-child attachments. We will discuss why most therapies, drugs, schools and social service programs do not help children become happy, cooperative, compassionate human beings. Most importantly, we will learn how to:

- Help children heal from insecure attachment and trauma,
- Guide and discipline children nonviolently,
- Find alternatives to traditional schooling, and
- Seek out alternative treatments, such as Eye Movement Desensitization and Reprocessing (EMDR), Neurofeedback and holistic, body-centered therapies that are likely to help behaviorally challenged children.

## Putting away blame: Feeling compassion for ourselves, our children and our ancestors

When families struggle with a child who is acting out in some manner, it is easy for parents to blame their child, blame the other parent, or blame themselves for the child's problems. Schools are often the first to place blame on children and parents, yet rarely do they blame their developmentally inappropriate teaching methods. Our society, too, blames children for their problems, as seen in the punitive, harsh reactions to children's behavior in the form of tougher and tougher "therapeutic" and juvenile justice programs. Parents, too, are blamed by social service agencies, yet are denied commonsense services that would meet their basic needs for mentoring and education that could prevent traumatic parent-child relationships.

Social service agencies betray children by failing to prevent damage done to children by intervening only when a child is reported to be severely abused. Society then punishes children for their symptoms later. Although commonsense would say that social service agencies should offer voluntary preventative services and education to each family who is having a child, and certainly to every child who is suspected of being maltreated, *these agencies often refuse to intervene even in cases when a child is known to be suffering neglect or abuse for years!*

In learning about the natural way that humans were meant to develop and learn, it is easy for us to blame our own parents, our children and ourselves for the way that we were raised and for the way that we act and react to one another. We can instead begin to realize that "civilized" societies have been indoctrinating our ancestors for thousands of years in parenting and cultural practices that have driven us further and further away from our natural instincts of parenting and learning.

We can understand that we are especially influenced by 340+ years of Puritan, industrialized parenting, passed down through our great-great-great-great (etc.) grandparents. This old religious/work-ethic parenting paradigm is responsible for why we no longer breastfeed our babies, wear them in a sling, comfort crying older boys, cosleep with our children or allow them to learn at home, in nature and out in the community with us. This influence is why we react with violence and punishment when children upset us, why we believe that they must obey us, why we strive to "socialize" them as young as age two, why we try to wean them from dependence so young, why we strive to make them grow up so soon, why we take the play and the childishness out of their lives so early, increasingly, with each generation that is born.

Many of our grandparents survived terribly abusive childhoods as the norm. They parented and influenced our parents by their own wounds, trying to be better than generations before them. As parents, we are also influenced by the wounds of how we were parented even as we strive to parent less harshly than previous generations. It is more helpful for us to view ourselves, our children and our ancestors with the empathy and compassion that will allow us to learn and grow and not blame.

Empathy is the ability to understand and feel from the perspective of another, whether or not we agree with their actions. While not denying or condoning the practices that have done harm to children, we can choose to view ourselves, our parents and ancestors with an understanding compassion; the kind of compassion that will allow us to understand what is wrong with our culture's way of treating children. This empathic insight will help us to take the actions we need to take in order to treat children in a way that is in harmony with nature's intent for their needs and development.

It is my hope that you will not skip parts of this book. Each point in this book, even if it sounds obvious, is important to the whole. Each chapter and section is written in a particular order to help readers understand how every piece of natural, attachment parenting fits together to create the desired result: A secure parent-child attachment that allows parents and children to live together in harmony, without constant conflict.

It is my hope that after reading this book, the books and resources you read afterward will support and enlighten you in finding ways to connect with your children. It is my hope that these ways of connecting are in harmony with your children's needs and development. It is my hope that after reading this book that you will practice tuning into your heart, your parenting instincts and what your children are telling you they need and not rely on "experts" and institutions to raise your children.

# Chapter 1
# Alarms in Nature

## *How does nature communicate that something is wrong?*

Nature has a variety of alarm signals that protect and serve the creatures that display them. Alarms are the forms of communication that animals display to alert parents, companions and predators that they are experiencing or sensing a need, a threat or a danger. In nature, animal parents instinctively respond immediately to the alarms of their young. They do not view responding to their young's needs as a choice, an inconvenience or as a moral or behavioral issue. They respond because they *must* respond. They respond because there is an innate understanding in each organism that it is anti-life to go against the best interests of their offspring.

**Animal alarms:**

- Hissing
- Growling
- Scratching
- Yelping
- Raising hair
- Spraying a scent
- Flattening ears
- Howling
- Whining
- Barking
- Mewing
- Bleating
- Calling
- Posturing
- Snapping
- Nipping

## *What would happen if an animal parent failed to respond?*

If an animal parent made a choice not to respond to its young, viewing the alarm as manipulation, misbehavior or as an inconvenience, the wellbeing, life and optimum functioning of the young would be endangered. Many people would laugh at the idea of a mother bear rolling her eyes and scolding her cub for disturbing her with an alarm signal. We recognize that in the animal world, animals don't have a choice; an animal parent's inconvenience is not an acceptable reason for them to fail to respond to their young. We know that nature built instinct into animal parenting to keep animal mothers of all species, from insects and reptiles to birds and mammals, in harmony with whatever needs they must meet for their offspring.

## Human alarm signals

As "civilized" humans, we have a cultural tendency to categorize ourselves apart from animals. In doing so, it is easy for humans in civilized cultures to deny that much of how we live is not in harmony with our needs or with how nature intends humans to live. Although we realize that an iguana kept in a cage is not living in harmony with its nature or needs, most people in our culture are completely unable to see that a baby in a crib or a child sitting at a classroom desk is equally out of  harmony with his or her nature and needs.

Humans *are* in fact animals, and are born with some of the most sophisticated and intense alarm signals in nature. Human mothers are also equipped with instincts and intuition about their children's needs, and can naturally respond optimally to their children's alarm signals if they are not conditioned to do otherwise. Let's look at the earliest and most primitive human alarm signal...

## The alarm of the human infant:

- Crying

In our culture, it is common to hear infants wailing and screaming in grocery stores or other public places, strapped into plastic carriers, with their embarrassed parents either ignoring their screams or shushing them with words. We observe very little action by the shopping-inconvenienced parents towards discovering and meeting the infant's need. *Although the distress of the infant is excruciating, as evidenced by the intensity of the alarm signal,* we often observe a strikingly cavalier and apathetic attitude towards that signal by passers by, who ignore the baby as calmly as the parents.

What is the purpose of the human baby's alarm? What happens when mothers, fathers and caretakers fail to respond to this alarm? As in the animal kingdom, the human infant's alarm signal is the infant's way of communicating distress to the parent. There is a physical or emotional need that the infant is experiencing that is distressing the infant and threatening the infant's optimal functioning. There is a danger to the wellbeing, and the infant's natural instinct is to cry in order to attract adult attention to meeting the need. The infant's cries and screams will intensify until the need is satiated. If the need is not met promptly or if the need is not met at all and the infant finally ceases the alarm signal out of exhaustion, damage has been done to the infant's ability to attach, trust and experience safety and calm. The brain will begin to wire itself for insecure attachment, distress and anxiety rather than joy and calm.

Jean Liedloff, researcher of tribal cultures explains in her book, *The Continuum Concept*, how serious it is it when human parents ignore the alarm signals of their babies: "Nature does not make clear signals that someone is being tortured unless it is the case. *It is precisely as serious as it sounds.*"

Just as animals continue to display alarm signals as they grow older and into adulthood, human youth continue to give us alarm signals when they have an unmet need or something in their lives is not in harmony with their optimal development.

Some of the alarms of children:
- Talking
- Crying
- Whining
- Yelling
- Pouting
- Tantruming
- Withdrawing
- Clinginess
- Defensiveness
- Sarcasm
- Hyperactivity
- Depression
- Anxiety
- Rage
- Distractibility
- Fidgeting
- Oppositionality
- Harassing
- Defiance
- Refusing
- Disrespect
- Threatening
- Aggression (verbal, physical, sexual)

- Destructiveness (vandalism, breaking toys, stealing, etc.)
- Self destructiveness (self mutilation, substance use, sexual promiscuity, bad relationships, suicidal gestures, etc.)
- Challenging
- Over compliance

The distress cries and acting out behaviors of youth, like the cries of an infant and the behavioral cues of animals, are nature-based alarm signals. Their alarm signals warn us that something in the child's body, immediate circumstance, life or environment is distressing to them physically or emotionally and is threatening harm to their optimal development.

When we fully understand that crying and concerning behaviors are the natural alarm signals of children, we will be less likely to, in good conscience, punish, medicate or force children into compliance with distressing, unnatural circumstances. We will begin to realize more and more as we look around our society, that from the hyperactive toddler to the rageful 17 year old, punishment, force, bribes, manipulation and medication do not make distressed children happy, cooperative or compassionate; nor do those reactions fill the voids and satiate the needs children are trying to alert us to with their alarm signals.

In the next chapter, *Recipe for a Happy Child: What Children Need to Thrive*, we will get a preview of the human attachment cycle. We will then dissect children's basic physical and emotional needs and how parents must respond to those needs in a healthier way. Lastly, we will discuss some of children's higher level needs and why those needs can only be satiated if the basic needs are fulfilled. We will learn why meeting children's needs at all ages is the cornerstone of a secure parent-child attachment.

# Chapter 2
# Recipe for a Happy Child: What Children Need in Order to Thrive

*Definitions:*
> **Physiological needs**: Physical needs.
>
> **Psychological needs**: Emotional needs.
>
> **Homeostasis**: a feeling inside that everything physically and emotionally is balanced and feeling good.
>
> **Satiated**: a feeling that a need, such as hunger, has been met and satisfied.

## *What do children need in order to thrive?*

When I've asked individual and groups of parents what they believe children need in order to thrive, I am amazed at how many parents list concepts such as "discipline", "structure", "religious faith" and "limits" *first*. Most of the parents who list these very abstract concepts have children who appear to be unhappy, disconnected from their parents and lacking those very concepts their parents say they need!

Abraham Maslow was a mid-20th century American psychologist and author who was most famous for his pyramid-shaped diagram, "the hierarchy of human needs." Maslow proposed that human's most basic physiological and emotional needs must be met before humans can function well intellectually, socially and spiritually. Although seemingly obvious, Maslow's theory about human needs is still way ahead of its time: Although colleges and graduate schools continue today to teach Maslow's Hierarchy as a basic principle to all students of education, social work, psychology and philosophy, many of the teachers and professionals that "learned" it practice as if they never heard it. In our culture, we still expect that children must obey, cooperate, respect adults and "do well in school" even though we are not, as a culture, meeting their most basic physical and emotional needs.

But isn't picking up our baby several times per day, feeding our kids three square meals, sending them to school, getting them involved with sports, buying them the newest video game console and designer clothing, making sure they have good self esteem, do their homework, get a few hugs and a little quality time with us meeting their physical and emotional needs?

That's what our culture has trained us to believe.

## A secure parent-child attachment: Every child's most basic need

What is secure attachment? Most parents believe that attachment means *feeling love* for their children and assuming that their children "know" that they love them. Attachment is much more than just *feeling love* for your children; *it is the basic biological, emotional, social and intellectual blueprint of your child's life-long happiness and ability to cope with life and relationships.*

Secure attachment requires more than just sentimental feelings and involvement for a few early years; it requires deliberate, constant and compassionate *action*, putting your children's evolving *needs* as a *priority*, for their entire childhood.

Secure attachment is the result of a loving, responsive parent meeting a child's physical and emotional needs promptly the majority of the time, thousands upon thousands of times, over a period of years. Providing a healthy physical and emotional environment for the fetus to grow is vital to attachment parenting. Meeting an infant's needs immediately for the first three years of life is crucial for optimal brain development. However, for the attachment relationship to remain secure and for the child to remain behaviorally and mentally healthy, *the parent must continue this cycle* (in a developmentally appropriate way) *until the child has reached adulthood.*

A secure parent-child attachment is so vital to your child's physical, emotional, behavioral, educational, sexual and spiritual wellbeing that Chapter 3 is devoted to exploring it in greater depth. For now though, in order to get a basic understanding of how a child's basic physical and emotional needs fit into secure parent-child attachment, here is a preview of the basics of the human attachment cycle:

There are four steps in the human attachment cycle:

- **Step one: Child has a need.**
- **Step two: Child expresses the need.**
- **Step three: Parent responds to the child immediately and meets the need as soon as possible.**
- **Step four: Child feels homeostasis, calm, joy, satiated and TRUST in the parent and in the world.**

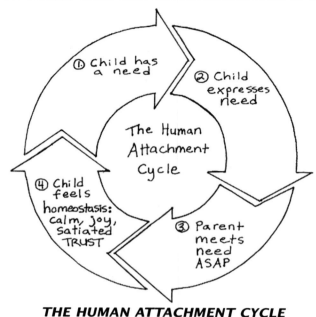

**THE HUMAN ATTACHMENT CYCLE**

This cycle starts again when the child's body or mind feels another need. When parents meet their child's needs promptly, consistently and fully, the majority of the time, a secure parent-child attachment will result and remain solid. Let's discuss in depth the basic biological, physiological and psychological needs that every child has and how parents can meet those needs. Keep in mind as you read, that meeting children's needs and providing them with environments where their needs will be met, *is the cornerstone of secure parent-child attachment.*

## Children's basic physical and emotional needs

Meeting basic human needs of the child: It seems so elementary! Yet, on a daily basis, children's physical and emotional needs are ignored, belittled, denied, responded to with delay or frustration and neglected by well meaning parents, teachers and other care-takers who honestly believe that they are doing the best for the children in their care. When adults have suffered a childhood in which their own most basic needs were not met, the buried rage, hurt and sting of the unmet needs can flare up when children request something of these adults.

Although we all strive to parent more lovingly than our own parents did, deny it as we may, our own unmet needs and psychological wounds will cause us to be insensitive and even mean at times to our children. It is our responsibility as parents to get the help and support we need in order to soften this reality so that we can develop the secure parent-child attachment that is vital for our children to grow up to be emotionally stable, compassionate and happy adults. Since it is our responsibility as parents to raise our children in the healthiest way possible, it is important to understand exactly what children actually need and how we can help meet those needs.

### A word about *wants*

Wants are not needs and are sometimes distractions for unmet needs. Examples of wants are:

- A Nintendo Wii
- Designer clothing
- Heelys roller-sneakers
- An iPod
- Candy and soda
- An electronic toy seen on TV
- Watching TV
- Going to a party
- Going to a dance
- Going to a fast food restaurant
- Getting to do what a friend gets to do
- Not having to do a chore

Here we will be discussing *needs*, which are:

- *Conditions of the body and mind that must be met if the child is to grow and function in an optimal way.*

### Basic physical needs

In children of all ages, from infancy through adolescence, the body is constantly trying to regulate, balance and process thousands upon thousands of internal conditions generated by all of the body's systems, every second! Naturally, this produces frequent physical needs all throughout the day. When infants experience physical needs, their bodies are consumed by an agony that they do not understand, nor have the ability to cope with.

A young infant does not know that she or he has a body separate from Mom. In fact, an infant does not realize that he or she even exists! *An infant is completely and fully helpless to provide any form of comfort and satiation to herself and uses cries and screams as a way to communicate the seriousness of the distress he is feeling.*

For toddlers, young children and older children, including adolescents, physical needs are distressing also, and are experienced as more intense and more anxiety-provoking the younger the child. However, for attachment to be secure, *it is vital for loving parents not to negate or ignore the distress, discomfort and anxiety generated by physical needs in older children and adolescents*, especially when those children are helpless to meet their own needs by the circumstances adults place upon them.

As humans, we should all be very acquainted with basic physical needs and the distress one feels when needs are waiting to be met. Unfortunately, my experience has been that too many parents and school teachers in our culture routinely treat children as if their bodies are made of plastic. They often treat children as if their bodies are not living, breathing, complex combinations of systems that have needs in order to function optimally. These adults may act as if they are *unaware* that the bodies of young people *experience pain and distress when those needs are denied.*

Let's clarify children's most basic physical needs:

#### ■ Air

Children need clean, fresh, outdoor air frequently throughout the day to replenish oxygen to the brain. Children need clean, fresh, smoke-free indoor air to maintain good health and minimize the risk of serious diseases.

#### ■ Food

Children must eat in order to be physically and emotionally healthy and develop optimally. Healthy food contains the various types of building blocks that every body part needs in order to function well, heal and fight off infection. Eating six small, healthy meals and snacks throughout the day will keep your child's blood sugar stable, leading to better health and behavior. Candy and junk food can cause blood sugar levels to drop, causing irritability, sluggishness and restlessness. Organic and all-natural snacks, vegetables and meats that are free of toxins, growth hormones and contamination are optimal for children.

#### ■ Hydration

Over 70% of the body is water. Water is essential to life. For optimal health, your child requires between four and 16 glasses of water per day— That is *four glasses of water for every 50 lbs of body weight* per day, depending on individual size and age needs! Poor hydration, and consuming dehydrating drinks such as soda, juice and coffee, will negatively impact your child's behavior and health.

#### ■ Elimination

Your child needs to always be free to use the toilet at any time throughout the day, in school, on car rides and at home. Your child's health and wellbeing can be severally compromised by being forced to "hold it" at school, or on car rides, leading to life-long digestive and urinary disorders. Make sure your preschool, elementary, middle and high school-aged children are *always* allowed to use the toilet at school. If your child uses the toilet infrequently, it is a sign of dehydration, poor diet or ignoring of bodily signals.

### ▪ Warmth/Comfortable temperature

For young children, temperature can be a life or death issue: Young children must be dressed warmly with hats, gloves and shoes in cold weather and kept cool in the hot weather. For older children, comfortable temperature means less behavioral and emotional agitation and sluggishness and less risk of hypothermia and heat exhaustion.

### ▪ Sleep

Children of all ages need adequate and restful sleep. Adolescent children's brains require that they go to sleep late at night and wake up late in the morning. School schedules do not respect this need. Respecting children's sleep needs leads to better health, better focus and less emotional and behavioral stress in the morning.

### ▪ Physical activity

Children's brains and bodies require constant, frequent, and continuous high energy physical activity all through out the day. Schools do not respect this need of children and limit or completely cut out outdoor play, especially in the middle and high school grades. The restlessness and agitation this causes children is severe. Children who cannot tolerate the restlessness and distress this causes them are labeled brain disordered and are given chemicals (medication) to subdue them. Frequent, high energy physical activity means less behavioral and emotional distress.

### ▪ Physical affection

Although this is also an emotional need, a child's body and brain require physical affection in order to develop optimally. Children of all ages who are comforted, hugged, caressed, held and rocked are more likely to act calm, feel joyful and exhibit more behavioral and emotional stability.

### ▪ Physical safety

Children need to feel physically safe in their own homes and lives. Children cannot feel or be physically and emotionally safe with parents and caretakers who yell, scream, threaten, hit, spank, smack, bully, grab, yank, pull, threaten, use sarcasm or otherwise hurt them in any way. As we will learn in Chapter 8, rough, physically and emotionally aggressive treatment of children is traumatic and will actually rewire their brains for very destructive physical, social, emotional and behavioral patterns.

### ▪ Physical comfort

Children have a lower threshold than adults for physical discomfort. The pain of unmet physical needs, an illness or an uncomfortable situation or environment can be excruciating to children. Yet, schools push children's bodies to the limits by denying their food, hydration, elimination and physical activity needs, forcing them to sit in hard, uncomfortable chairs, remain still for long periods of time, forcing them to stand and walk in lines, restrain their limbs to themselves and even deny them the comfort of touching their peers. Children who feel physically comfortable are more likely to act calmly, feel joyful and exhibit more behavioral and emotional stability.

### ▪ Good hygiene

When your child's body, hair, teeth and clothing are clean and presentable every day, she is less prone to illness, infection and harassment by peers. I suggest that younger children's routine include bathing/showering every other day, and older children shower and wear deodorant (if needed) daily. Children whose daily routine requires hand washing after using the toilet and before meals, and general good hygiene are more likely to be healthy and have a healthy sense of self.

### ■ Medical care

Regular doctor check ups and dental cleanings are essential to maintain good health. Children who are ill or suffer chronic medical problems need and deserve prompt, compassionate care and attention to their symptoms, pain, triggers and needs for rest and medication. Belittling or failing to respond to medical issues in children can lead to a more severe illness or even death. Children who feel good are more likely to feel calm, joyful and exhibit more behavioral and emotional stability.

### ■ Physical pleasure

Children need to feel joyful in their own skin without judgment. They need to be allowed to experience tactile, physical pleasure without shame, including the delight and comfort of physical affection with parents and peers, the rapture and joy of free play, and the very natural expression of sexual pleasure through self exploration and masturbation.

### Basic emotional needs

Children's emotional needs are as crucial and critical as their physical needs. In fact, studies of children in Romanian orphanages who were provided adequate care to their physical needs but not emotional needs show that a lack of physical affection and nurturance by an attachment figure can lead to "Failure-to-Thrive" syndrome. "Failure-to-Thrive" is a condition in which children's physical, emotional, intellectual and social development are severely stunted and delayed. Children in orphanages who received adequate physical care but not emotional nurturance have literally died from the neglect of their psychological needs.

*Emotional care, affection and nurturance are not "extras" that a child should earn for "good" behavior or get on the occasions when it is convenient or comfortable for the parent:* Emotional care, affection and nurturance are as vital and necessary to children from birth through adolescence as food and hydration.

Children's basic emotional needs, at all ages, include the need:

- To be securely attached to at least one parent,
- To feel loved and cherished by at least one parent,
- To be loved unconditionally,
- To feel connected to at least one parent,
- To be held,
- To be hugged,
- To be touched,
- To be caressed,
- To be rocked,
- To be comforted,
- To be respected for who they are,
- To be spoken to with respect,
- To be treated with respect,
- To be free of physical pain and harm,
- To be listened to and heard,
- To play freely and without structure,
- To be played with,
- To have daily one-to-one time with both parents,
- To be given eye contact,
- To be joked with,
- To be given verbal expressions of love and affection,
- To be given genuine expressions of pride and gratitude,

- To feel safe emotionally and physically,
- To feel safe to make mistakes,
- To have permanency,
- To visit other family members that they love, and
- To visit or live with caretakers who *can and will* meet their needs if we cannot or will not.

## Meeting our children's needs fully

### Fetal development

The secure attachment cycle begins in the womb! When expectant mothers provide their developing child with a healthy, calm, peaceful womb environment, secure attachment is already starting to take root! From the onset of your pregnancy through the entire nine months, you can foster a secure attachment to your child and promote physically and psychologically healthy fetal development by:

- Conveying emotionally that your child is wanted and loved,
- Eating a healthy, nutritious, organic diet,
- Keeping hydrated,
- Not smoking,
- Stopping all consumption of alcohol,
- Not ingesting any drugs that are not medically necessary,
- Reducing your anxiety and stress,
- Refraining from engaging in stressful situations,
- Staying away from people and places that cause you stress,
- Resting,
- Talking to and singing to your fetus,
- Taking vitamin and mineral supplements if approved by your doctor,

- Talking with your partner about attachment parenting if you haven't already done so,
- Having a support system to rely on physically and emotionally, and
- Having a positive, anticipatory frame of mind.

Other important attachment-related issues to consider before your baby is born:

- Consider giving birth vaginally if possible.
- Consider having a midwife help you deliver.
- Consider minimizing birth trauma by having a home birth or a hospital water birth.
- Before your baby is born, if you must birth in a hospital, *be sure you and your partner ensure that your baby is to be with you at all times and should not be taken from your arms* unless there is a severe medical situation that necessitates a separation.
- Before your baby is born, *make sure you make clear that you will not allow any doctor to circumcise your son, for any reason*! Circumcision is highly traumatizing to baby boys and disrupts secure parent-child attachment.

## Physical needs of infants and toddlers

Meeting the physical needs immediately and fully in our infants and toddlers is necessary and critical to optimal brain development and physical health. Our culture has tenaciously stuck to the ignorant parenting advice of the early 1900's to allow babies to "cry it out" and to not pick them up or comfort them when they cry. Facts about brain and physical development show very strongly that this advice is not just misguided and cruel; it is dangerous to the physical and psychological wellbeing of infants.

With the scientific knowledge we have in our culture about brain development, it is not acceptable for any professional to be instructing new parents to ignore the cries of their babies or to delay responses to the needs of their babies. In fact, it is unethical. It is also not acceptable to ignore crying babies or delay meeting babies' needs due to our own personal convenience, wants, feelings of tiredness, sluggishness or overwhelm. It is up to us as adults to find the support we need so that we can respond to our infants promptly and lovingly. If we choose to put our wants before our babies' needs, we will experience the results of our children's attachment-related problems in the future, including tantrums, acting out behaviors, oppositionality, mental health instability and less closeness to us as our children grow older.

### Are mothers expected to deny their own needs in order to cater to the needs of their babies and toddlers?

We will discuss in Chapter 4 how in peaceful tribal cultures, researchers have observed that children's needs are met immediately and lovingly *without* a lot of inconvenience to their mothers. For example, in peaceful tribal societies, infants are carried constantly by the mother, so the infant will breastfeed anytime he or she feels the need. This occurs conveniently while the mother is going about her daily business of working and spending time with peers. During the night time, when mother and father are sleeping, their baby is sleeping alongside of them, so the baby is able to breastfeed and feel comfort as much as needed, often without waking up the sleepy parents.

What a strong contrast to the hassles of Western cultural parenting which include parents running to pick up a screaming, crying baby left in a crib, strapping babies into carriers or lugging carriers around, hauling strollers out of car trunks, strapping the squirming baby into these devices while balancing the diaper bag over the shoulder, waking up several times in the night groggy and frustrated to tend to the screaming baby... No wonder mothers in our culture are so exhausted and resentful! I have often heard new mothers complain that they are unable to eat, take a nap, shower or run to the toilet because their babies scream as soon as they leave; in tribal societies, it is just a given that the infant accompanies the mother during all of these natural tasks, in a hassle-free, rush-free manner.

In the case of toddlers, mothers in tribal societies have a natural network of helpers, including older daughters and sons, their own mothers, grandmothers, aunts and friends. In our society, most mothers are isolated, live away from or aren't supported by their own parents and their peer support consists of the occasional "get the babies together" play date.

## Physical needs of young children, older children and adolescents

Meeting the physical needs of children in the first three years of life is of crucial importance to their brain development and health. However, meeting the physical needs of our young children and older children, through adolescence, is no less important regarding their health and attachment needs. In fact, meeting their physical needs solidifies the mother-child attachment and helps your child relate to you in a more cooperative, mutually respectful manner. Let's explore each need and discuss how parents can help children up through adolescence meet their basic physical needs.

### Air:
Parents have a responsibility to provide a healthy, smoke-free

environment for their child. Not only does smoking model smoking to children, it places children at medical risk for lung infections, asthma and lung cancer.

Parents can make sure their children are getting enough exercise, fresh air and outdoor play everyday. As parents, we have the responsibility to find an educational environment that respects children's need for frequent outdoor time.

## Food:

It is our responsibility as parents to provide children of all ages, adolescents included, with as much healthy, nutritious food as they need in order to grow and thrive. Most humans feel best when they eat several small meals and snacks throughout the day that are high in protein. Protein neutralizes the crash of natural sugars and contribute to physical and mental energy.

A healthy diet should include whole grains and a large amount of vegetables per day, especially leafy greens (not iceberg lettuce, which has no nutritional value). Fruits are also important, but should be paired with a protein to neutralize the natural sugars in the fruit. Organic and all-natural foods are free of the environmental toxins, pesticides, growth hormones, genetic engineering and bacterial contamination that is present in all mainstream vegetables, grains, meats and snacks. Some physical and behavioral problems in children may be a result of the toxins and growth hormones present in our mainstream food supply, including in meats, fruits and vegetables. Organic, all-natural foods are the cleanest and purest foods and are thus optimal for children's health.

I am shocked at how regularly parents allow fast food, sugary snacks and a frozen microwaveable diet to be the daily meals for their children. I am equally dismayed at children's minimal intake of vitamin-rich fruits and vegetables. *Children's brains and bodies cannot function at optimal levels without balanced nutrition.* Although a sweet treat or two daily is fine, many older children and adolescents barely get enough nutrition to function at a mediocre level. Their impairments can be seen in behavioral problems, sluggishness, tiredness, weakness, poor physical endurance, sugar cravings, overeating, depressive symptoms, frequent illness, growth slowness, obesity, thinness or injuries. In the case of toddlers, it is wise not to introduce candy in the first place.

Low blood sugar can lead to agitation, irritability, aggression, weakness, lethargy, tiredness, headaches and migraines. Eating six small, healthy meals and snacks throughout the day (balanced with a daily treat or two to satisfy a "sweet tooth") will help keep your child's blood sugar stable, leading to more stable health and behavior. As parents, it is our responsibility to make sure our children are in an educational environment that respects their need for frequent meals and snacks. I recommend that parents consult with a nutritionist to find the meal plan that is healthiest for their family and individual children.

## Hydration:

Your child requires approximately 4-16 glasses of water per day, depending on individual size and age needs. When your child is playing actively outside or inside, he or she needs to be hydrating frequently. Poor hydration, and consuming dehydrating drinks such as soda and coffee, will negatively impact your child's behavior and health. Most children that I have worked with over the years consume little or no water. Their parents buy or allow them to buy soda or sports drinks, which they drink throughout the day and with most meals. Most American young children are given juice or milk with each meal. Most juices have as much sugar as soda and thus are just as dehydrating as soda.

Although cow's milk has an abundance of the calcium that is vital for children's growing bones and muscles, cow's milk is hard on the digestive system and does not substitute for the body's need for water (raw vegetables are a better source of calcium).

Dr. Joseph Mercola recommends: "The simple way to calculate... [how much water you need] would be to take one quart of water for every 50 pounds of body weight. So... 64 ounces of water would... work for children and small women. The average adult is 150 pounds which would be three quarts of water, and many individuals are over 200 pounds which would be one full gallon of water. Let me make it perfectly clear that this is one of the most important health habits you could possibly do... Your exclusive beverage should be water."

## Elimination:

Of course, being well hydrated means that one is urinating more often, just as urinating infrequently is often a sign of dehydration. I will repeat a statement from earlier: Your child needs to always be free to use the toilet at any time throughout the day, in school, at home and on car rides. Your child's health and well-being can be severely compromised by being forced to "hold it" at school, or on car rides, leading to lifelong digestive and urinary disorders and unhealthy toilet habits. Likewise, if you have a child that "holds it" because he or she doesn't want to stop playing, encourage your child to use the toilet.

Our culture spends millions of dollars each year on laxatives and visits to doctors for urinary tract infections, incontinence, irritable bowel syndrome and other elimination disorders that result from our lifestyle which values denying the needs of the body. It is unfair and cruel that we set children up for these distressing problems. It is our responsibility as parents to be sure our children are in an educational environment that respects their very important health needs for hydration and elimination. In Chapter 6, Part II, we will be specifically discussing the health risks of forcing children to "hold" their bladder and bowel waste at *any* age.

## *Comfortable temperature:*

One of my mother's biggest pet peeves is seeing babies and younger children outside in cold weather missing gloves, hats, shoes, boots or even warm coats, alongside their warmly-dressed parents! Unfortunately, I see this everywhere in New England. I was once with a mother and her three year old son at a park on a cold January afternoon. The little boy had no gloves on, and I realized from holding his hand that his hands were icy cold. When I expressed this to the boy's mother, she answered casually, "My hands feel fine."

As parents, it is our responsibility to put ourselves in the skin of our children, who are younger, smaller and much more vulnerable than we are. This is the ability to feel compassion and empathy. Remember, the pain threshold of children is much lower than that of adults, but many times children ignore their bodily needs so as not to interrupt their play or because they do not like the feel of bulky winter gear.

In cold weather, it is important that we make sure our children have a hat, gloves and warm coat on to prevent frost bite and hypothermia. It is equally important to encourage the brave adolescent who goes out in 20 degree weather wearing only a "hoodie" to please wear (and zip up!) a warm coat and wear, at least, gloves. Likewise in very hot weather, be sure your child is dressed for the heat, stays hydrated, wears toxic-free sunscreen and comes indoors for breaks from the sun. Older children who are wearing jeans or three layers of black shirts in sweltering heat can be given a water bottle and gently reminded of the dangers of heat exhaustion.

## Sleep:

Bedtime is a battle every night in many American families. Many young children are up until nine or ten p.m. and then are expected to awaken at 7 a.m. the next morning. Adolescents are expected to stay up until late at night either working a job or doing homework, and then wake up as early as 5:30 or 6:30 a.m. the next morning for school. As I mentioned before, adolescent's brains require that they go to sleep late at night and wake up late in the morning, naturally, around 10 a.m. Our culture tends to belittle sleep, viewing naps as "just" for toddlers, and punishing groggy adolescents with late passes and detentions when they are unable to wake up in time for school.

I have worked with several adolescents who struggled with sleep patterns that caused them to be forced to repeat their grade in high school or to leave school to get the sleep they needed. In most cases, these children simply had an internal sleep pattern that required them to fall asleep at approximately 3:00 a.m. and wake up at noon, but it was seen as disabling by the culture. As parents, it is our responsibility to be sure our children's sleep needs are met by an educational environment that understands adolescent sleep needs. As we will discuss in a later chapter, homeschooling is often the most optimal educational environment for most of children's needs, including their sleep needs.

## Physical activity:

As parents, it is our responsibility to be sure that our children are allowed the frequent and continuous high energy physical activity throughout the day that they need. Children, especially boys, need mothers, fathers, grandfathers and yes, grand*mothers* to engage in physical or rough and tumble play with them! *Boys tend to feel closer to caretakers who can play non-structured physical games with them.*

Both boys and girls need not only the outlets but materials and space for healthy physical activity. Bikes, scooters, skateboards, bats, balls, racquets, water soakers and other active toys are important for children to have access to when outdoors.

The neurological, physical and emotional benefits to children of playing creatively, freely and with supervision in a wooded area, in a field, along the ocean and on natural trails are profoundly nourishing.

The type of physical activity children actually need, especially young children, is unstructured and free from adult direction. The obsession most American parents have with putting their children on organized sports teams is puzzling; not only are organized sports not developmentally appropriate for children under ten, there is little creativity or high energy physical activity actually occurring. Once the novelty wears off, many young children find the rules and lack of actual play time frustrating and lose interest.

Children who are allowed to spend more than an hour per day watching TV, playing video games and/or socializing online are missing out on valuable physical activity both inside and outdoors. TV, video game and Internet use can become compulsive, habitual and addicting. It is not physically, emotionally or intellectually healthy for children to be spending hours per day on passive, sedentary activities. Setting firm limits on screen time so that our children have enough time for physical activity is one of our responsibilities as parents.

Dr. William Pollack, author of *Real Boys,* stated at a conference that I attended that boys require *five or more* periods of intense physical activity per day. The fact that more parents aren't outraged at the lack of playtime and outdoor time in public school for children in grades K-12 is shocking to me. Despite the fact that most parents enjoyed three long recesses per day at least until the 6th grade doesn't seem to move them to take action to make sure their children's need for play and outdoor time is met daily.

The trend in public schools since the late 1990's has been to reduce recess to one ten-minute break per day, usually ending completely by the fifth grade. Children who fail to finish their schoolwork are often denied this one small break! Growing children as young as 10 years old through high school age are generally provided no outdoor play at all, or are expected to just stand or sit on a small area of the parking lot for 10 minutes after lunch with no actual physical activity. At one public school I observed, restless children ages 10-14 were expected to stand on a small paved area by a garbage dumpster for "recess" and were not to touch or play with the enticing snow that fell the day before, under the threat of detention. In many schools in the nation, thanks to standardized testing, outdoor time has been completely stopped for all grades.

As parents, we *know* this is unacceptable. Not only does this trend defy medical and child developmental practice, it is responsible for thousands of children being diagnosed with brain disorders and medicated for the distress children of all ages feel when they are expected to remain virtually motionless for six or seven hours per day. Additionally, once children arrive home from school, they are expected to do homework, which further limits their chances for unstructured physical activity.

## Physical affection:

This bears repeating: *A child's body and brain require physical affection in order to develop optimally.* One of your most important responsibilities as a parent is to provide your child a loving connection through physical affection. *A secure parent-child attachment is not possible without an abundance of loving physical touch* such as skin-to-skin caressing, hugging, cuddling, rocking, holding and kissing.

Infants and young children can actually die without physical affection. Infants and toddlers who receive an abundance of skin-to-skin contact and caressing have higher IQ's, more secure attachment and have more stable physical, emotional and behavioral health as they grow. Children of all ages, through adolescence, who receive regular, daily, warm physical affection from parents are more likely to have secure attachments to their parents and are more likely to be cooperative and stable physically, emotionally and behaviorally.

Children of all ages, girls and boys alike, need an *abundance* of physical affection from both mothers and fathers. Children who usually recoil and pull away from physical affection or who usually cling inappropriately despite receiving physical affection are *not securely attached.* Both types of children equally need and crave the comfort and love of physical affection, but the attachment relationship must be repaired slowly. We will discuss this more in Chapter 11 Parts I and II, including meeting the special attachment needs of adoptive children.

## Physical safety:

We must be willing and able to parent in a way that will not harm our children physically and emotionally. As parents, we are responsible for providing a physically and emotionally safe home environment. We must be sure that the people who we allow into our children's lives will be safe and not harmful or abusive to them. If we find that someone is acting harmfully to our child, even if it is a school teacher, our spouse or partner, we must put our child's wellbeing first and do what we can to be sure the situation changes immediately. If we are unable or unwilling to provide a safe environment for our child, we must seek out relatives, friends and helpers who are willing and able to help us provide a safe environment for our child.

## *Physical comfort:*

Children have a lower threshold than adults for physical discomfort, but will often develop desensitization to the discomfort when their needs are chronically ignored by parents and caretakers. As parents, making sure your child is physically comfortable is an important way of expressing to your child that his or her needs and feelings matter. That message will help children develop the ability to stay tuned-in to their internal signals and needs.

## *Good hygiene:*

Modeling, practicing and expecting good hygiene of your children is an important part of health and maintaining a positive sense of self. Too many of the youth that I have worked with have very poor hygiene. This impacts their overall medical and dental health, their sense of bodily awareness, their peer relationships and their positive sense of self. For infants and toddlers, cleanliness and hygiene are entirely our jobs; as children get older, they can gradually assume more and more responsibility for brushing and flossing their teeth, wiping their face after a meal, putting on clean and presentable clothing, showering, washing their face, brushing their hair and putting on deodorant. However, as their parents, it is necessary that we step in if older children are lax or neglectful about their hygiene.

## *Medical care:*

Part of parenting requires that we take good care of our children when they are ill, hurting or showing symptoms of a medical problem. A secure parent-child attachment remains secure when children trust that their pain or symptoms are taken seriously, soothed and medical care is sought. As parents, we can make sure our children have rest and proper medical attention when they are ill.

I have worked with many children who have suffered from chronic coughs, sprains, infected wounds, athlete's foot, acne, headaches, stomachaches and other untreated symptoms and were not taken to a pediatrician, holistic practitioner or to a specialist who could rule out more serious illnesses.

I have seen children struggle with severe symptoms of acute bronchitis, the flu, sore throat or colds and their parents do not take them to a health care provider. I have seen children with asthma denied their medication because parents did not want to "go through the trouble" of getting financial assistance to pay for it. I have seen children with severe allergies and asthma suffering in their own homes from animals that the children were allergic to–– because the parents would not part with their beloved pets!

I have seen children's chronic symptoms mocked, punished and called "faking" or attempts to "get attention" by parents who did not want to "bother with a specialist". I have seen children made to go to school when ill, during recovery, on the day of medical testing or procedures; not allowed the rest the mind and body needs in order to heal or fight infection.

## Physical pleasure:

As parents, we are responsible for responding to our children's experience of physical and tactile pleasure with support, information and non-shaming acceptance. We can allow them to experience joy when they experience the sensory world around them; we can smile on their expressions of affection between friends; we can allow them the joy of enjoying physical affection with us; we can make certain that our children are in an educational environment that approves of tender affection between friends and we can treat our children with respect when they find pleasure in their own bodies through self exploration and masturbation.

As parents, we are responsible for providing information to our children about their bodies, about bodily changes at puberty, about the appropriate places for self exploration and masturbation, about healthy physical boundaries with others, your sexual values and personal body safety. We are responsible for conveying this information to children in the way that they need it: Respectfully, sensitively, non-judgmentally and openly.

### The emotional needs of infants and toddlers

*Constant* skin-to-skin contact and emotional engagement through:

- Caressing
- Touching
- Breast feeding
- Eye gazing
- Massaging
- Playing
- Rocking
- Bouncing
- Cosleeping
- Excited, animated facial expressions
- Mirroring emotions
- Exchanging sounds and words

*...is literally the recipe for optimal brain development for infants.*

Babies who are stimulated in this manner, who are worn *constantly* on the mother in a sling, who feel the joy of *constant* skin-to-skin contact, who are allowed to wean from the breast at *their* pace...

- Are likely to attach securely to their mothers,
- Are likely to cry less,
- Are likely to squirm less,
- Are less distressed by being handed to another person,
- Are more comfortable exploring their environment when older,
- Are more secure,
- Are happier,
- More intelligent and
- More emotionally stable

...than babies who experience the typical low level of physical contact common in our culture.

## The emotional needs of young children, older children and adolescents

Children of all ages, including adolescents; both boys and girls, *also need and crave emotional care, affection and nurturance.* It is critical, in fact, to the brain development and emotional and behavioral well being of all children to receive *daily* nurturance, physical affection, verbal expressions of love, emotional safety and respect from their parents and caretakers.

Children of all ages, both girls and boys who receive:

- Hugs
- Cuddling
- Caresses
- Holding
- Rocking
- Rough and tumble play
- Loving eye contact
- Active listening
- Genuine expressions of love and gratitude
- And other types of physical and verbal affection...

...stay securely attached to their parents, are more cooperative, more respectful, more emotionally stable, more secure with separations, more self disciplined, more joyful, more compassionate and less clingy, less withdrawn, less anxious, less defiant, less swayed by negative peer influences and less aggressive than children who receive the typical low level of physical affection by parents common in our culture.

## The necessity of unstructured play

Play is such a basic necessity to the well being and overall development of children that I consider it to be a physical, emotional, intellectual, social and neurological need. Although our culture on the surface speaks sentimentally about the importance of play, the dangerous reality is that unstructured play is being phased out of children's lives, and at younger and younger ages.

Famous people from the early 1800's to today, from kindergarten founder Friedrich Froebel to child development experts such as Jean Piaget and Maria Montessori to the late children's TV icon, Bob Keeshan ("Captain Kangaroo"), have all echoed that "play is the work of children".

Although most people would agree in sentiment that play is the work of children, most people in our culture do not actually take that famous quote seriously. Unfortunately, adults in our culture, driven by the desire to drive children to excellence in every area of their lives, have filled children's lives so tightly with academics, homework, educational "toys", organized sports, classes, clubs, groups and electronics that there is little or no time during the day for children to just play. The trend since the 1990's has been to keep children as busy as possible with academic or structured activities; "free play" is treated as a waste of "learning" time.

Ironically, play is the very *way* by which children learn and develop intellectually, creatively, socially and emotionally! Removing play and replacing it with structured activities and "academics" is as upsetting to children's well being as removing healthy food from your diet and replacing it with a nutrition pill.

- Parent-child attachment is the blueprint and fuel for a child's physical, emotional, intellectual, creative, social and spiritual development...
- Play is the way the brain builds from that blueprint and uses that fuel to wire all of the potentials of a child's development.

In other words, *play is the way that children's brains are meant to learn.* Nature intended for human children to learn through play, just as other young mammals learn through play. The fact that children constantly play, prefer to play and will do anything they can to play, in every single culture of the world, at all ages, even in the midst of school schedules, structured activities, illness, war, natural disaster and the threat of punishment, shows adults that play is a basic childhood necessity. Children *must* play.

Here are some other important points about play:
- Play that is imaginative, creative, free, unstructured and child-led is optimal for a child's development.
- Children need to play dramatically and passionately, invoking fantasy and imagination.
- Older children require both solitary play and play with other children.
- Children of all ages usually love when the adults in their lives play with them, but at the children's direction.
- The most optimal toys and play materials for children and adolescents are toys that are used as props or are used for building, inventing or fantasy gaming.

- Fantasy play using themes of conquest, weapons, "good vs. evil" and fantasy "aggression" is age appropriate for older children. It is a cause for concern only if children are harming themselves or others (including animals), if they have difficulty empathizing with others, if they seem preoccupied with aggression and violence or if they are repeatedly reenacting a trauma.
- Electronic and "educational" toys usually take the creativity and the imagination out of play.
- There is no such thing as a "boy toy" or a "girl toy"— Children benefit from having a diversity of toys.
- Although a child can be too young to safely use a certain toy, there is no "certain age" to "outgrow" a toy— If your older child enjoys a toy or game, then it is serving his or her development.

Babies, young children, older children and adolescents all require play. As children grow older, their play changes, deepens and matures, but it ideally won't cease. As parents, it is important to understand that play is a necessity to our children's healthy development. It is our responsibility to make certain that unstructured play is restored as a priority in our children's lives.

## Children's higher level needs

When children's basic physical and psychological needs are met consistently, they feel secure and free enough to focus on higher level needs with joy, curiosity and excitement.

Remember Maslow's "hierarchy of needs" from Chapter 2? Maslow's hierarchy shows us that *basic physical and emotional needs must be met consistently in order for the child's brain to optimally focus on and sustain healthy development in higher areas of life functioning.*

Some of children's higher level needs include:

## Intellectual needs:

The desire to learn, explore and develop one's mind: Children are born passionate learners! They are curious about everything and learn so much by exploration! *Children's brains are designed to learn everything they need to learn on their own*, by exploring, using their hands and bodies, playing, asking questions, imitating others and requesting guidance when needed. Children only need the freedom, resources, tools and guidance that adults can provide for this purpose.

Our traditional school system does not educate children in line with their brain needs and development, and that is why most children in our culture lose their love and passion for learning that they were born with.

## Creative needs:

The desire to innovate, design, create, imagine and fantasize: Children are born creative and are natural inventors, artists, musicians, actors, writers, poets, dreamers and philosophers. Children require freedom, time, materials and resources in order to satisfy their creativity needs.

Unfortunately, our school system often destroys children's creativity by:

- Forcing learning,
- Forcing the creative arts as "subjects",
- Criticizing children's work,
- Doling out insincere praise of children's work,
- Burning out children with busywork, and
- Filling up their days with boring paperwork and assignments.

## Social needs:

Children's first and most important social relationships are in the family. Children learn how to function in cooperative, compassionate ways with peers and other people *by having their needs met first in the family.*

Children do *not* need same-age peers as our culture makes us believe that they do. Children *do not need* to go to day care, preschool or school. In fact, forcing children under seven to "socialize" with same-age children can actually impair the parent-child attachment and their ability to negotiate social skills later on.

Children, from toddlers to adolescents, benefit most from the social arrangements that peaceful tribal cultures live by:  Parent and adult supervised, mixed-age play groups of children, in which children can be caretakers and also look up to older mentors.

Older children, including adolescents, still need their family as their primary socializing relationship. If parents allow their adolescent's peers to be their *primary* influences, *the vital influence of the parent-child attachment relationship will be compromised.*

## Moral/Spiritual needs:

Children develop self discipline and the understanding of moral obligations to their fellow humans and animals, their society, their environment and to the world through the quality of the parent-child attachment relationship. Children also gradually develop spiritually in relation to the quality of the parent-child attachment relationship.

When children are treated with love and respect and their needs are met, their ability to develop a healthy spirituality is strong. When children's mistakes are responded to with understanding, guidance and an expectation of restitution and repair rather than punishment, fear-based tactics and violence, children develop accountability and self-discipline.

Children show the ability to feel empathy and compassion as early as infancy: When children are treated in loving, respectful ways and when they have a secure parent-child attachment, empathy and compassion for others will grow to include the world.

## Summary

The most critical parenting tool all parents must have if they wish for their children to be physically, behaviorally and emotionally healthy is the commitment to the secure attachment cycle. The cornerstone of a secure parent-child attachment is meeting a child's basic and then higher level needs from conception until the end of adolescence. Having physical and emotional needs met at all ages of childhood is critical to brain development and to the physical, behavioral and mental health of your child.

In the next chapter, *The Human Attachment Cycle*, we will learn why a prompt response to the cries of the infant and a compassionate, satisfying response to the needs and behaviors of children of all ages are necessary to a secure parent-child attachment. Most vitally, we will also learn that a secure parent-child attachment is the foundation for optimal physical, emotional, social, intellectual, sexual and spiritual development throughout the lifespan.

# Chapter 3
# The Human Attachment Cycle

## The secure attachment cycle

*Let's review:*

What is secure attachment?

- Attachment is much more than just *feeling love* for your children,

- Attachment is the basic biological, emotional, social and intellectual blueprint of your child's lifelong happiness and ability to cope with life and relationships,

- Secure attachment requires more than just sentimental feelings and involvement for a few early years,

- Secure attachment requires deliberate, constant and compassionate *action*, putting your children's evolving needs as a priority, for their *entire* childhood,

- Secure attachment is the result of a loving, responsive parent meeting a child's physical and emotional needs promptly the majority of the time, thousands upon thousands of times, over a period of years,

- Providing a healthy physical and emotional environment for the fetus to grow is vital to attachment parenting,

- Meeting an infant's needs immediately for the first three years of life is crucial for optimal brain development, and

- For the attachment relationship to remain secure and for the child to remain behaviorally and mentally healthy, *the parent must continue this cycle* (in a developmentally appropriate way) *until the child has reached adulthood.*

Remember, there are the four steps to the human attachment cycle, as indicated in the diagram.

- Step one: Your child has a need.

- Step two: Your child expresses her need.

- Step three: You, as the parent, *respond* to the child immediately and *meet his need as soon as possible.*

- Step four: Your child feels homeostasis, calm, joy, satiated and TRUST in you and in the world.

This cycle starts again when your child's body or mind feels another need.

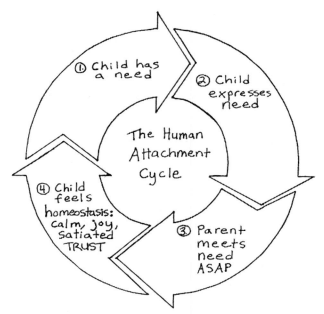

**THE HUMAN ATTACHMENT CYCLE**

Every step of the human attachment cycle is vital and necessary to the growing child, his development and to her ability to remain securely attached to you. Let's dissect each step and learn why:

## Step one: Your child has a need

As we learned in the previous chapter on children's needs, a child who has a physical or emotional need is experiencing *distress*. Depending upon the severity and urgency of the need, the child can be experiencing excruciating anguish or agony.

*When a child is experiencing a need, the need will gradually consume him until it is met.* When a child is consumed by a need, she is not focusing on *anything else but getting the need met*. As children grow older, they often appear to be able to multitask with unmet needs, or to "forget" the need, but the amount of energy, self denial and desensitization it requires is very draining and detrimental to their overall development.

## Step two: Your child expresses the need

Do you recall Chapter One's discussion of alarm signals in nature? When a child is giving us an alarm signal, he or she is expressing a need. Although not always as clear as a "check engine" light on the control panel of a car, children express their needs in a variety of ways, some methods more obvious than others. As parents, it is our job to be detectives and decipher the needs our children are trying to express to us by their alarm-like behavior.

Let's review and expand the list of alarms signals children use to express their needs to us:

- Directly telling us they have a need
- Asking us to help them meet a need
- Asking nicely
- Asking rudely

- Crying
- Whining
- Yelling
- Screaming
- Outbursting
- Pouting
- Tantruming
- Swearing
- Withdrawing
- Clinging
- Defensiveness
- Sarcasm
- Hyperactivity
- Depression
- Anxiety
- Raging
- Distractibility
- Fidgeting
- Squirming
- Oppositionality
- Harassing
- Defiance
- Refusing
- Disrespect
- Threatening
- Aggression (verbal, physical, sexual)
- Destructiveness (vandalism, breaking toys, stealing, etc.)
- Self destructiveness (self mutilation, substance use, sexual promiscuity, bad relationships, etc.)
- Challenging
- Over compliance

*It is most critically our responsibility as parents to not only decode that alarm signal, but to meet the needs our children are expressing to us.*

### Step three: You, as the parent, respond to your child immediately and meet the need as soon as possible

*Children whose physical and emotional needs are met promptly, consistently, regularly and with caring are less likely to express their needs using negative, disrespectful behaviors than children whose needs are denied, delayed, neglected or met with frustration and negativity.*

Did you notice in this four-step attachment cycle, that step three is the one step where you can take action? This is also the vital step that literally builds the foundation for a child's physical, emotional, behavioral, intellectual, social, sexual and spiritual health and development throughout life! Although that sounds daunting, it is a responsibility that we as parents must take seriously.

Children seem to have needs all of the time; is it possible to meet their needs all of the time?  If we set up a pattern from infancy of meeting our children's needs fully and consistently, the relationship will be strong enough to withstand the stresses of the times when it isn't possible for you to respond immediately and meet their need right away.

If we respond to our children's needs with care and love *most of the time* and meet their needs *most of the time,* we are:

- Providing relief,
- Easing their distress,
- Soothing their anxiety and preventing harmful stress hormones from flooding the blood stream,
- Helping our children stay joyful,

- Solidifying the relationship,
- Showing respect to our children,
- Showing unconditional love to our children,
- Conveying the depth of our love for our children,
- Conveying the solidness of our commitment to them,
- Conveying to our children that they won't be left alone with their distress,
- Conveying to our children that we truly care, understand and cherish them,
- Conveying to our children that their needs matter,
- Allowing their bodies to return to a state of calm and optimal functioning,
- Allowing their minds to return to a state of calm and optimal focus and functioning,
- Allowing our children the freedom to attend to higher level functions,
- Allowing the brain to continue its normal development without the potential for traumatic neurological damage,
- Teaching our children how to treat others, and
- Teaching our children how to parent in the future.

In short, we are conveying an affection, love, tenderness and soothing *that is deep enough to shape the kind of men and women our children will become and how they will, as adults, affect and impact our world.*

### Step four: Your child feels homeostasis, calm, joy, satiated and TRUSTS in you and in the world.

When a child's physical and emotional needs are responded to, promptly met and taken seriously, the child's distress subsides and the child associates the resulting warm feeling of comfort and satiation with the parent. The attachment deepens, the body and psyche (emotional mind) are in a healthy state and the child learns:

- To trust her parents,
- To trust that his needs are important,
- To trust that her needs will be met again,
- To trust that he is important and cherished by his parents,
- To trust that her world is safe,
- To trust that his body and its functions are wonderful,
- To trust that her life and her world are joyful, and
- To trust in the security of his parents.

This four-step cycle starts again when the child's body or psyche feels another need. When the child's mother or father responds *consistently* in a loving, prompt manner and meets their child's needs over and over in this cycle, secure attachment results.

## The attachment disruption cycle

Disrupted attachment is the result of a parent who fails to meet a child's physical and psychological needs, or delays in doing so, causing the child to become distressed.

*If the delay or failure to meet a child's needs happens many times or most of the time, the attachment cycle will be disrupted.* The cycle may even become disrupted if *one incident of failure to respond is traumatic to the child.* Meeting a child's needs in the first three years of a child's life is *critical.* However, if a healthy cycle is broken in later childhood, including during adolescence, the attachment relationship will be disrupted and the child will be insecurely attached.

This is the way parent-child attachment becomes disrupted:

- Step one: Child has a need.

- Step two: Child expresses the need.

- Step three: Parent ignores child or fails to respond to child's need immediately.

- Step four: Child feels distress, pain, fear, rage, depression and DISTRUST in the parent and in the world.

The attachment cycle is now disrupted.

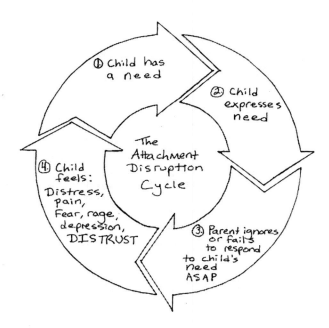

The attachment cycle disrupts or derails when a parent does not respond to their child's alarm signal and fails to meet the need promptly. When the next need arises, the previous need doesn't dissolve; instead, the first need is now magnified in intensity, which also magnifies any subsequent needs...

### The disrupted attachment cycle: An emotional train wreck
When the child's body or mind feels a new need on top of a previously unmet need, the cycle becomes emotionally disastrous, like an emotional train wreck. The original unmet need is like a disabled train, stuck to the railroad track: One of two things will happen:

1. If the parent *delayed* in responding to their child's need, the child will still be feeling residual distress, pain, fear, rage, depression and distrust. So, when the next need, or "next train", comes along, the child's distress INTENSIFIES! The fluidity of the cycle is jammed, and the "trains" experience a serious delay.

2. If the parent actually *ignored* their child's alarm signal and *refused or failed* to meet their child's need, the child will *still* be experiencing the need, but in a much more intensified, magnified way: The "train" is disabled and stuck on the track. When the next need comes along, the distress builds to an even more severe degree. The cycle is at a dead-lock, and the "new train" smashes right into the original "train", creating a wreck.

The "train jam" or "train wreck" status of the cycle doesn't stop the body and brain from experiencing more and more needs... To the contrary, the "trains" keep coming and coming and the jam either magnifies in severity or the "train cars" will keep careening into the "trains" in front of them, causing a twisted wreck. Eventually, the child must numb himself to his need, or even deny that he is feeling the need, in order to function.

## The danger of chronic stress

There is even more potential harm to children to consider: With each need that goes unmet, depending on the intensity of the need:

- The child's stress increases, causing his or her body to continually release powerful stress hormones, such as epinephrine (adrenaline), norepinephrine and cortisol, into the bloodstream and tissues.

- Chronic stress inhibits or rewires the two parts of the child's nervous system that regulate anxiety and calm:

- When the part of the nervous system that generates stress stays on, and keeps releasing stress hormones and chemicals into the child's bloodstream and tissues, your child will feel chronic anxiety.

Let's look at these two parts of the nervous system:

The *sympathetic nervous system* generates our lifesaving "fight-or-flight-or-freeze" panic reaction to a danger. However, this system is meant to be:

- Immediate,
- Of short duration, and
- Acute (used occasionally).

When a child experiences *distress* that is chronic and on-going:

- The body stays flooded with the powerful stress hormones that are intended to be released only for instant "fight-or-flight-or-freeze" reactions,

- The rest of the systems of the body stay in "standby" or slow mode rather than functioning at full capacity, and

- The brain becomes wired to use the sympathetic nervous system constantly.

*The parasympathetic nervous system* calms the body down after the "fight-or-flight-or-freeze" danger passes by releasing calming hormones into the bloodstream and tissues. This system:

- Gives the sympathetic nervous system the "red light" to stop working,

- Gives the rest of the body's systems the "green light" to return to normal functioning, and

- Allows the person to emotionally calm down and seek reassurance and comfort.

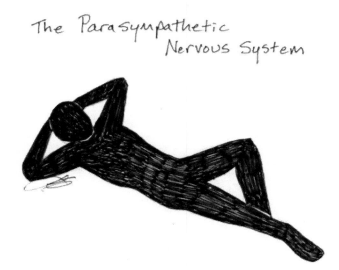

The Parasympathetic Nervous System

When a child experiences *distress* that is chronic and on-going:

- Parts of the parasympathetic nervous system atrophy (wither away), and

- The parasympathetic nervous system cannot put the brakes on the sympathetic nervous system anymore.

A chronic flood of the stress hormones in a child's body can cause a number of health problems such as:

- Digestive problems
- Urinary frequency
- Respiratory problems
- Headaches
- Insomnia
- Decreased endocrine (hormone) system function
- Decreased immune system function (leading to frequent illness)
- Inflammatory conditions in the body
- Blood sugar imbalance
- Decreased thyroid function
- Weight gain
- Decreased bone density
- Decreased muscle tissue
- High blood pressure
- High cholesterol, and
- Future heart disease

A chronic flood of stress hormones in a child's body can cause a number of behavioral and mental health problems such as:

- Decreased cognitive/learning function from atrophy of brain cells
- Anxiety
- Restlessness
- Hyperactivity

- Depression
- Agitation
- Aggression
- Mania

## <u>Meeting needs is NOT "spoiling"</u>

- *Delaying your response to your child's needs does NOT teach your child "to delay gratification"!*
- Ignoring or refusing to meet your child's needs does NOT teach your child to "be tough," "to be independent," "to grow up" or "to learn patience"...
- In fact, the distress, anxiety, anger and disrupted attachment that result *will actually cause children to "learn" to act in the opposite way...*

*You cannot "spoil" your child when you meet his or her needs.* Children become "spoiled", or materialistic, when the secure parent-child attachment cycle is broken and material objects are used as substitutes for basic needs. When children are insecurely attached, they will crave any type of small pleasure or novelty that will temporarily ease the distress of years of unmet physical or emotional needs. Most parents of "spoiled" or materialistic children notice the following things:

- How quickly their child tires of the new object;
- How the craving for new objects seems endless;
- How sour and "ungrateful" they become while, or right after, going someplace fun;
- How no matter how much you give, it is never enough; and

- Your child would rather buy something than just be with you.

These characteristics of "spoiled", materialistic children are usually symptoms of chronic, unmet needs from a disrupted and insecure parent-child attachment. All humans, including the many "spoiled", materialistic adults in our culture, will attempt to fill the holes left by their unmet needs in any way they can. Buying objects, gorging on junk food, using substances such as alcohol, tobacco and other drugs and craving unhealthy relationships to meet early needs are all people's heart-breaking attempts to fill the void of a disrupted, insecure parent-child attachment.

## <u>Numbing: When children's needs are chronically denied</u>
Remember:

- A child who is feeling a physical or psychological need is experiencing *distress*.

- Depending upon the severity and urgency of the need, the child may be experiencing excruciating anguish or agony.

- *When a child is experiencing a need, the need will gradually consume him until it is met.*

- When a child is consumed by a need, she is not focusing on *anything else but getting the need met.*

- As children grow older, they often appear to be able to multitask with unmet needs, or to "forget" the needs, but the amount of energy, self denial and desensitization it requires is very draining and detrimental to their overall functioning and development.

For infants, toddlers, young children, older children and adolescents, unmet needs eventually consume the child and every system of the body. When the child's needs are chronically delayed or neglected, after a point, an infant or child of any age will:

- Dissociate (emotionally withdraw from the present experience and turn inward),

- Numb themselves physically and emotionally,

- Develop a desensitization to the need, and

- Develop an abnormally high threshold to pain and distress.

When a child is experiencing distress, anguish, agony, dissociation, numbing or desensitization, she or he:

- Cannot feel close to the parent or caretaker who is causing the distress,

- Cannot feel that he and his needs are important,

- Cannot be focused on the myriads of tasks that she could be focused on,

- Cannot function at an optimal or even adequate level, and

- Cannot feel a desire to cooperate with the parent or caretaker who is causing the distress.

Children of *all* ages who are forced to physically or emotionally numb themselves from chronic distress may resort to desperate behaviors to try to regain a sense of feeling, such as:

- Constant rough play

- Self harming (hitting self, falling, banging head, scratching self),

- Self cutting

- Self mutilation

- Suicidal gestures or attempts

- Bullying others (people, animals)

- Harming others (people, animals)

- Vandalism

- Erratic, manic, out of control behavior

- Dangerous risk taking

- Obsessive materialism

- Substance use

- Sexual aggression or promiscuity

## Nature intended for children's needs to be serious issues

Children's needs are very serious issues. *Nature intended needs to be serious issues*, because the physical and emotional well being and survival of the child is at stake. As we discussed earlier, in the animal kingdom, animal parents do not put their convenience first, nor do they see their children's alarm signals and needs as behavioral or moral issues. Depending on the type of creature, an animal parent MUST meet the young one's needs, in whatever forms those needs may take for a particular species, or the young one will die. Here are some examples:

- A mother ichneumon wasp's responsibility is to bore a hole into a tree and lay her egg in the exact location as a certain type of grub. When her baby hatches, the baby will have the food it needs in order to survive and grow on its own.

- A mother Galapagos land iguana's responsibility is to embark on a long trek through dangerous and difficult rocky terrain, then dig a hole in which to lay her eggs in a safe location. When her eggs hatch in the safe location, her babies will have a greater chance of survival, as they are born ready to take care of themselves.

- A father penguin's responsibility is to guard and protect his egg at all costs while the mother travels for four months in frigid terrain to locate food. The father must endure death-defying extremes of freezing cold, wind and snowstorms in order to protect his unhatched baby. The mother must travel a seemingly impossible distance, despite enduring near starvation.

- A mother dolphin is responsible for nursing her calve as often as needed, from thee to eight times per hour.

- A mother elephant's responsibility is to comfort and reassure her child and remain in almost permanent physical contact with her calf 24 hours per day for many years.

- A mother panda's responsibility is to hold, cuddle, lick and nurse her cub for much of the day, and engage in play-fighting with him or her as the cub grows older.

- A mother grizzly bear's responsibility is to be ferocious in defending and protecting her young!

- A mother bonobo's responsibility is to nurse her young for four years, carry and protect them for several years and provide a great deal of physical affection.

Captivity, illness, or birthing more offspring than the mother is able to nurse can cause animal mothers to engage in actions that put the well being of their young in danger. What are the circumstances in our culture that cause human parents to have a difficult time meeting their children's needs? What actions or circumstances in a child's life will disrupt secure parent-child attachment?

## Circumstances and actions that disrupt secure attachment

- Industrialized cultural parenting
- Teen parent
- Immature parent
- Parent with few or no supports
- Birth trauma
- Infant placed in incubator after birth
- Circumcision
- Failure to respond to infant's cries immediately
- Bottle feeding
- Breastfeeding for less than $2^1/_2$ years
- Crib sleeping
- Child left alone at night
- Minimal skin-to-skin contact
- Minimal or no eye gazing
- Lack of physical affection
- Lack of 1:1 time and attention
- Restricted movement due to swaddling
- Depressed mother
- Mother has flat affect or blank face
- Angry mother
- Absent father

- Non-responsive parent
- Sarcastic mother or father
- Apathetic mother or father
- Shaming parent
- Aggressive, violent parenting (spanking, threats, abuse)
- Punishment
- Corporal punishment (spanking, shaking)
- Other types of abuse (physical, sexual or emotional)
- Neglect of physical and emotional needs
- Abandonment
- Developmentally inappropriate parenting or caretaking
- Forcing developmental tasks
- Day care
- Lack of support in upsetting situation, injury, illness or other trauma
- Parent will not admit mistakes and make restitution
- Out-of-home placement (foster care, group home, adoption)
- Loss of parent or loved one
- Death of parent or loved one
- Unexpressed grief
- Witnessing domestic violence
- Forced to go to school
- Forcing learning or "lessons" (at school or home)
- School stressors
- School-related interference with home life, such as homework
- Pain/Illness
- Hospitalization

- Poverty
- Homelessness
- Labeling rather than healing causes of symptoms
- Negative peer influences
- Substance using parent/Infant born addicted

## Disrupted attachment types

Attachment theorists John Bowlby and Mary Ainsworth studied attachment in the mid 1900's. Their research concluded that there are different types of insecure or disrupted attachment. Modern theorists have updated the original models as new information about infant and child brain development has been discovered. Here is a brief look at the three types of disrupted attachment and some of the major characteristics of each type:

**Avoidant attachment pattern** = Children learn to suppress, deny or withhold their feelings.

Children with this pattern may:
- Act friendlier to strangers than to parents,
- Act more interested in material objects than people,
- Act distant and cold,
- Act charming and superficial,
- Avoid intimacy and connection,
- Have difficulty showing appropriate emotions or may try to stifle emotions (i.e.: not being able to cry for a loss),
- Be unable to be honest and direct about emotions,
- Appear calm, collected and unconcerned,
- Act sullen, withdrawn, depressed or apathetic,
- Act indifferent or aloof,

- Act angry,
- Act passive-aggressive,
- Act aggressive, hostile and antagonistic,
- Act oppositional and defiant,
- Have to always be right,
- Be socially isolated or may bully peers,
- Not seek comfort or support when needed,
- Push away parents or avoid parents,
- Show a lack of empathy for others,
- Find humor or pleasure at the distress or misfortune of others, and
- Show distress when parents leave, but show little interest when parents return.

This pattern is likely the result of parents who:

- Had parents who were physically and emotionally aggressive towards them as children;
- Had to suppress or deny their feelings as children;
- Are hostile, angry, sarcastic and controlling with their children;
- Threaten or punish their children for showing anger, tears and testing behaviors;
- Show an intolerance for their children's emotions;
- Show an intolerance for their children acting upset at them;
- Become upset at their children when their children are upset;
- Act too fragile to handle their children's distress;
- Have difficulty empathizing with their children and their needs;

- Are physically and emotionally threatening and aggressive to their children; and
- Do not protect their children from other hostile, aggressive adults.

**Ambivalent/Resistant attachment pattern** = Children learn to exaggerate their feelings and are preoccupied with their unregulated emotional states.

Children with this pattern may:

- Act clingy and overly "needy",
- Act both clingy and rejecting,
- Act dramatic,
- Act unfocused,
- Act anxious and overly focused on fears,
- Act hypervigilant,
- Act hyperactive and "out of control",
- Act demanding,
- Overwhelm peers and caretakers,
- Throw tantrums and have rage outbursts,
- Act immature,
- Act regressive,
- Act physically and verbally aggressive,
- Act overly pleasing,
- Become very distressed at separation,
- Be labeled as "manipulative",
- Act so preoccupied with their own emotions that they are unable to notice or empathize with the feelings of others, and

- Show distress when parents leave, but may push away the parents when they return.

This pattern is likely the result of parents who:

- Have unmet emotional needs from their own childhoods;
- Are preoccupied with their own insecurities and needs;
- Expect their child to meet their emotional needs;
- Expect their child to show love to them;
- Often put their own needs and wants before their children's needs;
- View meeting their children's needs as an inconvenience;
- Have few resources and little support;
- Are depressed;
- Act caring and nurturing sometimes and distant and withdrawn at other times;
- Meet their children's needs sometimes and make their children wait to have their needs met at other times;
- Act caring or playful with their children in front of other adults and act impatient, withdrawn and sluggish when alone with their children;
- Ignore their children's needs or delay in meeting their needs
- Have difficulty empathizing with their children;
- Cannot tolerate their children being upset;
- Have difficulty understanding their children's needs, distress or experience of a situation;
- May not protect their children from hostile, aggressive adults (partner, spouse or teacher); and
- Are emotionally and/or physically neglectful towards their children.

**Disorganized attachment pattern** = Children learn a mixture of denying and suppressing their feelings and exaggerating their feelings

Children with this pattern may:

- Show a mixture of both Avoidant and Ambivalent/ Resistant patterns of behaviors.

This pattern is likely the result of parents who:

- Had abusive and neglectful childhoods;
- Show both hostility and caring towards their children;
- Ignore their children's needs then lash out when their children show distress by crying, protesting or acting out;
- Act loving and concerned towards their children some-times but show lack of empathy and understanding about their children's needs, distress or experience of a situation at other times;
- Act physically and verbally threatening or aggressive towards their children but also act affectionate, loving and caring at other times (i.e.: "spanks" or grabs children when angry, then later gives hugs and kisses);
- Use fear, shame, humiliation and withdrawal of love to punish their children;
- Are permissive at some times and punitive at other times;
- Create a chaotic, unstable, unpredictable environment for their children; and
- Are both neglectful and abusive.

## Now that we understand why our children are acting out, we can work on healing our children...

Many people reading this book will be considering by this point that their children's behavioral and emotional "problems" are probably related to breaks in the secure parent-child attachment cycle. Some of us will be moving in the direction of questioning whether our children *really* have a genuine brain disorder that requires powerful drugs—or if they are, instead, suffering the affects of many years of unmet basic needs and unmet higher level learning needs.

Many of us, when we realize this, will feel overwhelmed with guilt, sadness and shame for the needs we were unable to meet in our children. Many of us will feel grief, depression and anger at how our parents were unable to meet our *own* childhood needs; needs that still burn within us after many decades. These are normal and healthy feelings! These feelings mean the most important thing can happen: Healing and change.

Please remember that our "civilized", industrialized culture has passed down a neglectful philosophy of parenting for thousands of years, through our ancestors, that has taken humans further and further away from our natural parenting instincts. At this point in history, in industrialized cultures, the saturation (and ubiquity) of this neglectful parenting philosophy makes it nearly impossible for parents to keep the parent-child attachment secure without knowledge of nature's intent. Now that we are gaining the knowledge, we can begin to fill our children's voids and repair the damage to the parent-child attachment... and we can seek out healing and fulfillment for our own unmet needs.

In order to learn about how nature intended humans to parent and why our culture isn't doing it, we will learn in Chapter 4 about the parenting instincts of cultures that are generally peaceful and nonviolent...

# Chapter 4

# Parenting and Educating the Way Nature Intended

*"Today, humans are the only species in creation living out of balance. We covet our position as masters instead of servants of one another. We have forgotten that service to others is the rent we pay for our room here on earth."* –Muhammad Ali

*"We are not at present meeting the needs, in anything approaching an adequate manner, of the newborn and infant young who so precariously depend upon their new environment for survival and development..."*
-Ashley Montagu, anthropologist

*"'...Nature doesn't ask your permission; it doesn't care about your wishes, or whether you like its laws or not. You're obliged to accept it as it is, and consequently all its results as well...'"*
-Fyodor Dostoevsky, from <u>Notes from Underground</u>

*Definitions:*
  **Indigenous peoples**: Native cultural groups who inhabit the land that their ancestors lived on before it was colonized by settlers.

  **Tribal cultures:** A group of indigenous families and people who share a culture and a close-knit interdependent community which benefits all members.

**Interdependent:** Each person in a tribe has a responsibility. The functioning of the whole tribe is dependent upon everyone helping one another and doing their part.

**Industrialized cultures:** Cultures that are primarily driven by production of goods and services, making money, growing the country's economy and increasing technology.

**Violence:** Using physical or verbal aggression and force to express anger, to get one's way or to cause pain to another.

## Peaceful tribal cultures vs. industrialized cultures

Many researchers of human cultures report that human beings were not always violent, mentally ill, warring and domineering of children and of each other. Child maltreatment, abuse, neglect and murder, they state, have not always been the norm. Raising children by using our culture's common tactics of controlling, hitting, yelling, dominating, punishing, teaching by force, and coercing by manipulation and reward did not always exist. According to the evidence left behind by early tribal cultures, human parents likely were originally very securely attached with their children. Likewise, researchers state that the societies that attached well to their children were generally nonviolent, mentally healthy and cooperative, with equality between men and women!

Cultural geographer, James DeMeo, offers a well-researched theory that the origin of the controlling, domineering child rearing patterns that we use in our culture today began approximately in the year 4,000 BCE.

What happened to the peaceful tribal people in 4,000 BCE? According to DeMeo, several major changes affected people's emotional stability and their parenting:

- In a very large area stretching from North Africa into Central Asia, the lush rainforests began to dry up and turn to desert;

- The desert conditions created extreme stress for people, due to lack of food and hydration, extreme temperatures and difficult terrain;

- Instead of a peaceful society in which the sexes enjoyed equal status, men began to take on a domineering, warring role in relation to the stress;

- Breastfeeding, baby-wearing and high mother-child affection and attachment was gravely reduced or abandoned as stressful conditions worsened; and

- Many infants and children were abandoned and left to fend for themselves.

It makes sense that with such traumatic environmental conditions, the stability of the family, the tribe and the culture was severely damaged. Children were now likely growing up with disrupted attachments, neglect of their basic needs and abuse and growing into dysfunctional, violent, domineering adults. According to DeMeo, over the centuries, the new angry, stressed out, domineering culture began to spread and taint other tribal groups all over the globe.

Although most of the world has been industrialized now, there are still peaceful tribal societies that reportedly exist today. Tragically, these nonviolent cultures are threatened by extinction because of the greed of big corporations who are stealing and destroying their habitats. These cultures and others that still existed 100 years ago have a lot to teach us about how nature intended us to parent.

It is important to note two points:

- No culture is perfect or idyllic.
- Industrialized cultures do show a high level of unresponsiveness to human needs. However, there are many progressive movements in industrialized cultures that work hard to heal humanity.

It is important to keep in mind when studying world cultures that every culture has at least one practice that people in another culture may find unacceptable. There will always be stressors or traditions in every culture that will cause some people in a culture to behave aggressively or in less optimal ways. There will always be controversy in the fields of cultural study about whether or not a tribe is truly nonviolent. In today's world, it is rare that tribal cultures have not been infected by outside influences. However, the tribal cultures that remain the most peaceful and the most mentally healthy generally treat their children in natural ways.

This chapter focuses on the contrast between peaceful tribal cultures and the *dominant* philosophies of industrialized cultures. As we will see below, the common natural parenting and natural learning ways that most peaceful tribes live by are very opposite to the dominant parenting and schooling philosophies in our culture.

## Reportedly, in most peaceful indigenous cultures:

- Children are welcomed and cherished;
- Newborns are birthed in a gentle, peaceful environment with a midwife and are immediately placed upon the mother's breast;

- Newborns remain naked and on their mother's bare skin at all times;

- Infants are held constantly in a sling on Mom's body or in arms for one year;

- Mothers breastfeed children for *at least* two and a half years or up to six years. Children often wean *themselves* (the average breast weaning age world wide is four years and two months);

- Mom responds *immediately* to the cries of her infant and child of any age;

- Infants have constant skin-to-skin contact with Mom;

- Infants feel constant, intense motion while in the sling of an actively working Mom;

- Children cosleep with parents;

- Young children are with or near Mom all day;

- Mom keeps her young child near her as she works in the community with other adults and children;

- Parents and the tribal culture are respectful of children's development as part of nature and allow children to develop at their own pace (including developmental tasks such as sitting, crawling, standing, walking, weaning, toileting, reading, writing, maturing, growing up);

- Parents are generally nonviolent to children;

- Parents generally do not punish children;

- Parents accept the full range of emotional expressions from children, including anger and crying;

- Parents and tribal members provide all children with high expectations based on strong community modeling;

- The older child's day consists of meaningful play with

children of all ages, imitation of adult work and strong, important community involvement;

- Children are allowed democratic freedoms (they are free to form groups of mixed aged children and can explore and learn on their own);

- Adolescents and young adults remain interdependent members of the family and tribe and remain close to the family. Independence is at a youth's pace;

- Caring, mutual sexual relationships between adolescents are healthy because of secure parent-child attachment and are acceptable in the culture; and

- Close, nurturing family and community relationships, enriching, enjoyable team work, leisure and play are the culture's priorities.

## In industrialized cultures:

- Children are viewed as an inconvenience to the freedom of the parents;

- Newborns are birthed in the stressful, unnatural environment of hospitals and are often carried away and placed in an incubator or bassinet when born after Mother gives a brief kiss;

- Newborns are isolated in bassinets alongside other distressed, screaming newborns and swaddled with blankets;

- Infants, once they go home, are isolated in strollers, carriers, playpens or swings;

- Infants are bottle feed, missing vital nutrients, skin-to-skin bonding and eye-gazing;

- If infants are breastfed, it is brief breastfeeding. Mothers forcibly wean children (the average breast weaning age in the USA is less than one year);

- Infants and children are left alone to cry or there is a delayed response;

- Older children are mocked ("don't be a baby") when they cry;

- Infants are wrapped in cloth and isolated in plastic carriers most of the day, neglected of vital skin-to-skin contact;

- Infants are either kept motionless in cribs or carriers or they are isolated in swings and strollers, which provide weak, unnatural motion;

- Infants are isolated and left alone in cribs;

- Children are isolated and left alone at night in separate beds;

- Infants and young children are separated from their mothers and from their community by being put in daycare or preschool;

- Infants and children of all ages are forced to "progress" in their stages of development (Sitting, crawling, standing, walking, toileting, reading, writing, maturing, growing up) ;

- Parents believe they must "train" or "teach" their children developmental tasks (such as toileting) and use punishment for "failure" and rewards for "success";

- Parents hit ("spank", smack, whack, belt, whip, etc.), yell at and threaten their children;

- Parents use criticism, punishment and rewards or are permissive;

- Parents show poor modeling and there is no community or tribe to reinforce modeling of acceptable behavior;

- Children spend 13 to 15 years in school, isolated from their parents and communities;

- Children are forced to "learn" in school and are completely dominated by the school (even during after school hours);

- Children have a severe lack of play time and the freedom to direct their own interests;

- Children are denied learning by imitation of adults in the community;

- Children are not important, active participants in community life;

- Children are dominated by their parents and schools and form rebellious cliques, groups or gangs. These groups exclude others and often use harassment or violence to compensate for lack of power in their lives;

- Adolescents and young adults are pushed "out of the nest" at 18 and are expected to move away and be independent of their parents whether or not they are emotionally ready;

- Healthy, mutual sexual relationships between adolescents are often not possible because of early childhood neglect and trauma and are strictly forbidden by the culture; and

- Materialism is the priority. Working long hours at a stressful, unfulfilling job, away from family, is an acceptable way to live, with little time for "recreation".

## Meet the cultures: Highlights of some peaceful, nonviolent tribal cultures

The tribal cultures featured next are described by researchers of anthropology and human culture as generally peaceful, emotionally and mentally stable and nonviolent. In all of these cultures,

- Infants are carried on the skin at all times during the first year,

- Children are breastfed for at least two and a half years (and up to six years),

- The cries of babies and children are responded to immediately,

- Affection is freely given to children, and

- A child's day consists of play, physical activity and imitating adult activities at their choosing.

Following are more parenting highlights of ten tribal cultures that are reported to be generally peaceful:

## The Aka of The Congo

Afrol News.com summed up a report from *FatherWorld*, the journal of Fathers Direct, a group who published a worldwide study on fathering. The Akas have been named "the world's best fathers", the article began: "On average, Aka father(s) hold or are within arms' reach of their infants 47 percent of the time—almost as much as Aka mothers." They continue, "An Aka daddy uses every opportunity to be in close contact with his infant. Aka fathers often take the child along when they go drinking palm wine or during other social activities. They may hold the baby close to their bodies for a couple of hours at a time". For more information, please visit: www.afrol.com/articles/16592

## The Efe of The Congo

Mothering magazine's book, *Natural Family Living*, summed up the observations of sociologist Jean-Pierre Hallet, who lived with and studied the Efe for over 45 years: Efe "mothers and their babies are never separated for the first year. Babies are carried naked on the mother's bare chest or back, maintaining skin-to-skin contact. The babies nurse continually, weaning at about *five years*. Young children sleep between the father and mother. The Pygmies show a great deal of physical affection for each other. Children are not criticized and do not need to be controlled— they simply follow their elder's lead. The Pygmies are self respecting and totally secure. They lead a cooperative, joyful lifestyle that is wholly free of aggression".

## The Fore of New Guinea

*Organic Parenting*, an essay on Primal Spirit.com by Geraldine and Gaetano Lyn-Piluso, highlights the observed attachment parenting practices of several peaceful tribal cultures. Regarding the Fore, they report: "At roughly 30 months of age, Fore children begin to explore their environment and to make contact with other community members without the presence of their mothers. Their parents remain available, but it is now the child's responsibility to seek them out when the need is felt."

E. Richard Sorenson writes in *Learning Non-Aggression,* edited by anthropologist Ashley Montagu, that mothers in the Fore tribe serve as secure bases in which children could check back with them for encouragement and reassurance while exploring their environment. The Fore mothers did not, however, attempt to stop or control their children's exploration, nor did they jump up to trail their children.

The Lyn-Pilusos add, "This is contrasted by our society's practice of forcing and pushing children to act independently. [Our society's] children seldom truly become "independent" because of the lack of parental security and the lack of control and power experienced by the children."

Sorenson further describes:

- That the infant's "basic physical and emotional needs were quickly and readily fulfilled" at all times.

- The older infant was seated in the mother's lap all day as she worked and was in constant skin-to-skin contact with her.

- Punishment and chastisement were not used with children.

- Children rarely fought or aggressed against one another.

- Affection was used to respond to children who were angry or who did occasionally lash out.

- In areas where the Fore tribe was stressed due to land overpopulation, aggression began to manifest.

For more information, please visit: www.primalspirit.com/ps3_1lyn-piluso.htm or read *Learning Non-Aggression.*

## The Kaingang of Brazil

Lyn-Piluso and Lyn-Piluso, authors of *Organic Parenting* report: "Among the Kaingang of Brazil, tactile stimulation is an integral part of their lives. Mothers hold their babies close to their breasts at all times, making skin-to-skin contact a constant event in the first nine months of a baby's life and a regular occurrence thereafter. It is common for them to show affection by hugging, stroking, caressing, and kissing. None of this is hidden but is simply a part of everyday life. Besides receiving constant attention from adults, children will approach adults knowing that a gentle caress or cuddle will result. The Kaingang children have been described by Julius Henry (1964) as lying "like cats absorbing the delicious stroking of adults" (p. 18). Touching of this sort is also apparent in adult life."

## The !Kung of the Kalahari Desert

Patricia Draper writes in *Learning Non-Aggression*, that the !Kung "have a special way of handling anger and physical assaults by one child against another. When two small children quarrel and begin to fight, adults don't punish them or lecture them; they separate them and physically carry each child off in an opposite direction. The adult tries to soothe and distract the child and to get him interested in other things. The strategy is to interrupt misbehavior before it gets out of hand. For older children, adults use the same interventionist technique."

Regarding this, Lyn-Piluso and Lyn-Piluso in *Organic Parenting* state, "[M]ixed messages are what our society gives children. Our children are preached to about the horrors of violence, yet are shown that violence "is necessary" by "heroes"... Western parents usually react themselves with anger and often aggression during the child's normal expression of childhood aggression. Our children are scolded, preached to, and lectured about the "badness" of their actions. To get their point across, parents may hit children. Unfortunately, what our children learn then is that hitting, and aggression, rightly follows anger."

Draper reports that when an older child lashes out against a younger child, that child is "scolded". However, when a child lashes out against a !Kung adult, the adult reacts with humor and does not appear to express anger towards the child. She described parents gently deflecting a thrown object, but not giving attention to the tantrum. She observed that in cases when a parent was becoming angry, *another adult* in the vicinity would carry the child off in another direction. Draper states that this prevents adults from lashing out against children.

## The Muria of India

According to James DeMeo, the Muria were "characterized by the presence of a high level of body pleasure, for infants, children and adults, with a low level of trauma, anxiety, psychopathology, and violence..." The Muria had "a Ghotul", a "house and social institution set up and maintained by children of both sexes, and from which adults were generally barred from entering." *Age appropriate*, child-led sex play was allowed in the Ghotul. Unfortunately, the Muria tribe has been oppressed and eroded by former prime ministers of India and the Ghotul was banned. The culture now suffers from poverty, murder, suicide and other industrialized problems. They now dwell in the slums of African cities as their rainforests have been destroyed. I highly recommend reading DeMeo's book, *Saharasia* for more information.

## The Semai of Malaysia

Robert Knox Denton reports in *Learning Non-Aggression* that Semai look down on their neighboring Malays (who are more industrialized) for hitting their children. Denton states that the Semai explain, "Malays hit hit hit their children. We love our children. That is why our children are strong and healthy, and Malay children like baby rats." Denton reports that the Semai view all forms of physical punishment as dangerous and harmful to children. They reportedly view hitting a child synonymously with *killing* a child. As a society, "violence is clearly defined as non-Semai behavior."

Denton states, "even if a child wanted to become violent, it would have no very clear idea of how to proceed." He explains that children play a game in which they "square off with each other, assume dramatically threatening poses and flail away at each other with large sticks. The terrible blows they smite, however, always freeze about an inch from their target..." He adds that adults sometimes make a similar gesture in a teasing manner when children are acting too rambunctious.

Denton also discusses the concept of "bood", which means "not want to". If a parent asks a child to do something and the child says, "I bood", the request is dropped. Semai parents do not force anyone, including their children, to do anything against their will. In fact, when disagreements arise in their tribe, large committee meetings are held, sometimes for days at a time.

For more information, read *Learning Non-Aggression* or Robert Knox Denton's book, *The Semai, a Nonviolent People of Malaya*.

## The Temiar of Malaysia

The Temiar website, *Temiar Web*, states, "by the time they become adults, Temiars have learnt to feel anxious that their actions might cause someone else harm... The Temiar also see other beings as more similar than different, or in other words, more like themselves than not, and show the respect due to oneself to other people they interact with... Instead of alienating flowers, trees, or cicadas as inherently different from humans, Temiars stress their similarities." Please visit www.temiar.com for more information.

## The Trobriand Islanders

Before the Trobriand islanders encountered religious missionaries and industrialized influence, this culture was characterized by high parent-child affection, strong involvement by fathers, an emphasis on spontaneity and play, an openness to children's natural sexual play with peers, equal relationships between men and women and strong, monogamous marriages.

"Trobriand adults exhibited a high degree of emotional health, and a lack of neurotic, antisocial behaviors or sexual pathology", James DeMeo states in *Saharasia*. The exceptions were the chiefs and their children, who were restricted in their freedom, allowed less time to play, sex play wasn't allowed between peers and older youth were forced into arranged marriages. Not surprisingly, says DeMeo, the chief families acted quiet, obedient and docile and suffered from social, emotional and marital problems!

## The Yequana of Venezuela

"The Yequana infants, from birth until they voluntarily begin to crawl, spend virtually all their time in their mothers' arms. A mother might ask another adult or child to hold her infant for short periods of time, but this is only done if the infant agrees," state the authors of *Organic Parenting*.

Jean Liedloff, author of *The Continuum Concept*, lived among the Yequana for an extended period of time. She states that in the Yequana tribal culture, a mother's love is unconditional for both girls and boys; a father's love is constant. His approval depends upon how the child follows social norms, but he does not "make" or force a child to do anything. He patiently assumes that the child will learn by the very strong cultural example of the elders.

She reports that unlike the dangerous environment of our culture, the entire tribe is available to watch over and help children if needed. Yequana mothers do not give commands, nag children to "be careful", "stop climbing", "get down from there", "stop running", "don't touch that", or express fears of them getting lost. The Yequana reportedly appear to trust in the child's instinctual ability to do what is in their best interest. For example, Liedloff writes, "a Yequana tot would not dream of straying from his mother on a forest trail, for she does not look behind to see *whether* he is following, she does not suggest that there is a choice...; she only slows her pace to one he can maintain. Knowing this, the [child] will cry out if he cannot keep up..."

Children are reportedly provided with small versions of canoes and paddles and adult tools such as bows and arrows, grating boards and cooking utensils. Children are allowed to play at and practice adult work as much or as little as they wish. They are not forced to stay at it or do it a certain way. Play is truly the work of Yequana children, who gradual begin to participate in the meaningful work of the adults, voluntarily. Yequana youth spend most of the day swimming, canoeing, going on trading trips in groups and engaging in constant, active play and learning with mixed age groups or alongside their elders. I imagine all of these children would be put on stimulant drugs if they were forced to sit quietly at desks in America's public schools!

In Yequana society, full expression of emotions is reportedly the norm. When a person experiences pain, even adult men and women will wail and scream in the arms of their spouse, with no shaming behaviors from others or attempts to stop the person's crying. Leidloff noted that when she provided medical attention to Yequana children and adults, they would scream and cry freely in pain, but never pulled away during the procedures. They were comforted by their mothers or spouses if needed. They *emotionally* recovered very quickly, because no one told them, "be a big boy", "you're okay", "it's nothing to cry about", "what a wuss" or "you're crying like a big baby"!

Liedloff recalls, "One Yequana boy came up to me clinging to his mother and screaming at the top of his lungs from a toothache. He was about ten years old... It was clear that he was making no attempt to suppress his reaction to the pain or his need for the [instinctual] comfort of his mother's arms... [His friends] did not have any difficulty accepting his sudden departure from their gallant ranks into infantile dependence upon his mother; there was no hint of mockery from them..."

The tribe is so cohesive that even "for orphaned *adults*, there is a custom that provides for the adoption into another family," states Liedloff. [Italics mine]

Unfortunately, the Yequana have suffered much intrusion by religious missionaries and visitors from "civilized" societies; they even wear Western clothing now. For more information, please visit:

www.everyculture.com/South-America/Yekuana-Orientation.html or read Liedloff's book, *The Continuum Concept*.

# Lessons from the animal kingdom

The most important examples of natural, attachment parenting are from our fellow humans who have lived, or are still living, in natural ways. However, since humans are members of the animal kingdom, below are a few short lessons that our animal relatives can also teach us about the crucial importance of natural, attachment parenting:

## Carrying vs. caching species

Here is even more evidence that the cries of human infants are meant to be answered immediately: Which mammals are humans most like?

- *Caching (hiding) species*: Mothers, such as deer, must hide their babies in burrows or nests for long periods of time to protect them from predators while the mothers forage for food. Caching mothers nurse their young infrequently so as not to attract predators. When the mothers leave, *their babies must remain silent and still, so as not to attract predators.*

- *Carrying species*: Mothers, such as gorillas, carry their young with them at all times and sleep cuddled up to them. Babies must nurse frequently, and mothers nurse babies until babies wean on their own. *If there is a separation between mother and baby, the baby cries out and will cry until mother reconnects.*

Very obviously, we are carrying mammals—We are meant to carry our babies with us at all time, breastfeed until our babies wean themselves and cosleep with them. Our babies are meant to cry when we put them down or walk away, *as an alarm signal that they need to be with us.* To read about Dr. N. Blurton Jones' research on carrying vs. caching species of animals, please visit The Natural Child Project's website: www.natural-child.org/peter_cook/ecc_ch1.html

## Marsupial theory
Mammals that carry their young in a pouch after birth are called marsupials. Marsupial babies are helpless when born and go through an important stage of development when they are in the pouch.

According to research published in 1958 by Dr. J. Bostock, human babies who are carried on their mother's bodies may be going through a stage of "external gestation" or development like the marsupial babies in the pouch. The human infant is born helpless. After the natural carrying period, approximately one year, the infant is mobile and less helpless, like the marsupial baby who is ready to leave the pouch.

## Rhesus monkeys
When Rhesus monkey infants were denied skin-to-skin contact, affection and breastfeeding from their mothers in a science experiment, they showed the same behaviors as many children

in our culture who have been diagnosed with all of the faddish mental illnesses of our time. Interestingly, the monkeys who were provided a soft "mother" doll to hug and cling to had less behavioral problems than the monkeys who were allowed to feed from a plain wire structure. When both dolls were set up for them, the baby monkeys would even cling to the soft "mother" doll even if the wire "mother" was the only one equipped with the bottle!

Normal Rhesus monkeys raised by their mothers receive constant nurturing, nursing and mutual playing. When they grow up, they are affectionate and nurturing to their young. However, in the science experiment, when the baby monkeys raised by the dolls in the science experiment grew up, they treated their own babies in an aggressive, abusive manner, acting violent, psychotic and depressed. The monkeys "raised" by the wire "mother" were the most mentally ill and aggressive.

## Bonobo primates

We share 99.1% of our DNA with a highly intelligent primate called the bonobo! Bonobo mothers nurse their young for four years and carry them for up to ten years! The infants do not engage with peers for a year and a half, as mother-child attachment is the primary focus. Mothers play frequently with their young, especially games that foster eye contact. The facial expressions of Bonobos are highly intense and they are extremely affectionate with one another. Mother bonobos, like human parents, are known to gently tip the chin of a child upward to enhance eye contact! The mother-son attachment in bonobos is very strong and affectionate and is life long. Sons live with their mothers even after they are fully grown. Females separate from their mothers earlier than males, at about seven years old, and join a neighboring group of bonobos.

In bonobo society, there is no violence against the young by males or by females. Adult males and females share co-dominance in their groups, with the society being more female-centered. Although bonobos are highly sexual, sexual violence is not part of their culture. In fact, researchers suggest that bonobo partners regulate their sexual acts through sensitivity, by reading the eye contact of one another. Bonobos appear to be our closet mammal link to the qualities of altruism, empathy and compassion. These qualities are apparently fostered in bonobos the way they are fostered in humans, beginning with a secure parent-child attachment.

Clearly many of our mammal relatives, like people in peaceful tribal cultures, can help us as industrialized humans re-learn what we have lost: The instinctual ability to respond to our children's needs and form strong parent-child attachments.

# Chapter 5
# How Children Develop

*Definitions:*

**Developmentally appropriate:** Natural for the child's physical and emotional age.

**Psychosocial development:** A child's natural development emotionally and socially.

## How attachment affects development potential

Nature teaches us that the security of the parent-child attachment and how well our children's physical, emotional and higher level needs have been met determines how well children develop:

- Physically
- Emotionally/psychologically
- Intellectually/cognitively
- Socially
- Sexually
- Spiritually and morally

If we have a secure, nurturing attachment with our children, our children will develop to their fullest potentials in all of these areas of development:

- **Physical development:**

  - Our children's physical growth is more likely to be just right for their genetic blue print;

  - Our children are more likely to be physically healthy;

  - Our children are more likely to develop habits that keep them healthy;

  - Our children are more likely to be physically active; and

  - Our children are more likely to develop good hygiene.

- **Emotional and psychological development:**

  - Our children are likely to be affectionate, engaging and friendly;

  - Our children are likely to be emotionally secure when we are with them and when we are not with them;

  - Our children are likely to be comfortable expressing the full range of emotions, including happiness, joy, sadness, anger and frustration;

  - Our children are likely to be emotionally stable and calm and are able to express emotions appropriately, fully and to the appropriate people; and

  - Our children are likely to treat themselves with respect and show a positive outlook about life.

- **Intellectual and cognitive development:**

  - Our children are likely to learn with ease at their own pace and show natural strengths in various areas;

  - Our children are likely to develop a strong passion for certain interests and request help and guidance in areas of difficulty;

  - Our children are likely to be confident, focused, curious and excited about learning, following through on many interests while leaving behind things that do not interest them; and

  - Our children are likely to crave learning and naturally will want to increase knowledge and skill.

- **Social development:**

  - Our children are likely to make friends and keep close friendships over time;

  - Our children are likely to be comfortable and friendly in social situations and balance their own needs and wishes with the needs and wishes of friends;

  - Our children are likely to become skilled at reading basic social cues such as facial expressions and body language; and

  - Our children are likely to feel comfortable and confident playing with children of a range of ages; same age, younger and older than themselves.

- **Sexual development:**

  - Our children are likely to have a healthy curiosity

about the human body and sex and will feel secure in asking us questions when they want information;

- Our children are likely to feel comfortable and positive about their bodies and their functions; and

- Our children are likely to be sexually responsible, internalizing their parent's values and making choices based on those values.

■ **Spiritual and moral development:**

- Our children are likely to be kind, caring, sensitive, compassionate and peaceful with others;

- Our children are likely to be empathic and compassionate towards all people, animals and the natural environment and want to alleviate the suffering of others;

- Our children are likely to be genuine with their feelings of interest in others and friendship, caring and compassion for others;

- Our children are likely to be cooperative based on the security of the parent-child the relationship. They are likely to develop a sense of responsibility and self-discipline based on an internal sense of moral principles of respect for themselves, others and all living things; and

- Our children are likely to be genuinely spiritual, whether religious or not, and feel a developing sense of connection to a higher spiritual purpose.

If the parent-child attachment is disrupted, several things are likely to go wrong in a child's individual development (depending upon the severity of the attachment disruption):

- **Physical development:**

   - Our children's physical growth may be slow or stunted;

   - Our children might be small, skinny, overweight or out of shape due to physical or emotional neglect;

   - Our children may be sickly or have many illnesses;

   - Our children may have many habits that put their health at risk;

   - Our children may dislike physical activity or act sluggish; or

   - Our children may refuse to keep good hygiene.

- **Emotional and psychological development:**

   - Our children may be emotionally withdrawn and pull away from physical affection;

   - Our children may be emotionally needy, clingy or act younger than their expected age;

   - Our children may be emotionally stunted, unable to express emotions other than anger or depression;

   - Our children may be emotionally explosive, unstable and erratic, unable to regulate emotions;

   - Our children may be self destructive, self harming and negative; or

- Our children may be aggressive and bullying towards others.

■ **Intellectual and cognitive development:**

- Our children may seem to exhibit difficulties learning, processing and understanding information;

- Our children may excel in one area and seem "behind" in another area;

- Our children may be restless and unfocused, easily frustrated and unable to commit to learning or doing something new; or

- Our children may be "burnt out" from forced schooling.

■ **Social development:**

- Our children may have difficulty making or keeping friends;

- Our children may act in odd or awkward ways, isolate from others, harass others or become dominated by others;

- Our children may not know how to read basic social cues such as facial expressions and body language; or

- Our children may only be able to play with children significantly younger or use negative attention-seeking behaviors.

■ **Sexual development:**

- Our children may be preoccupied with sexual themes

due to sexual trauma, due to being shamed for masturbating or for same age sex play, or due to parents
not providing them with information about sex;

- Our children may be ashamed of their bodies and their
  bodily functions ; or

- Our children may be sexually promiscuous and risky,
  they may become teen parents or they may contract a
  sexually transmitted disease.

- **Spiritual and moral development:**

  - Our children may act antagonistic, insensitive, aggres-
    sive, violent or cruel;

  - Our children may exhibit apathy (not caring about the
    feelings or experience of another) for certain people,
    groups of people, animals, natural environment and
    for the suffering of others;

  - Our children may be polite, charming or exhibit sur-
    face niceness rather than deep compassion and empa-
    thy for people, animals, the environment and for the
    suffering of others;

  - Our children may develop obedience out of fear but
    not self-discipline or an internal sense of moral princi-
    ples based on respect for themselves, others and all
    living things; or

  - Our children may follow religious rituals and go
    through the motions because they are forced to, but
    feel no real sense of connection to a higher spiritual
    purpose.

Each individual may experience development at a developmentally normal, accelerated, delayed or stunted pace, dependant upon other variables such as:

- Physical health

- Genetics

- Temperament/Personality Type

- Brain function (cognitive deficits, abilities, neurological issues)

The secure parent-child attachment relationship will help all children, regardless of their abilities and capabilities or challenges and impairments to reach their individual highest potentials.

## Trust vs. mistrust and other important tasks

Learning a few basics about the developmental stages of childhood is helpful for us as parents as we learn about nature's intent for children. Children of all ages are learners, thinkers, creative inventors, artists, researchers and philosophers. In order for their brains to reach adulthood, the young brain must undergo *major developmental changes* in order to become capable of:

- Adult level reasoning,

- Adult level understanding,

- Adult level responsibility, and

- Adult level self control.

The young brain is not yet capable of a mature adult's level of development, thus the young person *naturally* acts in ways that do not reflect mature adult level reasoning, understanding, responsibility and self control. This seems obvious! However, many adults mistakenly believe that the behavior produced by the developing brain is *bad* and must be punished.

Punishment, threats, lectures and nagging cannot speed up brain development, any more than it can speed up physical growth! Yet, children and adolescents continue to be punished for behavior that is *developmentally appropriate*. Children who are gifted, articulate or who appear older than their age are often expected to act more maturely than they are capable. Adolescents physically appear adult-like, and may even be taller or larger than their caretakers. People might assume that adolescents are adults because of their mature appearance. Unfortunately, their normal spontaneous, risk-trying and curious actions are often pathologized, and viewed as "impulsive", "irresponsible" behavior. In reality, their behavior is *appropriate and necessary to their age and developmental stage.*

According to child developmental psychologist Erik Erikson, humans all have a special task to complete at each stage of development. In the 1950's he came up with a theory that consisted of eight tasks or stages of human psychosocial development, from birth to death. We will look briefly at a simpler version of them:

- **Age range: Infancy**
- **Task: Trust vs. Mistrust**

<u>**What it means:**</u> If a child's basic human needs are met in this critical first year, the child will have a strong, internal feeling of trust. The child will be able to trust people who have earned his trust. If a child's needs are not met constantly and the attachment cycle is disrupted, the child will develop an obsessive, bottomless feeling of being unable to trust anyone.

- **Age range: Toddlerhood**
- **Task: Autonomy vs. Shame and doubt**

<u>**What it means:**</u> Toddlers begin to realize that they have a will of their own. If their parents allow them the freedom and safety

to explore their world without punishment and without hearing a constant "no", they will develop a sense of self. If parents react to their toddlers with anger, frustration, punishment, hitting or control, toddlers will develop a deep sense of shame and doubt in themselves. This is likely to manifest in oppositionality and angry acting out.

- **Age range:     4-6**
- **Task: Initiative vs. Guilt**

**What it means:** Children at this age begin to have some social and personal challenges and responsibilities, including behavioral expectations. If parents are strong models for their children and the attachment relationship is secure, children will feel motivated to take initiative (doing something without being asked). If children at this age are forced into social situations (such as day care and school) or are expected to accept responsibility that is not developmentally appropriate, they will develop a sense of anxiety and guilt. This may manifest in children acting perfectionistic or children not wanting to assume any initiative.

- **Age range:     6-12**
- **Task: Industry vs. Inferiority**

**What it means:** Children during this stage of life are masters of exploration, imitation and making, building, learning and creating things! The work of children at this age is playing, exploring and *doing*. Unfortunately, in our culture, some of the most active and busy years of most children's lives are spent sitting quietly in a building, listening to adults, doing hours of paperwork or sitting in front of a TV screen or computer monitor. This is the opposite of what children of this age range need for their development!

If children feel motivated and encouraged to learn and explore and do both on their own and with adult guidance, they will develop a sense of accomplishment. If adults force children to "work" and confine them to school-like conditions, one of two things tends to develop: Children may act busy doing the things adults tell them they must do in order to please the adults in their lives. Or, children may develop a sense of inferiority, incompetence and "disability" when they are unable to measure up to the adult's wishes or developmentally inappropriate schooling expectations.

- **Age range:    Early and mid-adolescence 13-18**
- **Task: Group Identity vs. Alienation**

**What it means:** Youth at this stage are developing emotionally and morally. They are figuring out who they are and how they relate to others. Intellectually developed youth at this stage are capable of advanced, deep and abstract thought called "formal operations". This advanced stage of brain development causes youth to naturally question everything. There is a focus on peers and romantic relationships may begin to develop in the mid to late teens.

Youth of this stage who have the solid foundation of a secure parent-child attachment are likely to form healthy social and romantic relationships. They are also more likely to accept their parent's guidance and consider their parent's moral principles at this challenging stage of life than youth who have insecure parent-child attachments and neglectful, permissive or angry, controlling and judgmental parents.

Traditional school is dangerous at this stage of life, because the conditions of adult power and control over children lead youth to form cliques and peer groups which can be very toxic and cruel. Also, when adolescents could be exploring their world, traveling, contributing and apprenticing as active members of the community, they are confined to six years of school.

### <u>Young adulthood and secure attachment</u>

Erikson's stages have been updated in modern years to include a later adolescent stage for ages 19-24, called Identity vs. Identity confusion. This is the stage when young adults become focused on what their purpose is in life and what they want to do to contribute to the world. A young adult who has the secure base of a lifelong parent-child attachment will make the transition to adulthood and adult-level purposes, relationships and responsibilities naturally, not trying to hold onto immaturity and irresponsibility. Erikson's later stages, from young adulthood until death, will also be easier for adults to negotiate if they had a secure, loving foundation.

## A brief word about temperament

Why is one child's personality so different than another child's? They may have different *temperaments*. Temperament is a person's inborn way of responding to their environment.  In the 1950's, researchers Stella Chess and Alexander Thomas developed a theory about temperament. They found that there are three ways that children respond to situations and to people in their lives: (The names of the categories have been updated with more positive language.)

- <u>Adaptable</u> – These children have calm and upbeat personalities, approach new situations positively, adapt easily and their natural body rhythms tend to be regular.
- <u>Slow-to-warm-up</u> – These children have low intensity personalities, can seem shy, are slow to approach new situations, are slower to adapt and react with less intensity than "Adaptable" children.
- <u>Spirited</u> – These children have high energy, high intensity personalities, may adapt slower to new situations and their natural rhythms may change frequently.

Respecting our child's temperament needs will help us prevent conflicts before they begin. Our child's temperamental characteristics are more likely to be stable if children have a secure parent-child attachment. Likewise, an insecure parent-child attachment can *exaggerate aspects of a child's temperament, causing children to exhibit symptoms of unstable behavioral and mental health.*

In Chapter 6, Part I, we will discuss traditional schooling, including day care. Although these are two of the most universal and unquestioned requirements in industrialized culture, they are also two of the most harmful disruptions to secure parent-child attachment and to children's natural development.

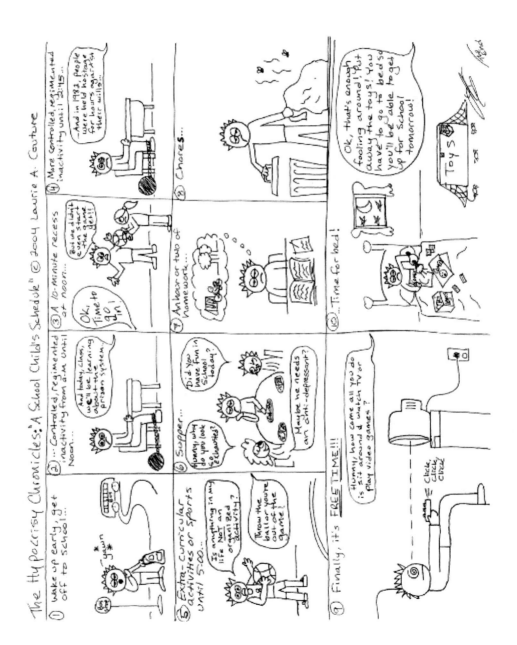

# Chapter 6  Part I

# How School and Day Care Harms Children and Secure Parent-Child Attachment

*"It was no doubt noticed that, when given a choice, most children prefer not to do school work.... Most children don't like textbooks, workbooks, quizzes, rote memorization, subject schedules, and lengthy periods of physical inactivity. One can discover this - even with polite and cooperative children - by asking them if they would like to add more time to their daily [school] schedule. I feel certain that most will decline the offer."*
-Earl Stevens, writer and columnist

*"When we grew up and went to school,*
*there were certain teachers*
*who would hurt the children any way they could;*
*by pouring their derision upon anything we did,*
*and exposing every weakness, however carefully*
*hidden by the kids...*
*We don't need no education; we don't need no*
*thought control;*
*no dark sarcasms in the classroom;*

*Teachers, leave those kids alone! Hey! Teacher! Leave*
*us kids alone!*
*All in all it's just another brick in the wall...*
*All in all you're just another brick in the wall."*
  -*The Happiest Days of Our Lives* and *Another Brick*
  *In the Wall by Pink Floyd, 1979*

*Definitions:*
  **Traditional Schools:** Public schools, religious private schools or
  other private schools that run similar to public schools.

  **Democracy:** Every person has a say and equal power in a group.

  **Self-directed learning:** Each learner takes responsibility for
  his/her education and leads it in the way that is best for him/her.
  The learner follows what is interesting and necessary to the individual's life.

  **Regiment:** Strictly controlling someone or a group.

## Dangerous to the parent-child attachment

*"This morning I went with a friend to take her son to*
*school and when we were walking back out she said*
*she'd seen a lot of mothers crying last week dropping*
*their children off to their first year of school... 'Why do*
*all of those mothers cry?' She didn't answer. She*
*knows, I think, it's because they're all overriding every*
*instinct they have for their child's well-being."*
  -*Anonymous, as quoted in* <u>Walking on Water</u> *by*
  *Derrick Jensen*

*"The implicit message of [our cultural] practices is that*
*relationships are not a priority; work is the priority.*
*Relationships have become a kind of 'treat', encapsu-*
*lated in the concept of 'quality time'."*
  -*Sue Gerhardt, psychotherapist and author*

Most parents in our culture were raised to believe that children must go to school. When their young children reach a certain age, most parents believe that school is what is best for children and that it is where children belong. Most parents believe that sending their children away for the day "will give them an education" and "socialize" them. In fact, many parents are so anxious about wanting their babies to "get ahead" academically and socially that they are sending children to daycare in infancy and to "pre-K" at three years old, hoping that very young children will have four years of "education" prior to kindergarten! Not only is this developmentally inappropriate, it is detrimental (harmful) to a secure parent-child attachment.

The younger a child is when she is forced to separate from her mother, the more likely it is that the parent-child attachment will be disrupted. As we learned in the previous chapters, in the first year of life, children are intended by nature to be in near constant skin-to-skin contact with their mothers, and also with fathers, siblings and others family members. When an infant is left in the care of strangers, away from the mother, competing for attention along with several other infants, left alone in highchairs and cribs, the damage to the attachment cycle can be *excruciating* to the infant: *Suddenly, his mother is gone, and his entire existence is longing, distress and despair.*

The fear, longing, anger and distress that toddlers and very young children experience when forced to go to school is no less harmful, although they are more likely to eventually resign to the fact that they have no choice. Because the secure parent-child attachment becomes disrupted, behavioral and mental health problems may begin to manifest. The fact that three year old toddlers are being expelled from *preschool* for violent behavior and *prescribed powerful drugs for symptoms of a disrupted attachment* is testimony to the suffering these little ones endure by being apart from their parents.

By the time children are six years old, almost every one of them is in school. Children at six are expected to separate from their parents without a problem. The natural instinct to cling and protest the unnatural separation is answered with more force and shaming by the parent or even a parent sneaking away when the child turns around. A more securely attached child may show excitement for school because it is something new that the child expects to be fun. However, when the novelty and fun of school wears off, eventually every school child resigns himself to the inevitable fact that he is stuck going to school everyday. Like we learned in our discussion about the disrupted attachment cycle, the school child learns to numb her feelings or he shows his distress by acting out in a variety of ways.

Children at six are also expected to spend several long hours, five days per week, sitting still at desks, ignoring their instincts for:

- Comfort from their parents,

- Meeting bodily needs,

- Exploring, and

- Energetic playing.

At the end of the school day, their time, their parents and play are *still* not theirs: Now, (beginning in some schools as early as preschool), first graders must deaden their instincts, needs and wishes some more and force themselves to do *homework*! Often, homework creates major conflicts between parents and children, causing another source of pain in a child's life.

And so goes the cycle for the next eleven years or longer, depending upon if a child is forced to repeat a grade. By the time children graduate, there is no time left to make up for all of the lost time that could have been spent with family. There is no time left to make up for all of the lost time that could have been spent playing, exploring, creating, dreaming, building, inventing, reading, writing and learning on their own.

Not many parents realize that that's exactly what the United States government wanted when they first instituted public schooling in 1852.

## Dangerous to democracy

*"Most children's early experiences are undemocratic. Their human rights, including free speech, are ignored... Children do not need to be taught about oppression; they are oppressed. They do not need to be taught about human rights abuses; their human rights are trampled on every day they are in school."*
    -Wendy Priesnitz, author and magazine editor

*"The nightmare of schooling is costing our kids, our families, and communities dearly in every way... [Public school] is a system that nurtures the worst in humanity and simultaneously suppresses individuality and real community."*
    –Matt Hern, author

*"The truth is that schools don't really teach anything except how to obey orders."*
    -John Taylor Gatto, author and former New York
     City high school teacher

*"School is a prison and I can't afford the bail."*
    -12 year old middle school boy, 2001

### *Public school is a way to keep people ignorant and in control...*

Imagine a fairy tale country that has a government based on freedom, democracy and basic human rights for all. Now, imagine that to prepare the children for the rights and responsibilities of living in this free, democratic country, the government institutes a surprising new law: Beginning at the age of five, children in the country are forced for 13 years to be hostages, confined to an institution run like a prison and a dictatorship!

In that institution, children's movement and bodily functions are controlled and regimented. Children cannot get out of seats or out of rooms without permission. Calls to parents are forbidden except in emergencies. Children have no right to question the daily program regimen, no right to challenge the dictator's ideas or actions, no right to have any say over rules, the discipline or how they are treated. Children have no right to independent study, or to have their own learning styles and learning needs respected. The children can only go out for exercise for 10-20 minutes once or twice per day, but that stops totally around the age of 10. Visiting hours with family and friends and free time spent playing or learning on their own is limited by all the boring work children are forced to do. Children are taught that the democracy exists, but are not allowed to take part in it.

Strangely, at the age of 18, children in that country are released from the institution. They are expected to be ready to function in their free country and go on to advanced education and careers. They are expected to be self-motivated, free-thinking, innovative and assertive individuals. They are expected to live like they were living in a democracy all those years, with rights and freedoms.

Now imagine that this fairy tale is not a fairy tale. Imagine that this institution really does exist... because it does: It is the very real way that public school has been operating for the past one hundred and fifty years!

Forced public schooling, or confinement education, did not exist as long as many of us assume: In 1650 the New England colonies attempted to create forced schooling to keep the colonists in line, but too many parents said "no way!" to the idea.

In the early 1800's, an influential secret society began researching the Prussian system of forced schooling. Prussia was a very powerful and authoritarian government in the region of what is now Germany, Poland and Russia. The Prussian government had developed a mass childhood education system so that they could grow an obedient group of people to conform to the Prussian goals of conformity and service to the government, military and to the mines. Former New York City high school teacher, John Taylor Gatto, writes that the Prussian government believed that "the government is the true parent of children".

In 1852, the American secret society, known as "The Order of the Star Spangled Banner", was successful in passing a law for forced mass schooling in Massachusetts, just like Prussia! Even though most parents fought it, some even with guns, Gatto writes that within the next 50 years, every state followed suit.

Famous people in the early world of schooling such as Horace Mann, John Dewey and kindergarten founder, Friedrich Froebel, all were supportive of an institution that would control education *to prevent people from becoming too knowledgeable and powerful*. Gatto writes that in the early days of education, reading was actually *discouraged*! Dewey reportedly believed that when children learned from their parents, communities and on their own, people become "dangerous because they become privately empowered, they know too much, and know how to find out what they don't know by themselves without consulting experts".

## What was the American government *thinking*?

- Schooling was influenced by the idea that self-directed learning created "dangerous", free-thinking, intelligent people who would make sure the government never became more powerful than the people.

- Schooling was influenced by the false idea that children would never learn on their own (even though they had been learning on their own for centuries!).

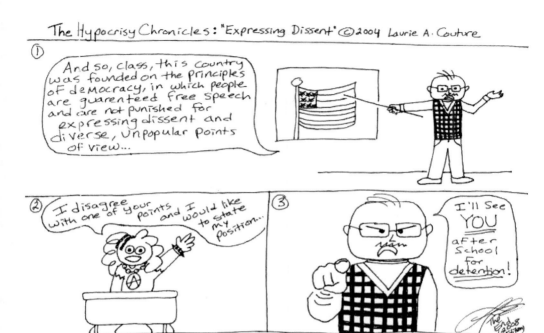

- Schooling was influenced by the idea that parents cannot teach their own children.

- Schooling was influenced by the idea that only "experts" can teach.

- Schooling was influenced by an idea that isolating children from their parents would limit free thinking, ensuring a more malleable (controllable) and willing labor force.

- Schooling was influenced by the work ethic of the 1800's which valued passive obedience to an authority.

- Schooling was based on preparing children for lives of service to hard labor in factories, mills and the military.

- School discipline was influenced by harsh religious views of children as bad and in need of punishment and control.

- Schooling was influenced by a lack of knowledge of child development.

- Schooling was influenced by adults showing little concern for the physical, emotional, social and intellectual needs of children.

- Schooling was influenced by adults who had no knowledge of the parent-child attachment cycle or nature's intent for how children learn best.

*"All the time you are in school, you learn through experience how to live in a dictatorship. In school you shut your notebook when the bell rings. You do not speak unless granted permission. You are guilty until proven innocent, and who will prove you innocent? You are told what to do, think, and say for six hours a day. If your teacher says sit up and pay attention, you had better stiffen your spine and try to get Bobby or Sally or the idea of spring or the play you're writing off your mind. The most constant and thorough thing students in school experience- and learn- is the antithesis [opposite] of democracy."*
    *-Grace Llewellyn, author*


*"The great purpose of school can be better realized in dark, airless, ugly places... It is to master the physical self, to transcend the beauty of nature. School should develop the power to withdraw from the external world" -William Torrey Harris, U.S. Commissioner*
        *of Education 1889-1906*

## Dangerous to a child's development

> "The most important piece of technology in any classroom is the second hand of a clock. The purpose is to teach millions of students the identical prayer: Please God, make it move faster."
>
> -Derrick Jensen, author and environmentalist

*"Today's schools have too little to do with learning and too much to do with control, indoctrination, and destruction of the human spirit."*
   *-Steven Harrison, writer*

*"...The whole idea of children sitting motionless at desks listening to the same material being presented at the same rate was appalling... I began to see first grade as a violent shock to the healthy human organism"   -George Leonard, author*

*"Schools...demand that our kids spend twelve (twelve!) years of their natural youth in often morbidly depressing and oppressive environments..."*
   *-Matt Hern, author*

## But isn't school good for children?

Almost everything about the controlling, "one size fits all" environment of traditional school is opposite to what nature intended for a child's development. Some of the reasons why traditional school is detrimental or harmful to children are:

- Traditional school's structure, demands and curriculum are not in line with children's developmental or learning needs;

- Public school is becoming more and more focused on cramming facts into children according to a curriculum *designed by the government*, not even by teachers!

- Public schools are cutting all of the things about school that used to be enjoyable: Free play, recess, art, music, drama, fun events, field trips and hands-on activities.

They've added increased homework for all grades and started homework for children as young as *preschool* age!

- Traditional school regiments children's basic physical needs and fails to allow children to respond to their own needs when *they* feel the need;

- The physical body is denied not only liquids, snacks and elimination, but exercise and rest in traditional school;

- Almost half of the states in the USA *still permit teachers to legally assault children with paddles* in public school;

- Traditional schools do not take into consideration that there are seven different intelligences (we will discuss them later);

- It provides no time for solitude, small child-led group meetings and independent study;

- Traditional school does not allow children to direct their own learning based on talents, interests and abilities;

- Traditional school fails to function as a democracy to prepare children to participate in a democratic society;

- Traditional schools are institutions based on control, order and punishment for non-compliance;

- When a child develops a special relationship with a special, caring teacher, the child will usually not have that same teacher the next year, nor will that child be allowed to carry that relationship on outside of school;

- Mistakes are not viewed as learning experiences, but as failures or infractions;

- Children's effort and performance are graded according to the subjective opinions of a teacher;

- Grades are permanent, undisputable and are used to divide and "track" children according to performance;

- Traditional school labels children who cannot conform as "learning disabled" or "behavioral problems";

- Traditional school isolates children from their families;

- Traditional school isolates children from the community;

- Children are forced to take busy work home after being confined for six or more hours in school;

- Homework further isolates children from family time, play time, social time and time for pursuing one's own interests;

- Children's knowledge is "tested" by using standardized tests that are not designed to measure anything but how well a child tests and how well a child can recall isolated facts. This does not demonstrate a child's knowledge, intellect, experience, creativity or moral development;

- Traditional school isolates children from taking part in contributing their ideas and talents to society;

- Learning is considered to be about "getting the right answer" rather than about the process of how to ask questions and where to find answers;

- Discovering answers from peers or parents is called "cheating";

- Traditional school is responsible for thousands of children being prescribed drugs for their exuberance, boredom or due to the teacher's inability to provide a stimulating learning environment;

- Traditional school isolates children from interacting with people of various age groups;

- Traditional school creates a climate for children to isolate themselves into exclusive groups in order to establish a sense of power and territory in a hostage-like system (similar to prisons);

- Traditional school's insensitive, control-based practices offer little opportunity for children's voices to be expressed, leading to rage, rebellion and revenge;

- Traditional school is an outdated institution based on the factory work ethic of the early 1900's; and

- Traditional school has refused to modernize to meet the creative and intellectual needs of children.

## *Nature's intent is for children to learn by playing, imitating and doing*

Going to school is a very new idea in the whole history of humanity. When we discussed peaceful tribal cultures in chapter four and how they raise their children, do you recall any mention about tribal parents sending their children to day care or school?

In the peaceful tribal cultures that we discussed, children are around their families and community members all day, for their entire childhood. Children in the tribal cultures we discussed spend their days doing what nature intended for their education: Playing hard, socializing with parents and mixed age groups, imitating and trying the different types of work done by the adults and community members, accompanying parents and community members on hunting, trading and building treks and preparing for and participating in community events such as festivals and celebrations. Tribal children learn language and communication skills by *communicating* with their families, friends and community members. No one forces the children to sit at desks and learn artificially. *No where else is childhood more natural than in peaceful tribal cultures!*

The most advanced subjects and topics can be learned *without* school. In fact, children who are allowed to learn naturally, at their own pace:

- Tend to have a secure parent-child attachment,

- Tend to be confident, secure learners,

- Tend to believe they can learn anything they want to learn,

- Tend to delve deeper into subjects that interest them than children forced to follow a teacher's curriculum,

- Tend to keep and constantly develop their creativity,

- Tend to keep and constantly re-energize their passion and love for learning,

- Tend to know how and where to find information and knowledge that they want and need,

- Tend to be active members of their local communities,

- Tend to have friendships that are genuine and enduring, based on mutual interest, not how "cool" one's clothing or material objects are,

- Tend to be involved with many different educational programs and events in the community during the day,

- Tend to out perform public schooled children in several areas,

- Tend to be several years ahead of their public schooled peers in several areas, including maturity, social skills and moral development,

- Tend to be happier, calmer and more emotionally and behaviorally stable than public school children, and

- *Can and do* get into Harvard, if that is their desire!

Natural learning is in line with:

- A secure parent-child attachment,

- A child's physical, emotional, social, intellectual and moral needs,

- A child's natural development,

- Active play, and

- A child's interests and abilities.

Traditional schooling doesn't measure up to *any* one of those important childhood needs! How could we have become so convinced that school is good for children?

## High school: Keeping youth immature

High school is an institution that keeps adolescents imprisoned in a system that:

- Does not allow them to pursue the careers they wish to pursue,

- Nor does it allow them to be active members of the community beyond a menial job or a few hours of "community service".

Although many adolescents are capable of taking college courses or starting their own businesses years before they are released from high school, they are denied these "real world" experiences. Bored and tired of mindless busywork, high school-aged children stay caught up in the negative peer culture that keeps then dependent upon pop culture and preoccupied with immaturity.

## Dangerous intellectually and creatively

*"Everybody in my class thought [my] comic books were really funny, except for one person – my teacher! I remember one teacher who used to rip up my books and tell me I'd better start taking life more seriously, because I couldn't spend the rest of my days making silly books. Fortunately, I wasn't a very good listener... One day my principal took me out of class and said to me, 'I know you think you're special because you can draw, but let me tell you something: artists are a dime-a-dozen. You will never make a living as an artist!' Those words haunted me for many years. How delightful it was to prove him wrong!"*
    *-Dav Pilkey, author and artist of children's books*

*"...Education has become one of the chief obstacles to intelligence and freedom of thought."*
    *-Bertrand Russell, English philosopher, mathemati-*
    *cian, and writer*

*"One had to cram all this stuff into one's mind for the examination, whether one liked it or not. This coercion had such a deterring effect [upon me] that, after I had passed the final examination, I found the considera-tion of any scientific problems distasteful to me for an entire year."    -Albert Einstein*

*"I hated school so intensely. It interfered with my freedom. I avoided the discipline by an elaborate technique of being absent-minded during classes."*
   *-Sigrid Undset, 1928 Nobel Peace award winner*

## Three different learning styles, one teaching style

Humans learn through their senses. Each individual is wired to learn best through a certain sensory channel, or a combination of sensory channels called learning styles. The four learning styles are:

- Visual = watching

- Auditory = listening

- Kinesthetic = doing

- Combination of two

If children are to learn something to the best of their ability, children must learn it through their own learning styles. Most children, especially boys, learn by doing or by a combination of watching and doing. Traditional schools do not accommodate the learning needs of kinesthetic learners, because the very nature of traditional school is to control movement, exploration and sound. Traditional schools teach primarily by lecture and talking, expecting children to listen. Traditional schools sometimes incorporate books and writing on the board, which caters to visual learners who learn by reading. However, this won't work for children who learn by watching someone *do something* – by *watching actions*.

Unfortunately, this auditory and combination of auditory and visual style of teaching only works for some children, usually girls with a lower intensity temperament. For high intensity children, especially boys, who are kinesthetic learners- learners by doing  – there is very little accommodation. Instead, kinesthetic learners who cannot conform to school are labeled as "learning disabled", or as having a brain disorder such as "ADHD" or some other mental illness diagnosis. It is tragic to imagine that your child might be diagnosed as *disabled* and given a brain-altering *drug* simply because he is a very natural kinesthetic learner!

## Eight different types of intelligence and a "one-size-fits-all" school

Children are not stretch gloves; when it comes to learning, it is impossible for one size to fit all! How come schools still try? Happy, curious, energetic, exploring, active children are danger-ous to the smooth, orderly function of an institution that is designed to hold large groups of children in one area, with a low ratio of adults. Any human need that goes outside of the routine of sitting, listening, walking in a line or doing something by the bell or schedule is not likely to be accommodated. When order is the most primary rule, anyone who cannot conform to the way the school operates is a threat to the order. Instead of *accommodating children's needs*, children are expected to *accommodate the school and the teacher's way* of doing things!

It is inconvenient, then, that intelligence is not as simple as regurgitating facts from a school textbook, or pounding out the right answers on a test or parroting back to the teacher the answers she feeds a group of children sitting at desks. It is even more inconvenient to traditional schools that Howard Gardner discovered that there are at least eight different forms of intelli-gence, not just *one* like scholars previously believed!

## The eight intelligences

- Linguistic: The intelligence of reading and writing.
  - Examples: Researchers, writers, scholars, public

speakers, politicians, comedians, radio personalities, attorneys.

- Logical-Mathematical: The intelligence of numbers and math.
  - Mathematicians, scientists, accountants, computer programmers, engineers, business persons.

- Spatial: The intelligence of pictures, images and art.
  - Artists, graphic designers, webmasters, sculptors, art therapists, inventors.

- Bodily-Kinesthetic: The intelligence of the body and hands.
  - Athletes, dancers, actors/actresses, dancers, mechanics, surgeons, carpenters, seamstresses, sculptors, artists, firefighters.

- Musical: The intelligence of music and rhythm.
  - Musicians, singers, DJs, musical therapists, sound mixers, sound engineers.

- Interpersonal: The intelligence of understanding people.
  - Therapists, counselors, social workers, life coaches, salespersons, activists, anthropologists, doctors, spiritual leaders, philosophers.

- Intrapersonal: The intelligence of knowing yourself.
  - Small business owners, entrepreneurs, therapists, counselors, inventors, philosophers, poets, artists.

- Naturalist: The intelligence of the natural environment and natural sciences.
  - Scientists, doctors, veterinarians, naturalists, wild life rescuers, forest rangers, activists, animal caretakers, arborists.

Many people have a combination of two or more intelligences.

## The intelligences that traditional schools recognize

- Linguistic: The intelligence of reading and writing.

- Logical-Mathematical: The intelligence of numbers and math.

Children who are both linguistically and logical-mathematically intelligent are traditional school's most valued students. If your child is primarily artistically, musically, kinesthetically, interpersonally, intrapersonally or naturalistically intelligent, he or she is likely to be labeled "learning disabled", brain disordered ("ADHD") or mentally ill for not being attuned to the two intelligences that traditional schools value.

The children who suffer the most in school are children who learn primarily through the body, through creating, through social relationships and through daydreaming and thinking. These children may have exceptional talents and abilities, yet may still be considered learning disabled, brain disordered or mentally ill because their intelligences are considered to be "hobbies". Their natural intelligences are not recognized or valued as academically "acceptable" by traditional schools, educational evaluators, psychologists, psychiatrists and counselors.

How many mangled, ruined lives have been caused by schools not accepting children's intelligences and learning styles as real and valid? How many children grew up being told that they were "stupid", "incompetent", "disabled" and "failures" simply because they had an intelligence or combination of intelligences that the school did not recognize as "academically acceptable"?

How many potential inventors, artists, writers, musicians, athletes, human and environmental rights activists, philosophers, dreamers, poets, sculptors, veterinarians, comedians, interior

designers, animal sanctuary caretakers and small business owners has the world never known because their school experiences
were traumatic and damaging to their passions, motivations,
ambitions, dreams and self confidence?

What did you want to be when you grew up? Did you follow your
dreams? Why or why not? What about your children? What are
their dreams? What has school been doing to those dreams?
What will school do yet to those dreams? Will your children
become who *they* really dream of being someday?

> "...The force-feeding process [of schooling] is so relent-
> less that many students gag on it. They tune out or
> leave school, and in some cases, become permanently
> soured on learning."      -Wendy Priesnitz, author

## Dangerous to the health and body

> "Schools are physically injurious— for the body, which
> at this early age is inseparable from the soul."
> -Leo Tolstoy, writer and education reformer

It is natural for children to be physically active for most of the
day. It is natural for children's bodies and minds to generate
physical and emotional needs constantly throughout their day.

It is unnatural for growing, developing children to spend the
better part of 14 (or more) years of their lives primarily sitting
still, taking orders and doing boring, tedious paperwork that has
little to do with their real lives and interests.

*It is not the intent of nature for children's bodies to be put in
distress by adults. Children's bodies are not adapted for the*

*chronic physical and emotional stress of adults denying or delaying meeting their needs.* It is not the intent of nature for children to be continually forced to sit with unmet needs, desensitizing themselves to their body's natural signals. Over time, over years, maybe decades into adulthood, the negative affects of the chronic neglect and abuse of the body's natural functions catches up to individuals.

Not only is traditional school developmentally inappropriate and intellectually inadequate, the environment is dangerous to children's health and growing bodies. In traditional public schools and religious private schools, it is common practice for teachers to:

- Regiment or control children's movement, and

- Regiment or control children's bodily functions.

Do you remember our discussion of children's basic physical needs in Chapter 2? We are going to look at how traditional schools cause children physical and emotional distress by ignoring and denying children's most basic physical needs:

## Air

- Children from first grade to 12th grade spend the majority of each weekday confined to the indoors. Although fresh air replenishes the oxygen in the brain, making children better able to learn, children are kept indoors, regardless of how beautiful the weather. Children in the later grades are often not even allowed one outdoor break per day.

## Food

- It is recommended by doctors and dietitians that people eat between six and eight small meals per day to keep blood sugar levels stable and metabolism high. However, in traditional schools, children are not allowed to eat when hungry. Instead, they are only allowed to eat at morning snack time and lunch time. By middle school, snack breaks have usually ended, so older children must go without food from breakfast until noon, with no snack break in the afternoon. When blood sugar is low, brain function, learning, mood and behavior are negatively affected.

## Hydration

- It is recommended by doctors and dietitians that for optimal health, people drink approximately *four glasses of water for every 50 lbs of body weight* per day, depending on individual size and age needs. That means that a 50lb child should drink at least four glasses of water per day and a 200lb youth should drink approximately 16 glasses of water per day! In school, children are lucky if they consume two glasses of liquid all school day. If that liquid is soda, juice or coffee, it is actually dehydrating and doesn't count as a glass of water. Children are taught to ignore their thirst signals and are often not allowed to get a drink of water during class. Dehydration affects brain and body function, learning, mood and behavior negatively.

## Elimination

- This is one of traditional school's best kept secrets: *Children are usually not allowed to go to the bathroom when they feel the need!* In fact, *most teachers view toilet use as a privilege, not a right!* Most teachers in elementary grades have regimented bathroom times when all children are expected to urinate or defecate on schedule. If children need to use the toilet at a time that is not convenient for the teacher, they are likely to be told "no" or told to "wait".

- In middle and high school, children are often not allowed

to go to the bathroom at all during class. They are expected to use the toilet in the three to five minutes between
classes, and also grab books and walk to class. If they are
late, they are often punished. Some high schools lock
school bathrooms or issue a certain number of passes to
children. Some teachers *reward* children who do *not* use
their bathroom passes and *punish* students who cannot
wait to use the toilet!

- Many of the youth that I have worked with over the years
  report to me that they are afraid to drink water during the
  school day because they might have to use the toilet during class. Some youth have told me that they "hold it" all
  school day because they are afraid to ask the teacher to
  use the toilet for fear of being embarrassed in front of the
  class if the teacher says "no". These certainly aren't safe or
  healthy habits! Some youth report being punished with
  detentions for even *asking* to use the toilet!

- Unfortunately, the number of children from kindergarten
  through 12th grade who are forced to sit in pain, wet or
  soil themselves, leave class without permission, urinate in
  trash cans or take other drastic measures is upsetting. I
  call this problem, "forced retention of bodily waste"—forcing children to hold their bodily waste. Forcing children to
  ignore their natural bodily signals and hold poisons in
  their bodies can lead to a long list of urinary and digestive
  health problems. In Part II of this    chapter, we will discuss this subject in more detail, as there is virtually nothing written about the subject anywhere else. I believe parents need the information in order to protect their children's health.

## Warmth/Comfortable temperature

- Many middle and high schools have arbitrary dress codes that restrict youth from wearing clothing that is appropriate to the hot weather. For example, although girls are allowed to wear skirts and sleeveless shirts, boys are not allowed to wear shorts or sleeveless shirts in some middle and high schools. Despite this rule, many older schools do not have air conditioning in the classrooms that could keep children and teachers comfortable.

## Sleep

- School schedules do not respect the biological fact that adolescents naturally fall asleep later at night and wake up late in the morning. Ironically, even though younger children naturally wake up earlier in the morning, school starts later in the morning for the lower grades! At precisely the age when adolescents need to sleep later in the morning, schools expect them to be at school as early as 7:30 a.m.! Late arrivals are usually punished with detentions.

## Physical activity

- It is incomprehensible to me that teachers and school administrators do not realize that children's brains and bodies require constant, frequent, and continuous high energy physical activity all through out the day. Schools cause great distress to children by limiting or completely cutting outdoor play, especially in the middle and high school grades. Schools reportedly do this in order to cram more lecture and paperwork into children, falsely assuming that it will increase their standardized test scores.

- Denying children the primary way they learn- through active, hands-on play and physical activity- is not only

developmentally inappropriate, it is harmful to their education. The restlessness and agitation this causes children
is severe. Children who cannot tolerate the restlessness
and distress of sitting still at desks most of the day are
labeled as learning disabled, brain disordered or mentally
ill and prescribed drugs. Although frequent, high energy
physical play and activity is the best way for children to
learn, traditional schools see active play as a waste of
time. They further demonstrate this view by forcing children to do even more school work *at home*, when children
could be playing!

## Physical affection

- Even young children are expected to function for several
  hours of the day without the physical comfort and affection of their parents and family members. Physical comfort
  and affection regenerates and re-energizes us. Although
  many loving preschool and kindergarten teachers cannot
  help but give hugs and affectionate caresses to the heads
  and faces of little ones, teachers in elementary, middle and
  high school are generally instructed not to touch children.
  Caring teachers fear giving students affectionate pats on
  the back, or a comforting hug or a shoulder rub because
  of sexually abusive teachers who have betrayed the trust
  of children. However, children of all ages, including
  depressed, angry and hurting adolescents who are suffering at home, may crave healthy affection from a special
  teacher.

- Children are also denied affection and playful roughhous-
  ing with peers at school as well, causing school to be a
  place of tactile deadness. Young "lovebirds" are banned
  from holding hands; girls are told to stop braiding one
  another's hair and boys are punished harshly for playfully

wrestling or mutually batting at one another as they laugh. Children become touch-starved during the day, and evidence it with constant attempts at touching, smacking, poking and grabbing at each other for fun or to antagonize others.

## *Physical safety*

- The conditions we have mentioned so far in this chapter certainly do not create an environment of physical safety. Even more shocking is the completely legal practice of teachers, coaches and principals hitting school children with paddles in both public and private schools! In almost half of the 50 states in the USA, mostly in the southern part of the country, teachers, coaches or principals are allowed to assault children by hitting them on the buttocks with a wooden board.

- Children are assaulted for everything from missing basketball shots to talking out loud to fighting. Even more shocking are the laws that protect schools from legal action even when they cause severe injury to children such as bruising, hematomas, pelvic or tailbone fractures, damage to the genitals or internal organs, psychological and sexual damage and severe pain! In fact, Irwin A. Hyman states in *The Case against Spanking* that in Texas, the law states that schools may legally hit children with paddles "up to deadly force"!

- Although people in New England and other non-paddling states are shocked beyond words when they learn that "schools still hit kids", they don't realize that children are often yelled at, insulted, mocked and rough-handled by teachers in non-paddling states and denied use of the toilet. There have been cases of children being verbally harassed in front of peers by teachers or physically attacked by teachers and school staff. In one private school in Massachusetts for children with Autism, developmental disabilities and "behavioral problems", children receive *electric shocks* for noncompliance or for symptoms of their disabilities!

- Sexual exploitation is the most egregious assault that an adult can do to the body and spirit of a child. When school teachers and staff betray the trust, innocence and psychological health of children by using them sexually, one of the most tragic crimes has been committed. Children are vulnerable and helpless in school, even when they are physically larger and stronger than their teachers. Strict rules and force are applied if children break school codes by defying a teacher. Children can be seen as "being in subordination" for questioning a teacher or speaking up for their rights. Sexually abusive teachers and school staff, like sexually abusive parents, take advantage of their powerful positions by trapping children into complying with and keeping quiet about sexual situations.

- Both male and female teachers have sexually assaulted boys and girls of all ages, from preschoolers to 12th graders. Sexual assault can take the form of very inappropriate physical boundary breaking (fondling, inappropriate kissing, sexualized comments to the child), touching of the genitals or breasts or rape.

- School sexual assault commonly takes the form of a school teacher (or staff person) who has taken advantage of an adolescent's developmentally appropriate sexual feelings towards the teacher by engaging in statutory rape ("sex" with a youth under the age of consent). Youth with abusive, traumatic home lives are more likely to be targeted for sexual assault by school teachers and staff.

## Physical comfort

- Schools push children's bodies to the limits by denying their food, hydration, elimination and physical activity needs, forcing them to sit in hard, uncomfortable chairs, remain still for long periods of time, forcing them to stand and walk in lines, restrain their limbs to themselves and even deny them the comfort of touching their peers. Children who feel physically comfortable are more likely to act calmly, feel joyful and exhibit more behavioral and emotional stability.

- Respectful, caring teachers and staff will often bend the rules to allow children the comfort of a fun environment, such as having class or special services outside in warm weather, in the cafeteria, in a circle, on stacks of pillows or in the gym. However, they put themselves at risk when they continually bend the rules in the interests of their students. Besides these few treasured teachers, very little about school is conducive to physical comfort.

## Medical care

- In some schools, children are penalized for illnesses, medical problems and medical and mental health appointments, being forced to make up work or classes for taking care of their physical and mental health.

- How many adults would tolerate doing work on a sick day? Yet children who are recovering from the flu, bronchitis, abdominal pain, chicken pox, broken bones, asthma attacks, migraines or even major surgeries are expected to keep up with their homework—even though they are supposed to be *resting*!

## Dangerous socially and emotionally

*"School days, I believe, are the unhappiest in the whole span of human existence."*
  *-H.L. Mencken, writer and social critic*

*"Even when most people still supported the schools in principle, hundreds of parents...were telling or writing me that most of their worst anxiety dreams were still school dreams, or that every time they went into their children's school, for whatever reason, they could feel their insides tighten up and their hands begin to sweat."   -John Holt, author and educator*

*"Would Eric Harris and Dylan Klebold have become "the monsters next door" (as Time Magazine dubbed them) if they'd had another way to go? At school they were harassed as "dirtbags" and "faggots" and pummeled with bottles and rocks thrown from passing cars. Did they go there because they wanted this abuse? No, we understand perfectly well why they went there: they had no choice in the matter. They "had" to go, compelled by law and social pressure. If they'd had another way to go, they would have disappeared from Columbine long before their only dream became a dream of vengeance and suicide."*
  *-Daniel Quinn, author*

Not only are most traditional school environments harmful to children in the ways mentioned earlier in this chapter, but the toxic peer culture at traditional schools can be emotionally and socially devastating for some children, even deadly.

When children are forced into a situation in which they:

- Have little or no power,

- Are almost totally controlled by adults,

- Are influenced by adults who are abusive, indifferent to their feelings or are neglectful of their needs,

- Are influenced by adults who model disrespect of children,

- Will be punished for trying to assert their needs and wishes,

...children are likely to form an underground peer world that the adults cannot control. This peer world is almost always in the form of cliques, exclusive groups or gangs that are based on having some level of psychological or physical power and control over others. Cliques and exclusive groups are not to be confused with clubs and groups that children form based on mutual interests and friendship— such groups are usually positive, enriching, enjoyable and emotionally fulfilling for all members.

Cliques, exclusive groups and gangs exclude others based on fears, stereotypes, hatreds and prejudices. Traditional schools are where these "Lord of the Flies"-type cliques flourish. Cliques force excluded children to form groups of less powerful youth. Cliques make sure that children in those groups stay in their groups and don't penetrate into the clique or exclusive group. It is almost impossible for teachers or school staff to end or stop these cliques. (In some cases, teachers or a bully's parents even join in on the harassment!) Cliques, exclusive groups and gangs are one of the only ways children can find power in a traditional school setting.

## Why do children harass others?

- They likely have a disrupted parent-child attachment;

- They may be the victims of physical and emotional neglect or physical, sexual and/or emotional abuse at home;

- They may be harassment victims themselves;

- They may be unable to express their emotions in nonviolent ways;

- The adults in their lives have likely passed down prejudices, hatreds, stereotypes, and a lack of compassion for others;

- They may have been influenced by the relentless sarcasm and disrespect they see on TV and in other media;

- They are likely in a situation in which they have very little power over their lives;

- They may have a fragile sense of self;

- They may feel a grandiose sense of self; and

- They may have a lack of empathy and compassion for the suffering of others.

I am surprised and disappointed at the number of parents who are aware that their children are suffering harassment or isolation at school and don't take fierce and serious action to protect their children! Despite being aware that their children suffer torment by peers (and teachers), sometimes for years, they don't remove their children from school.

How many of us would tolerate a work environment where we are shunned and rejected and are called painful names, mocked and laughed at for our clothing, shoes, hair or our looks? How many of us would tolerate being aggressively gossiped about; rumors about us spreading like wildfire amongst our coworkers through whispers, instant messaging, web pages and notes? How many of us would tolerate being targeted at work for cruel pranks designed to destroy us socially and emotionally for the laughs of others? How many of us would tolerate having our weaknesses discovered and deliberately struck with the sword of exposure and verbal battery? What if the harassment was daily, relentless and constant for months or years?

Most emotionally healthy adults would indignantly refuse to be treated so disrespectfully and would likely take legal action or search for another job. However, in the case of children, who are trapped in their school situation like hostages, their parents may tell them:

- "Just ignore them."
- "Just walk away."
- "Tell them nicely to stop."
- "Toughen up."
- "Let it roll off you."
- "Names can't hurt you."
- "You have to learn to deal with it yourself."
- "You must be doing something to annoy or provoke them."
- "If you treat people nicely, they will be nice to you."
- "I'm sure it's just a misunderstanding."

Many schools have "anti-bullying" policies that put them in compliance with the law. However, when text messages can spread cruel rumors to an entire school with the press of a cell phone button, punishing a few students has almost no positive effect and can even inflame the harassment.

Despite the fact that many of the infamous school shootings of the past several years were a result of children who endured severe harassment at school, many teachers, parents, professionals and authors still refer to peer harassment as "teasing". The word "teasing" belittles the pain and humiliation that harassment victims feel and the seriousness of the actions. Words like "teasing" and even "bullying" make peer harassment sound like a normal part of growing up. It isn't. Verbal harassment can escalate to physical violence at any time. It is deeply emotionally and socially harmful to children and can cause lifelong damage to a person.

### Why are certain children singled out?

Young people are singled out for endless reasons in public school, most having to do with whether or not an individual is considered "cool" or powerful. Here are some common, specific reasons why harassers target peers for harassment... Harassers target the victim for:

- Not having the "right" clothes,

- Not having the "right" brand clothes,

- Not wearing the "right" clothes the "right" way,

- Not having the "right" hair cut,

- Not having the "right" material possessions (cell phone, video game system, MP3 player, car, bike, trading cards, toys, etc.),

- Liking the "wrong" type of music,

- Liking the "wrong" music group/artist,

- Appearing "too smart",

- Appearing too "weird", too different or too unique,

- Not being a "jock" or "preppie",

- Not being wealthy,

- Being of a younger age or lower grade in school,

- Belonging to a certain group,

- Being shy or isolated,

- Being wild, creative, "hyperactive" and spirited,

- Being witty and intelligent,

- Being overweight,

- Being underweight,

- Being seen as unattractive,

- Delayed puberty,

- Premature puberty,

- Not being "tough" enough,

- Being of a different race or culture than the dominant demographic of the school,

- Not having a girlfriend or boyfriend,

- Being perceived as "gay",

- Being bisexual, gay or transgendered,

- Being seen with the "wrong" person,

- Being a virgin,

- Refusing to try substances,

- Being seen being nurtured by parents in public,

- Not being rebellious enough,

- Etc...

Being treated in this manner is detrimental to the spirit and heart of children. Peer and adult harassment has the effect of rejecting, shaming, humiliating and hurting the very being of children, causing them to feel worthless, ugly, defective, rageful, anxious, depressed, self-hating and helpless.

*Harassment has tragically driven many targeted and tormented children to seek escape by fantasizing about, attempting or actually committing suicide and homicide. It is incomprehensible to me that children's lives are being tragically cut short because "going to school" is considered more of a necessity in our culture than protecting children!* Harassment by peers and by adults is no laughing matter!

## Harassment is detrimental to harassers and bystanders, too

Harassment is also detrimental to the young people who harass others and to the bystanders who watch the harassment and laugh but do not comfort or advocate for the victims. Harassers dehumanize people and desensitize themselves to the suffering of others. Their illusion of power is only aggression, not a strong, positive, internal sense of confidence. Bystanders who fail to comfort or advocate for victims are learning to deaden their compassion and empathy for others... For both harassers and bystanders, healthy spiritual and moral development becomes stunted.

Is your child the victim of peer harassment? It is important that we take action as our children's protectors and voices. In a traditional school setting, children are very limited in how they can advocate for themselves. Despite the increased attention to the problem by the media and despite statements by school officials that they "have a no-tolerance policy for bullying", most schools do *not* take children's complaints about harassment seriously enough without an adult's intervention. If schools do take the issue seriously, attempts at school to "peer mediate" or suspend harassers tends to spread the harassment like a virus. Unfortunately, often the only way severe harassment will cease is when parents and their children take legal action against the most prominent harassers or when the victim leaves the school.

If your child is repeatedly a target of harassment, are there any unmet needs that your child needs you to help fulfill? Is the parent-child attachment secure? If your child lacks confidence and assertiveness, it is possible that your child has unmet emotional needs. You can start the repair process by being a strong and supportive advocate for your child by taking serious action and removing your child from the school.

Is your child bullying and harassing others? This is a sign of a child who is suffering serious unmet needs and likely a disrupted parent-child attachment. It is vital that you decode what your child needs and then do your best to make sure those needs are met. Your child has closed herself down to her sense of compassion and empathy for others. As parents, it is our responsibility to help our children learn and reconnect with their natural sense of compassion and empathy. Children cannot learn empathy and compassion unless their parents show empathy and compassion *to them* and to other people.

Lastly, what media influences are exacerbating the problem? If your child watches TV, plays violent video games, hangs out online and becomes preoccupied with pop culture, he will find plenty of sarcastic, apathetic role models for treating people in disrespectful ways.

Is your child a bystander who laughs along and fails to comfort the victim? Your child may fear becoming the target of harassment unless he laughs, joins in or walks away. She may feel that her social status would be in jeopardy if she was seen comforting the victim or taking the victim to get help later on. Instilling a moral and spiritual responsibility in our children to respect all people and to help or comfort people in need is our responsibility as parents. Unfortunately, cultivating in our children empathy and compassion for others and a responsibility to protect and help others is severely lacking in our culture. Most importantly, children cannot develop empathy, compassion and a healthy moral and spiritual sense of helping others unless *they* are treated with empathy, compassion and tenderness.

### *Prevention doesn't require more programs*

Preventing peer harassment doesn't require more programs and tougher punishment... *more of the same will give us more of the same*. Preventing peer harassment requires us as parents to:

- Meet our children's needs,

- Prioritize secure parent-child attachment,

- Cultivate empathy and compassion for others,

- Model a strong spiritual and moral duty to helping and respecting all people,

- Model and show that disrespecting others is unacceptable to you,

- Find alternatives to traditional school to prevent children from being forced to form cliques, exclusive groups and gangs because they lack power over themselves and their lives, and

- Find alternatives to traditional school to prevent your child from being forced to conform to cliques and exclusive groups to avoid harassment.

For information about youth sub-cultures, please see the section, "When angst becomes a sub-culture" in Chapter 10.

## A word to the "gem" teachers

Most of us remember you: You are those few special teachers who make traditional school livable, tolerable and fun. You are the teachers who think that the most important classroom rules are *mutual* respect between teacher and students, making kids laugh and having fun. You don't yell, don't punish, don't enforce arbitrary rules and you don't have adult temper tantrums when your students challenge your authority.

You are the teachers who love to get children involved with playing, exploring and thinking on a deep level. You are the teachers who take time to discover the passions of your individual students. You care for all of your students, even (and especially so) those most offensive to you.

You are the teachers who buck the system, advocate for your students, take students under your wing and genuinely care about their lives and needs beyond the curriculum. You are the teachers who always give bathroom and water fountain passes, you look the other way when students sneak a snack and you are light on kids who horseplay because you understand that children don't leave their living, breathing, needy bodies at the door to the school. You step in to spare students from punishment and you even put your job on the line to stand up for justice.

You are the teachers who entered the field because you truly love children. You are "gem" teachers. You are probably too humble to even *know* that you are "gems"; that's what makes you a gem.

This chapter does not negate the wonders that you have done and do; in fact, it is you who make it possible for children to pass through their school prison sentences with a sense of humanity, inspiration, fondness, connection and affection. In other words, a relationship with you makes school worth the tedium and heartache.

Although as gems you probably wouldn't want to abandon your students, your talents would be better suited by fighting for the right of children to play and learn in freedom. I challenge you to read former New York City high school teacher, John Taylor Gatto's books and other books listed in Chapter 12. I challenge you to consider using your insight and knowledge of the "inside" workings of traditional schools to educate parents, community members, law makers and other teachers about the need for alternatives to traditional schooling.

## Alternatives to traditional school

It is impossible for children's development to meet natural, optimal levels if they spend 14 years in an institution that treats them like prisoners. As parents, it is our responsibility to provide the best learning environment possible for our children within our means and circumstances. We will discuss alternatives to traditional school in greater depth in Chapter 11. Here is a brief preview of what alternatives are available:

- Unschooling (child-directed curriculum)
- Homeschooling
- Democratic schools
- Montessori schools
- Waldorf schools

- Other non-traditional private schools
- Charter schools
- Early college
- Internet correspondence schools
- Independent study at a traditional school
- Part-time attendance at a traditional school

# Chapter 6 Part II

# Schooling—More About Dangers to Health and the Body

*"Traditional school schedules... reflect our culture's denial of the needs of the human body. An examination of these schedules is likely to uncover rigid toileting schedules in lower grades and only short breaks allotted between classes in upper grades."*

  *-Cheryle B. Gartley, President, Simon Foundation for Continence*

*"The denial of bodily functions is so deeply ingrained in our culture that it is actually possible for people to be cruelly unsympathetic about the need to use a toilet, even though they have probably been in similar situations themselves."*

  *-Rebecca Chalker and Kristene E. Whitmore, M.D., authors, Overcoming Bladder Disorders*

*"Do not be surprised if the school seems more intent on shielding an abusive, incompetent teacher than in protecting children who are under the control of that teacher."*    *-Jordan Riak, child advocate*

# Protections for adult workers, not for school children

Using the toilet in traditional schools is often viewed as a *privilege*, not as a basic need or a right. Unfortunately, even though this problem is very common in schools, pediatricians, urologists, gastroenterologists, social workers and the media have done very little to protect children.

Occupational Safety and Health Administration (OSHA) codes protect adult workers, including teachers, from their bosses denying them the right to use the toilet. OSHA and other human rights organizations such as Amnesty International, believe that denying a person use of the toilet when they need to use it is a human rights violation.

Unfortunately, children have no political voice and they rarely tell their parents about this embarrassing problem, so most school teachers are able to neglect children's basic needs without legal consequences. In fact, in some books and teachers' websites, teachers *brag* about delaying and denying children's use of the toilet and list doing so as a good classroom management "tool"! Here are some web quotes from teachers:

**Teachnet.com** "Classroom management "How-to" tips":

- "I never let a student go to the bathroom when they ask".

- "If they need to use the bathroom, sharpen pencils, etc. during class, they need to give me a card. When all three cards are gone, they lose a recess for every time they need one of those things. It allows for three 'emergencies' a week".

- One teacher requires that children must pay "five dollars" to use the toilet and water fountain unless they bring in "doctors notes". She also suggests docking recess time for time spent using the toilet and water fountain!

- "Our school has a really good policy regarding bathroom use and passes in general. At the beginning of the school year, each student is given a handbook that has 2 pages for passes... One page is for 1st semester and the other page is for 2nd semester. There are roughly 20-25 slots for each semester. In order to get out of class, to go use the restroom, go to their locker, library, etc., they must have this handbook. If they don't have it, then they can't go. It's as simple as that. If they fill up their 1st semester side in the first quarter, then they aren't allowed any passes the second quarter. If the student loses his or her book, they have to buy a new book. Ours cost $5 each. The office staff will then pro-rate the number of passes they have left depending on the number of weeks left in the semester. If a student is caught tampering with his or her book or gets caught using another student's books, then they lose all passes for the remainder of the semester."

**EducationWorld.com** "Where educators go to learn":

- One teacher gives students "two bathroom passes" per term. She adds, "They may use them when the need arises, but get no more chances after the passes are gone".

**NEA.org** "Works for Me Tips Library":

- This teacher wrote that her students are "only allowed two passes every nine weeks and if they want to leave the room, they are required to use one of these passes... The students who choose to stay in class receive five extra credit points per pass not used."

- Another states, "...Each of my students may only have three passes every nine weeks. Each time they use a pass, I mark it on the list next to their name. After their third pass, they need to make up ten minutes of class during their lunch period."

The law protects adults from abuses like those listed. OSHA would never tolerate employer policies that stated that workers could only use the toilet for "three emergencies a week" and two visits per term. OSHA would say it is illegal for workers to be made to submit "doctor's notes" or pay bosses "five dollars" in order to use the toilet!

However, school children of *all* ages, in *all* grades have been forced to...

- Retain bodily waste to the point of pain,

- Wet and soil themselves,

- Attend school diapered,

- Urinate outside, in the stairwells, in bottles or in school garbage cans, and

- Accept punishments for using the toilet without permission

...because they weren't allowed the right to use the toilet when they felt the need!

In 2003, I struck up a conversation with a 13-year old boy who recalled an incident in the 6th grade when he needed to use the bathroom and was forced against his will to remain in the classroom:

"The teachers in my school won't let you go to the bathroom. Even at lunch time, if you ask to go to the bathroom, they say, "finish your lunch first". And then, after all that, you still have to sign out to go! It's hard to explain, but there are a couple of nice teachers that let you go in class when they are sitting at their desk and aren't explaining something. Last year, I had Mrs.___

who is wicked strict. One time I had to go to the bathroom really bad... I raised my hand and asked her nicely, 'can I please go to the bathroom, I really have to go', but she said no. I waited like five minutes and raised my hand again, 'I really have to go to the bathroom!' She said no again! Finally, after 15 more minutes, I was ready to pee my pants, and I raised my hand and asked again. She said no, and I said, "I'm going to piss myself!" She says, "That's really inappropriate!" and I said, 'Well, I'm going to piss myself if you don't let me go! I HAVE TO GO TO THE BATHROOM!' She made me go sit in the corner at another desk, *but wouldn't let me go to the bathroom*! After like a few more minutes, I got up, got my stuff, and she's like, "where do you think you're going?" and I just said, 'I'm outta here'... and I walked out."

## Medical risks

Forcing children to "hold it" is not in line with educational goals. Remember Abraham Maslow's "hierarchy of human needs" in Chapter 2? He stated that unless the basic needs of the body are met, the child can't function optimally on higher levels tasks.

Forcing children to retain their waste is also not in line with medical advice: Medical professionals recommend that people should drink several glasses of water per day, empty the bladder frequently, and empty the bowels when the need first arises.

There are serious health risks involved when children are forced to retain their waste.

Risks to the urinary system include:

- Urinary incontinence/Enuresis
- Urinary tract infection
- Overextension of the bladder muscle
- Weakening of the brain-bladder signals
- Incomplete voiding and frequency
- Bladder contracting against closed sphincter
- Urinary reflux
- Kidney failure

Risks to the digestive system include:

- Constipation
- Stool impaction
- Encopresis (bowel incontinence)
- Weakening of the brain-bowel signals
- Bowel obstruction

For more detailed information about these health risks and medical resources, please see Appendix C.


## Parents speak out!

The most active section of my website, ChildAdvocate.org, is the *Denial of Toilet Use at School* section, which offers parents information about health risks as well as actions they can take to protect their children. The section also offers families resources and a voice to tell the world about how teachers are abusing their power over children by forcing them to retain waste. Below are a sampling of the letters I have received from parents of children who have suffered this form of pain and humiliation at school (If you wish to skip reading the letters, please go on to Chapter 7):


*April 29, 2005 (Louisiana, USA)*
"Throughout my school years I can remember a couple of teachers who would not let anyone use the restroom. I guess it was not that big of a deal to me until today. I picked up my four year old son from pre-K and he told me that he had an accident. I thought that maybe [it happened] while he took a nap, and I told him that it was ok. That's when he told me what happened. He said that he was at recess and told the teacher that he had to use the bathroom and she said, "oh well". He said that he could not hold it in anymore and he used the bathroom on himself. The teacher then asked him if he went in his pants and he said "yes". She responded "oh well" again. She did not call me to get dry clothes. My embarrassed four-year old walked around school for three hours with wet pants."


*May 18, 2005 (California, USA)*
"My son goes to a private school in __, CA. He is in kindergarten.

He's at school from 8am to 3pm. The school has a bathroom policy for every grade K-8. Punishment varies from grade to grade. My son's class policy is that they can only go to the bathroom during recess or lunch time. If they go during class time their name will be written on the 'sad board' (your name is written on the 'sad board' if you did something wrong). I found out about this bathroom policy late last year because my son's name was put on the sad board. He told me that he went to the bathroom during class time so his name was put on the sad board. My son was upset and I was upset because I didn't think this was right. I spoke to the teacher about it and she said that they have to teach them 'bathroom discipline' so that it didn't interrupt the class...

Last week my [other] son was put on detention after school for the same reason. He used the bathroom during music class... I called the principal and told her this needs to stop. I couldn't get her to agree to change the policy or just get rid of it. So, I called my sons' doctor... She wrote me a note to give to the school. The bathroom rule is still in force for the rest of the children. Because of the actions I have taken this became a little war between me and the school. I don't know what else to do. I just want them to stop this bathroom policy."


*September 9, 2005 (Florida, USA)*
"My five year old daughter started going to kindergarten a few weeks ago. One day she had to use the toilet during nap time and the teacher would not allow it. Being a shy, conforming child, she obeyed the order and had to "hold it in" until she came home. She is five. I and my husband were outraged. I asked the teacher and she said that she could not allow it because "if she gets up then everybody gets up." She said they were supposed to use the toilet BEFORE the nap time. My daughter explained to

me that there were too many people in front of her in line that she did not get to use it then (23 kids in the class, ONE toilet). I had told my daughter that under no circumstances will she "hold it" again. My instruction is, if she has to go she will go ahead use the bathroom no matter what... I cannot believe a teacher could do this to a young child and justify it as if it was a right thing to do. I was born in Asia where we had very strict rules in schools growing up. However, I had never heard of or encountered such inhumane treatment to a child. I still cannot believe this is happening in the "freest" country in the world. In the US we would fight for 'humane rights' for people in other countries. We would fight for animal rights and send someone to jail for failing to feed their goldfish on vacation and we would deny our children of basic need of voiding the body waste? What is going on???"

*August 28, 2006 (Colorado, USA)*
"I would like to thank you so much for your website. Our family knows now that we are not alone in this battle. I wish I had access to this information ten years ago. My daughter was born with vesicoureteral reflux. We spent the first year of her life in and out of the hospital with incredibly high fevers and UTI's until the doctors felt she could undergo the surgery to correct the problem. Even after that the pediatrician told me that she would always be susceptible to UTI's...

On her first day of kindergarten she had an accident at school. Being a young mother, I had no idea that children would be restricted from using the bathroom... I didn't even think to ask about it. After that, and the years since (she's in 8th grade now) I have sent letters requesting that she not be restricted from using the restroom whenever she needs to...and without punish-ment. There have been more than a few times when I have had to come in and talk to a stubborn teacher who refused to understand. And this is with a child who has a medical condition. I always felt for the students who could not get a note from a doctor.... This was the case for my son.

Due to what I went through with my daughter I felt my son deserved the same dignity. Year after year I sent the same note, minus the medical reason, but loaded down with many of the same facts that you go over on your website. I have never had a problem with it until this year. His new teacher stubbornly refuses to allow my son to use the bathroom. The teacher tells me that the students are allowed to go at first recess; they have five minutes before lunch and recess after lunch. When I sent my yearly letter he informed me that after discussing his policy with the principal and the school nurse they are backing the teacher. I am going to a meeting this Friday with the teacher, principal and the school nurse and I am coming in armed to the teeth with all of the information and sources you have provided on your website. I feel more than confidant that my son, and most likely the entire student population, will be rid of this archaic 'rule' thanks to all the hard work you do."


*April 29, 2004 (Wisconsin, USA)*
"Please help. I have a seven year old son who was denied the right to use the bathroom. He ended up wetting himself. As a mother and a nurse, I am absolutely sickened this would ever happen. I have spoken with this teacher as well as the principal. Not effective. This teacher's policy is that a first grade child has to pay tickets to use the bathroom. My son didn't have any tickets so she wouldn't allow him to go. In my conversations with her she makes herself very clear that she isn't willing to change her "policy"... After I did confront her on this, she announced the situation to her entire class. Her statement was, "I'm not saying

any names, but someone wet their pants in class. You will still be paying me five tickets to use the bathroom"... If someone needs to use the bathroom, they need to use the bathroom. Not only do I have medical concerns, I have dignity and respect concerns. No one should be denied the right to use the bathroom..."

*April 17, 2001 (Oregon, USA)*
"My eight year old son was punished for using the bathroom during class time. He was made to write his name on the blackboard under a frowning face and then had to miss five minutes of recess time, during which he had to sit at his desk with his head down. The teacher refuses to call this a punishment. He claims my son is paying back "time" that he used to go to the bathroom. The principal believes it is the teacher's right to do this and the superintendent is backing him up. We are heading to an executive session with the school board to discuss the matter. I removed my son from that school and placed him in another district, where he is not punished for a bodily function. I am so angry that other children are still being punished in that classroom and I am working towards change, but it is hard."

*April 29, 2003 (California, USA)*
"My son is in a private Christian school in Los Angles, California in fourth grade. He lost his [right] to use the restroom, due to turning the lights off one day during recess... I have a meeting today with the principal and I have a doctor's note on file not to restrict his bathroom rights. The teacher is in disagreement with the doctor and has called this meeting to once again stop his rights to use the bathroom. He has a severe rash on his groin and has developed shingles, from possible result of stress from this teacher. Please help us! I know our children have rights I just do not know who to turn to?"

*April 5, 2007 (Oklahoma, USA)*
"My fifth grade grandchild attends ___ Middle School in ___, OK. She is prone to kidney infections, and has a family history of kidney stones and what used to be called Bright's disease. She was refused bathroom use even though she held it until her work was complete. I have had nothing but problems with this school all year and am now angry and fed up. The state department of education is absolutely no help. I am going to talk with the teacher, the principal and the superintendent and am also talking to her pediatrician. I do intend to take legal action if it happens again."

*October 20, 2006 (Florida, USA)*
"I have three children in ___ county, FL schools, and they lock the bathrooms. Just today I received a call from my oldest, 6th grade, that he had an accident in his pants. He was denied the use of the restroom. The teacher stated he didn't have a key, and that he would have to wait. I was outraged! Not only is it inhumane to deny a child the use of the restroom, but completely humiliating and traumatizing for a child to go through. And this is not the first incident. My younger two in elementary are rewarded for not using the restroom all day. My youngest, second grade... comes home with stomach cramps and has bowl problems because of it.

Teachers actually guard the drinking fountains and restrooms during class changes and dismissals, denying children to use them. I had witnessed this myself while picking up my son one day. We had walked past the teacher to get a drink when I was told we were not allowed (we got a drink anyway)! During this time a young boy, holding himself, asked if he could go to the bathroom. She simply stated, 'they're locked'... The school's explanation is its a "safety issue". Something needs to be done about this.."

*January 29, 2005 (South Carolina, USA)*
"My twelve year old son just received a suspension (all day), for using the restroom. His locker is directly across the hall from the restroom, and he had a locker pass, so after he was finished at his locker he quickly went into the restroom, as he stated he just couldn't hold it any longer. When I learned he was being punished for this, I went to the school and spoke with the Assistant Principal, and she was very annoyed with us for my refusing to allow my son be in ISS all day when that is not a behavioral issue, nor a reason to be punished. She demanded that he do it anyway, and I said absolutely not, that if that's the case he will go home with me. Now it is a truant day as I took him out of school, and they marked it as OSS [out of school suspension]. What can be done about this?"

*April 6, 2005 (Kentucky, USA)*
"I was wondering if maybe you can help us. My son is 12 years old and denied toilet use at school about a month ago. He wet his pants— he could not hold it any longer. We did not get a call from the school all day... We found out when he came home from school and had on different clothes. When I asked what happened to his clothes and he told us what happened we were very upset. We called the school. My husband had words and the teacher said it would not happen again. Well yesterday, my son asked to go to the rest room and the same teacher told him no! My son got mad, then the teacher told him to go ahead or 'you will wet in your pants like the last time' and then the teacher started laughing. This should not be accepted at ANY SCHOOL.

What can we do or where do we go to get this matter under control? "


*August 9, 2005 (Tennessee, USA)*

"I wanted to tell you that I found your website after my child had been denied the right to go to the bathroom today at school. This was the first day of school and my son asked the teacher if he could go to the bathroom. The teacher said he 'only let girls go since their bathroom was close to the room'. After about 20 minutes, my son could not hold it any more and started to have an accident... The teacher finally gave him a pass to go to the restroom. My son had to go search the restroom down and in the process wet his pants.

He is 12 years old and in 7th grade, first day in this middle school. No one showed them the bathrooms in orientation! He then went to the office, very embarrassed... They sent him to the guidance counselor's office, and he called me in tears. I went to get him and after the principal apologized and said it never should have happened, I said that I don't know if we will be back. I then went to the school board and requested that he be allowed to go to another zone for school. I spoke with the super-intendent. He also apologized and to me and to my son. We went and enrolled in another school this afternoon. I can't believe this is allowed to go on in the school system. I feel that it is a form of child abuse!"


*March 4, 2002 (Texas, USA)*

"...Our school district is threatening expulsion of my 13-year-old daughter because she left the classroom without permission to go to the bathroom. She asked permission from the teacher, who told her to "hold it". Five minutes later, my daughter asked again because she could no longer wait to visit the bathroom... The teacher refused to allow her to leave, but my daughter left anyway and went to the bathroom. The teacher has punished her with a detention for leaving to use the bathroom.

We will not allow her to be punished for this, so the school has stated that they will give her two days of detention. Further, they stated that, should we not allow her to serve the "double detention", they will elevate the punishment to an in-school suspension, and will expel her if she does not attend the in-school suspension. We are steadfast in our belief that our daughter should not be punished, much less suspended from school, for taking action in her own best interests when the teacher would not. We can not bring ourselves to give in to pressure from the school to allow our daughter to be punished for something they have no right to punish her for..."

*November 18, 2003 (Florida, USA)*
"... My [13 year old] son is in the middle of expulsion from a public school after relieving himself in a corner of the classroom. This was done is secrecy and humiliated my son, because he was not permitted to go to the bathroom. He requested several times; witnesses state at least three and up to six requests were made. I would love to get something into law that will give our children the same rights that OSHA has given adults. It is illegal for an employer to deny an adult the right to use the bathroom...."

*October 23, 2004 (North Carolina, USA)*
"...My 14 year old freshman daughter has just been given one

day of in-school suspension at __ High School. She repeatedly asked a first year male teacher, 'please, please, let me now go to the bathroom'. The teacher requested that she wait 10 minutes, she did, and then asked again. She was again told "no". She knew that she had started her period. She finally became so panicked that she told the teacher she had started her period and her parents would sue if she was not allowed to leave. She then left the room knowing she was about to have blood all over her bare legs. They have suspended her for being disrespectful. This is a straight "A" student for the most part [and she] has never... had any type of behavior issues..."

*Follow up letter 11/3/04:*
"...I have copied & pasted much information from [your] website and forwarded it to the numerous parents I have received phone calls from (after an article was printed in our local newspaper) whose children also have been denied this basic human right at this same school. One mother told me her daughter came home covered in blood after a teacher refused to allow her to leave class to go to the bathroom. Another parent told me her son was told by this same teacher to 'pee on the floor, he would be the one cleaning it up'.

Many parents have made their way around this issue by having their physician write a note to allow the student to always be allowed to leave the room to use the bathroom. This has worked well but is not the solution. Parents are astonished as to the amount of information I have been able to provide them... The response from 'going public' with the news article has been only positive to my daughter. She has been interviewed for her school newspaper article about this subject. 'Going public' was a leap for our family to take; my daughter realizes how many other students she has helped and also that we as parents value her and her rights... I am forever changed by this incident and will never stop advocating the rights of all children/students to never be denied this basic human right... "

*August 24, 2004 (Florida, USA)*
"I have a 14 year old boy who was forced to hold bodily waste by school officials in the state of Florida to try and force him to confess to allegations against him. They locked him in a room for two hours and wouldn't let him relieve himself until he confessed. To me this is a form of torture- something you would have seen in Nazi Germany, not Florida. He never confessed because he didn't do anything. When he finally got to a phone to call me, boy, were they mad at him because they knew when I got there I would put a stop to him being tortured... When I met the school board here one of the things I complained about was the maltreatment of my son. The school official who had done this quite proudly admitted his doing so to the board. The school board didn't care. They claim its common practice to use this form of torture on children here in Florida... How can schools get away with it?"

*January 2, 2003 (Massachusetts, USA)*
"My [high school-aged] daughter was recently denied use of the restroom at her school after a 90 minute testing block. My daughter, after taking her test, asked to use the restroom and told the teacher she was menstruating and needed to change. The teacher gave her the choice of taking a tardy. She had worked very hard for over a quarter not to receive any more tardies, as another tardy would lead to a Saturday school or ISS. I think this is simply abhorrent that a person has to make a decision like this. It simply should not be legal. Who is protecting our

students? The schools care about their rules and not about the individual students… The School Board protects their principals, the principals protects their teachers and so on. Who protects the students?"

*September 7, 2005 (New York, USA)*
"I live in New York State and today my child had her first day as a sophomore in high school. This evening she presented me with a printed page of three bathroom passes that were provided to each student in her Earth Science class and explained their use. Each child is given three free bathroom passes per month. They do have opportunities to earn more but, more importantly, if the passes are not used during the month they can be turned in and the child will receive an extra point on their grade… My child also informed me that she… will purposely not drink anything the whole day because using the bathroom is such a problem in all classes. She explained that each of her new teachers gave their own bathroom use policy and one just plainly said that they need to schedule their bathroom issues for any time other than his class and that if they left his class for any reason that they would be required to come back after the school day had ended to make the time up doubled. This was her chorus class!!!"

*February 11, 2003 (Texas, USA)*
"I'm writing in regards to your article about abuse in schools. The one that caught my attention was denying the use of the lavatory. My son is currently involved in just such an issue. My son is 16 years old and a junior in high school. He asked his teacher if he could go to the bathroom. She told him no. He continues to ask her several more times stressing that it was an

emergency, and she denied him. He told her that he felt like he was about to wet his pants and she again denied him. He told her that it was causing him pain from trying to hold it. She said no. He got up to go to the bathroom and she physically barred his way by standing in the doorway. He told her that he wasn't going to wet his pants and would rather go in a bottle that was in the waste basket. She told him to go right ahead but that he wasn't going anywhere. So he took the bottle from the trash, went to a corner and turned his back and urinated in the bottle. I was notified two days later by the principal. I was told that the teacher will only be getting a warning put in her file, whereas my son was punished for 3 weeks for his own abuse. My son is the victim here but is getting treated like the culprit... My son has been withdrawn from public school and placed in an alternative school."

*March 8, 2004 (Ohio, USA)*
"... My daughter has already served a three-day suspension from her high school for an unauthorized bathroom visit. She asked her teacher for permission to go and was denied. She explained to the teacher that she couldn't hold it and really needed to go and was still denied permission. Thank goodness that my daughter was strong enough and had enough courage to stand up for herself. She walked out of class and went to the bathroom and was given a three-day suspension. When the vice-principal brought my daughter in to talk to her the next day, she proceeded to call my daughter "immature" because she "couldn't hold it" and then accused her of lying about her whereabouts when she was told to go to the office. My daughter felt completely humiliated, simply because she had to use the bathroom...

I never in my wildest dreams thought I would need to get a note from my daughter's doctor stating that she should be excused when the need arises. It is pitiful what they put our children through... I, in fact, did appeal her suspension to the principal and the superintendent's office and both times it was upheld. I now have to appeal to the Board of Education next week. The interesting part about this rule is that it's not in the Student/Parent Handbook... I think that if all the parents at the school actually knew about the rule, they would be as outraged as I was. I gave both of my daughters permission to break that rule when they told me about it at the beginning of the school year. I knew there would be consequences for my daughter's actions, but hey, someone has to stand up and fight back."

*February 17, 2004 (New Jersey, USA)*
"My child who is in tenth grade in a New Jersey high school was given a pass in the beginning of semester as was every child, they were told [that if] for any reason it becomes lost or used up they are to be denied bathroom usage. He left it home one day and his teacher refused him the use of the bathroom. As his mom, I told him to excuse himself and go to the bathroom, not to ever hold it in (I had this experience myself in junior high about 17 yrs prior, so I know the scar of urinating on yourself in front of your classmates. I'm now in my 40's and still remember like it was yesterday). Well, he left the room, went to the bathroom and has received detention.

Tell me who has the right to limit the use of bathroom? [When they are young] children we teach them whenever you need to go, not to hold it in or you could have problems; now as pre-adults the schools systems are telling them, 'no you can not go unless I say so'. We want them to grow up with respect but, they get no respect back. That is why they carry such anger towards superiors... I hope that people start to help all children in this and any other unfair problems that arrive within our nation's schools. Our high school has 80 min classes and they want them to hold it in for that length of time. How UNFAIR."


*January 25, 2006 (Oregon, USA)*

"I have a daughter who is 17 years of age and in high school. She is only being allowed to use the restroom as follows: At the beginning of the year she is given two "potty passes" for the next six weeks. If she does not have any unexcused absences or unexcused tardies she is given one more pass for the next six weeks... After meeting with the vice-principal and the teacher I was told that my daughter is lucky because many other teachers have a much stricter policy. I am appalled, as both of my employers both happen to be civil rights attorneys. I took both of them to the meeting with me, as my daughter's legal representation.

This meeting was a waste of time. The school will not change the teacher's policy. The vice-principal told my daughter that if it was an emergency and she didn't have a pass, to just walk out of the teacher's classroom..., go to the bathroom and then go to his office. He would decide if it was the appropriate action... But this leaves it open for him to also punish her if he feels otherwise. Therefore, we came to no conclusion. That same night I called my local television station and we were on the news. I have also contacted the local newspapers and have an interview set up. My daughter went back to school today and students have come up to her telling her their experiences. I want this heinous abuse stopped and stopped now!"

*September 2, 2006 (Mississippi, USA)*
"My 17 year old son asked to go to the restroom at school four times during a class. When he was not allowed to go, he left class & went. The assistant principal called today to notify me my son would be suspended for one day for leaving class without permission..."

*To read more letters, as well as stories that have reached the media, please visit: www.childadvocate.org.*

# Chapter 7
# How Our Everyday Life Causes Emotional and Behavioral Problems

"In the Babemba tribe of South Africa, when a person acts irresponsibly or unjustly, he is placed in the center of the village, alone and unfettered. All work ceases, and every man, woman, and child in the village gathers in a large circle around the accused individual. Then each person in the tribe speaks to the accused, one at a time, each recalling the good things the person in the center of the circle has done in his lifetime. Every incident, every experience that can be recalled with any detail and accuracy, is recounted. All his positive attributes, good deeds, strengths, and kindnesses are recited carefully and at length. This tribal ceremony often lasts for several days. At the end, the tribal circle is broken, a joyous celebration takes place, the person is symbolically and literally welcomed back into the tribe."

- Jack Kornfield, author of The Art of Forgiveness, Lovingkindness, and Peace

Constantly, we as parents are conditioned to accept and live with so many beliefs, trends, habits, routines and practices that seem harmless but are actually harmful to our children's natural development. It is important that we, as parents, consider whether it is worth the potential harm to our children's development and to the parent-child attachment to continue to expose them to things in our culture that have been shown to be detrimental to children.

Let's discuss some of the attitudes, habits, routines, trends and practices in our culture that "everyone" seems to accept, but that can be harmful to our children and the parent-child attachment.

## How we view children

Historically, children have been, and are still, the most oppressed, exploited and victimized group of human beings on the planet. Children remain the most voiceless and the most discriminated against group of people in our culture. While every adult group in the United States has won basic human rights protections and freedoms, children remain the only group of human beings without the same rights to equality, respect, protection from bodily harm and freedom of speech.

If you are having difficulty believing this, ask yourself these questions:

- Why are children the only people in the United States and England that it is legal to hit?

- When your children make a mistake, do you respond to them the way you would respond to an adult?

- When we talk about hitting children, why do we use candy-coated words like "spanking" and "smacking" instead of the words "hitting" and "assault"?

- Do you speak to your children with the same respect that you would speak to an adult friend?

- Do you speak to your children with the same respect that you would speak to someone you are trying to impress?

- We are paid to go to work and we choose to work. Why are children forced against their will to go to school?

- When we are done work, our time is ours. Most of us are paid when we must take work home. Why are children forced to do homework on their own time?

- Why are children's basic physical, emotional and developmental needs not a priority in schools? Would you tolerate a boss or spouse telling you that you weren't allowed to go to the bathroom?

- As adult consumers, if we are unsatisfied with a service, we can "fire" the provider or take our business elsewhere. Why can't children, as the consumers in school, fire boring, punitive, cruel and uncaring teachers or "take their business elsewhere" at their will?

- Why are *children* removed from their own homes and placed in foster care when they are being abused, rather than their *parents*?

- Why are *children* forced to see or move back in with an abusive parent that the child doesn't want to see or move back with?

- Why do we view children as less entitled to basic rights and respect than adults?

## Discipline: How and what we model for ou children

In peaceful indigenous cultures, it is generally understood that children will naturally learn what they need to learn about appropriate behavior from strong family and community role modeling. Children are naturally wired to imitate the expectations of the society they live in, whether they live in a peaceful, cooperative tribal culture or an aggressive, materialistic, self-centered culture. Although they do require guidance to help them understand and make sense of how they fit into a cooperative family and society, children learn...

- Respect,
- Self-discipline,
- Responsibility,
- Cooperation, and
- Appropriate social behavior

...through a secure parent-child attachment and through the family and community modeling that is prominent in their lives.

Adults in our culture, from each generation, are very zealous about claiming that "children today" have "no values". These adults point out that many children in our culture act rude, disrespectful, aggressive, violent, selfish, materialistic, "spoiled", undisciplined, hyper-sexualized, apathetic and lazy. What the adults seem to be unaware of is that *most children in our culture have actually internalized our culture's values perfectly!* In other words, our children are actually behaving *just as they are being taught* by us and by our culture! The rude, disrespectful, aggressive, violent, selfish, materialistic, "spoiled", undisciplined, hyper-sexualized, apathetic and lazy behaviors that many industrialized children pick up are simply *the way our culture lives.*

Even if these aren't the values we want our children to live by, these are the values that we as parents and we as a culture actually pass on to them.

If we want children to grow to become happy, compassionate, respectful, cooperative, self-disciplined and responsible human beings, then we cannot preach one set of values to our children and live by and expose them to opposite values. In peaceful tribal cultures, it is expected that children will grow to act like the adults act in their culture. In our culture, it is expected that children should grow to act the way parents, teachers and authorities *tell* them to act, *even if most of the adults act opposite to how they are telling children to act!*

Let's look at the following negative behaviors and how our culture models them for children:

## Violence and disrespect

One of the biggest concerns that adults in our culture have about children is how disrespectful, aggressive and violent children are acting at younger and younger ages. Should this surprise us? *Parents begin teaching children to be aggressive and violent, sometimes before the age of two, by hitting or getting rough with children when they don't like something that they do.* Most of us were raised to believe that "spanking", "smacking" and other forms of hitting, pain infliction and rough handling are acceptable, harmless or even necessary ways to "teach" children "discipline'. Unfortunately, the only lessons that hitting and rough handling teach children are:

- Violence is an acceptable way for a stronger or more powerful person to get their way with someone weaker;

- To avoid more violence, I must be sneakier or more powerful and intimidating; and

- To avoid more violence, I must take out my rage and my revenge on someone else.

Likewise, we teach children to be rude, disrespectful and verbally violent by:

- Disrespecting our children's needs,

- Ignoring our children or their needs,

- Mocking or laughing at our children or their upset,

- Mocking or laughing at other people or other people's misfortune in front of our children,

- Speaking disrespectfully, sarcastically and rudely to our children,

- Speaking disrespectfully, sarcastically and rudely to other people in front of our children,

- Yelling at our children,

- Yelling at other people in front of our children,

- Making threats to our children and intimidating them,

- Making threats to others in front of our children,

- Calling children hurtful names,

- Calling other people hurtful names or "bad mouthing" others in front of our children

- Verbally fighting with our children,

- Verbally fighting with other people in front of our children,

- Allowing them to watch rudeness, sarcasm and disrespect modeled on TV and movies that target youth, and

- Allowing them to watch TV shows and movies that are intended for adults.

*Children will learn and do exactly what we model for them as parents.*

Children also learn and do what our culture models for them, too. If we as parents are nonviolent to our children and others, but constantly expose our children to bad examples in our culture, they will internalize those examples and follow them. Children receive their modeling about how to act in our culture from:

- The lifestyle their parents live,

- The types of outside relationships parents bring into the family,

- The way their school runs,

- The way teachers and school faculty treat children,

- The way their peers dress, act and talk to others,

- The way they see people dress, act and talk to others on TV and online,

- The advertising they see on TV, online and around them,

- The types of toys, video games, music, clothes, food and material objects we allow them to have, and

- The degree to which children see us involve ourselves in standing up for the rights of others.

Believe it or not, all of this is what "discipline" and learning are all about. If parents allow their children to witness disrespectful talk, sarcasm, aggression and violence at home, in school, on TV, online, and with peers, this will *naturally* teach children how to act in this culture.

## Selfishness and materialism

If parents, schools, peers, advertising, TV shows and movies model a preoccupation with individualism, selfishness, material objects, money and "independence", children will naturally take on these values. Our culture is saturated with the drive to get more and more, bigger and better and the latest, most up-to-date toys, gadgets and clothing; it is amazing that adults expect the average industrialized child to be anything *but* selfish and materialistic!

## Restlessness

Our culture is all about rushing and never having enough. From children's school schedules and extra curricular activities to the lightening speed video and sound bites on TV, children in our culture are taught to be bored quickly with anything that isn't fast-paced and intensely entertaining. People in our culture seem to have a generalized restless feeling of never having enough of some material object or commodity, such as time, money, entertainment, clothing, toys, electronics, TV, alcohol, medication or junk food. We pass this inner restlessness onto our children, causing them to crave what they don't have, and feel unsatisfied with what they do receive.

## Drugs

Adults in our culture are often hysterical about children using drugs, yet in our families and everywhere in our culture, children see drugs and drug-like substitutes for happiness promoted. Examples include:

- Seeing parents or family members who smoke, drink or use other drugs;

- Being forced to take psychiatric drugs for behavior or hearing about other children doing so;

- Seeing junk food, TV, video games, web surfing, IM-ing or shopping being used compulsively by parents, peers and people on TV and in movies; and

- Seeing advertising that promotes medication or fulfilling oneself with material objects.

## Hyper-sexuality

The media is so flooded with sexualized talk, images, innuendo and adult themes that TV shows and movies that target children are becoming increasingly developmentally inappropriate. The view our culture has of children and sexuality is psychotic: On one hand, the United States government pays for "sex education" programs in public schools that refuse to inform youth about safe sex, simply telling youth they aren't to have sex until marriage. This view point completely ignores the fact that some youth are or are going to be sexually active. There are even laws that make it a *crime* for youth under the age of consent to have consensual sex with other youth of the same age (while I don't recommend adolescents under the age of consent having sex, we need to ask ourselves why it is a *crime* for them to have consensual sex)!

On the other hand, our children are drowned from the toddler years onward with sexualized images, "dirty" talk, swearing, explicit music and adult-level themes in TV shows, movies and songs that are supposed to be *for children!* Sexualized clothing is now even being marketed to *toddlers,* and even *dolls* sport clothing fit for a dance club! Children are likely to be confused by the mixed messages they are receiving from parents who allow them to listen to explicit music and see TV shows and movies with adult themes, but tell them that they shouldn't be having any sexual contact with other children!

## Apathy

Apathy is showing indifference to or a lack of compassion for people, animals, the environment or about a situation. Apathy is the opposite of empathy, which is the ability to feel and experience what someone else is feeling, from *their* perspective. Apathy is also the opposite of compassion.

I thought *Wikipedia*, the online encyclopedia, defined compassion perfectly, as "a sense of shared suffering, most often combined with a desire to alleviate or reduce the suffering of another; to show special kindness to those who suffer. Compassion essentially arises through empathy, and is often characterized through actions, wherein a person acting with compassion will seek to aid those they feel compassionate for."

Unfortunately, in our culture, compassion for people and their suffering generally runs low, especially during a time of war. From bashing opponents in fiercely competitive sports games to making derogatory comments about a certain group of people, apathy seems to be a way of life for many people in our culture. There is even less compassion in our culture for the most voiceless people and beings, especially children, wild animals and our environment, most likely because children, wild animals, trees, rainforests and planets cannot vote or donate money to politicians. Most people in our culture are so burnt out at the end of a long work day that they "veg out" in front of their TV sets rather than advocate for the rights of children or fight the destruction of our natural environment.

Children watch and learn from the things we prioritize in our lives and from the way we talk about, view and treat other people. They also watch the media closely, seeing mostly sarcastic, selfish and mean-spirited characters harass, bully, mock and one-up others on TV and in movies. It is a rare children's movie or TV show that doesn't have at least one sarcastic, foul-mouthed, apathetic bully mocking and one-upping a weak-minded side-kick. When children are exposed to these models day in and day out, over time, they naturally pick up and assimilate this cultural modeling into their own behavior and values.

> *Children have never been very good at listening to their elders, but they have never failed to imitate them. –James Baldwin, author, activist*

## How we substitute ourselves

How often do we give our children imitations of parent-child connection or substitutes for what they really need from us? From bottles, pacifiers, stuffed animals and cribs to day care centers, schools, material objects, TV, Internet, video games, therapists and drugs, we seem to fill our children's entire childhoods with substitutes for our time and substitutes for a deeply connected, secure attachment with us.

We are so saturated by the toxic parenting expectations in our culture that when parents are describing the "needy" behaviors their children display, they do not see the very obvious clues and solutions imbedded in the children's behavior: Our children need *us*, not distractions or substitutes.

I discovered the following letter to *Wondertime* magazine written by a parent for the "Family Traditions" feature of the Fall 2006 issue — I felt that it was a perfect snapshot of the average American parent's lack of attunement with her child's basic, natural need for physical connection with her:

"When my son Max was small, he didn't sleep well. The thing that helped him sleep better was holding my hair. I had to sit on the floor outside his crib and let him hold my hair through the bars. Whenever he was upset, it was always my hair that soothed him. Around the time he was 2, I hit upon a better idea. I bought him a faux hairpiece at an accessories shop in the mall. He called it his "mama hair", and he sleeps with it to this day (he's four now). The original piece eventually looked like a dred-locked roadkill so we've replaced it several times, but it's still the only thing that soothes him in the nighttime." -*Letter from New Hampshire*

My heart winced at the longing this little boy was expressing for connection and physical closeness with his mother and the tragedy of his mother seeming unable to feel or listen to her nat-ural mothering instinct. Although Max's mother was well mean-ing, she seemed completely unaware that her son needed phys-ical closeness and connection with *her* more than anything. I can picture her sitting on the floor, her son gripping onto her hair through the bars of the isolating crib, his body and heart aching for skin-to-skin contact with her. Her hair "through the bars" was as close as he could get to her, and the essence of Mom was felt in the comfort of her hair. "Through the bars" was an accurate description; it calls up images of a barrier between child and nature, child and mother; seclusion, isolation, a cage and a *prison.*

When Max was two, Mom said she "hit upon a better idea" than having him hold onto her hair at night through the crib bars. She seems to be implying that giving Max *fake* hair was a better idea than soothing him with her own hair and her own body. Not only did Max miss the skin-to-skin contact of cosleeping with Mom, he then lost the little physical contact he had of holding her hair in his hand each night! The fact that Max has slept with the fake hair piece for four years implies that he is still not cosleeping. The fact that Max refers to the fake hair piece as his "mama hair" shows the extent of the need he is trying to meet for physical contact with mom, using a lifeless substitute. Mom ends the letter insisting that the fake hair piece "is still the only thing that soothes him in the nighttime." I wonder if Mom has ever tried the one thing that *would* truly "soothe" Max in the nighttime... *Cosleeping*?

In the same issue, in the "Growing up" section, there is a letter under the "Firsts" feature, titled "Off to Preschool". The last half of the letter reads,

"...As we walked the three blocks to school, Lucy waved to the shopkeepers, the trees, and the gargoyles peering down from the corner cathedral. We pass through this neighborhood every day, but that day, it felt like we were crossing into a new world. And, tucked into her backpack, out of sight of her classmates, were Lucy's blankie and pacifier. Just in case."

Lucy's Mom is right: Lucy definitely *was* crossing into a very "new world"; the world of unnatural separations from:

- Her parent/s,
- The attachment relationship,
- Self-directed learning,
- Having her basic needs met, and
- Freedom.

This is Lucy's first day of 14 years of being separated, for several hours per day, from the person nature intended for her to learn from and be physically close to during those 14 years. Lucy is given *substitutes* for:

- The comfort of her mother,

- The learning she could be doing on her own,

- The real-life social world of her family and neighborhood, and

- The trees she could admiring and climbing during the day.

She is given unnatural substitutes for mom, such as a school building, teachers, same-age classmates, a school playground structure, a blankie and a pacifier... "Just in case".

## How we force children to grow up

As with the many other areas we discussed, our culture has a bizarre double standard for children: We say that we want children "to be children", for children "to keep their innocence as long as possible", for adolescents to "wait until adulthood" to have sex and for children of all ages to turn away from violence. However we show children the opposite with our actions.

Most adults try to keep children "in their place" by dictating and scheduling their lives, treating them like property. Yet most adults also try to force children to "grow up" prematurely and show "maturity" and "independence" that isn't safe or in line with their natural development. It seems that parents in our culture are very quick to sever children's *natural* dependency, forcing them out into the adult world as early as possible.

## **"Miniature adult" trends and fads**

I have seen so many questionable trends in our culture that cause younger, preadolescent children to appear older and tougher than their age and even sexually provocative. These "miniature adult" trends and fads include:

- "Buzzed" or shaved haircuts, resembling the conformity of the military, for young boys (this trend is finally on its way out);

- "Teen-like" or sexually provocative clothing, even thong underwear and bras, for young girls;

- Clothing for both girls and boys with sayings, pictures and slogans which are sarcastic, hateful and even derogatory;

- Clothing for young children that promotes violence and materialism, such as "gangsta" outfits, designer logos, army camouflage or movie franchised clothing;

- Cell phones, TV's and MP3 players for young children; and

- Referring to children between the ages of 8 and 12 as "tweens".

## **Perverting childhood via the media**

Another serious concern I have is the number of children who are allowed to watch TV shows and movies and play video games that are intended for adults. I have seen parents on many occasions bring young children to dark-themed PG-13 movies. I have likewise seen children as young as eight brought into rated "R" movies featuring graphic sexual images, violence and gore.

From my work with children and families, it appears to be too common a practice for parents to allow their children, even young children, to watch gory horror movies and other adult-themed movies and TV shows. It is just as common for parents to buy or allow children to play rated "M" (mature) video games intended for adults. Although rated "M" games focus on heavy violence, detailed gore and sometimes explicit sexual images, many parents that I've talked to minimize the impact that these images have on their children or act as if they are helpless to stop their children from playing these games. Likewise with movies and TV shows, parents often justify that their children are "mature enough" to "handle" the adult imagery.

It is confusing to me why parents are allowing children under 16 to be exposed to images, dialogue and material that:

- *Is intended for adults,*
- Is explicitly sexual,
- Is graphically violent,
- Is frightening,
- Is potentially traumatizing, and
- Depicts sex, the human body and human relationships in a mocking or negative manner.

While children between the ages of eight and 15 may *appear* as if they are unaffected by images of horror, explicit sex and violence, these images can cause trauma to the developing mind. These adult images also may:

- Distort the reality of relationships,
- Exaggerate the danger in the world,
- Glorify violence and hatred of others,
- Increase anger and behavioral problems,

- Trigger past trauma,

- Desensitize children to the suffering of others, and

- May influence youth with attachment disruption to become involved with promiscuous sexual relationships, alcohol use and adult behaviors at a younger age.

Parents, we must ask ourselves, *what is the rush for our young children to grow up so fast and look and act so tough or provocative? What is the rush for our children to be exposed to adult-level images and subjects so soon?* Our children will be spending the majority of their lives being adults; won't there be enough time for adult-themed entertainment when they reach adulthood? What messages are we sending to our children?

As parents, it is important that we scrutinize the fads and trends that are pushed onto our young children and refuse to jump on the bandwagon of those trends that turn children into "mini-teens" or "mini-adults".

As parents, it is important that we view the movies, TV shows, websites and video games that our children want to watch or play *ahead of time*, to see if they are developmentally appropriate. Most rated "R" movies and rated "M" games are *not* appropriate for children under 15 or 16. Some youth are more mature and emotionally stable than others and some "R"-rated movies and "M"-rated games are less harmful than others. However, it is important to keep this point in mind: *If your children already have symptoms of emotional distress, aggression or other behavioral acting-out symptoms, allowing them to view sexualized or violent images is very likely to exacerbate your children's problems.*

# How we fail to allow children to grow naturally

We have seen that our children are living in a culture that constantly gives them opposite messages of what to do and how to live. In areas where children need innocence, dependence, time to develop and guidance, adults force children to act "tougher", more independent or responsible than they are capable. In other areas, when children need room to grow, experiment and direct their lives, adults keep a death-grip on their autonomy and freedom.

We are modeling crazy-making polarities to our children in so many ways. When this crazy-making modeling is added to the distress of an insecure parent-child attachment and unmet needs, we have a guaranteed recipe for behavioral and emotional instability. Here are some other ways that our culture refuses to allow children to grow naturally:

- We force children to go to school and do work for 14 years that they aren't interested in, and then we expect them to love learning, choose a career path and act ambitious.

- We take away children's choice to direct their education as they wish, and then we expect them to show responsibility, cooperation and self-discipline.

- We want children to be happy and carefree, yet we rush them through childhood and structure almost every hour of their day with homework, tutoring, school clubs, lessons and organized sports, rather than just letting them play and "be children".

- We want children to grow up to be "good citizens" in a democracy or "free country", yet very little about their lives looks like democracy.

- We want adolescents to respect us and take our principles, rules and values seriously, yet we may be slow to respect their passions and interests (such as playing in a band or being part of a gaming club), or their personal choices (such as hair, clothing and personal style).

- We rush adolescents out of childhood and dependency before they are ready— then, we may be perplexed and impatient when they cannot manage adult responsibilities late into their 20's because they are still trying to meet their dependency needs.

In order to keep the parent-child attachment strong and to meet our children's needs, it is important for us to consider how everyday life in our culture works against parent-child attachment and children's basic and higher level needs. When everyday life in our culture magnifies its worst features, children can become traumatized. Traumatized and unconnected children will manifest their angst through warning signals. Chapter 8 discusses childhood trauma and the behavioral and emotional symptoms of trauma.

# Chapter 8
# Child Trauma and Post Traumatic Stress Disorder (PTSD)

*"Injustice anywhere is a threat to justice everywhere."*
  *-Dr. Martin Luther King Jr.*

*"Society chooses to disregard the mistreatment of children, judging it to be altogether normal because it is so commonplace."*    *-Alice Miller, author*

*"You have a right to live a safe life from the threat of war, abuse and exploitation. These rights are obvious. Yet we, the grown ups have failed you deplorably in upholding many of them."*
*-Kofi Annan, former Secretary-General to the United Nations and Nobel Peace Prize winner, 2001*

*Definitions:*

**Age of (sexual) consent**- The youngest age that a child can legally give permission for another consenting person to have sex with him or her, for example, at age 16.

**Hypervigilance**- An exaggerated sensitivity and reaction to the possibility of threat or danger (modified from Wikipedia.org); may manifest as restlessness or anxiety.

**Cerebral cortex**- The thinking, conscious part of the brain, located at the front of the head, that regulates decision making, problem solving, control of behaviors and emotions.

**Temporal lobe**- The section of the brain located on the side of the head. This part of the brain processes sound and hearing, as well as artistic and musical appreciation. It contains the amygdala, a part of the brain involved with the "fight-or-flight-or-freeze" panic reaction and anxiety.

**Fight-or-flight-or-freeze reaction**- The life-saving process for getting the body ready to fight or run from a perceived danger or to become motionless to prevent danger. This process causes a person to have a burst of intense strength, split-second reactions, super speed or frozen stillness in response to a frightening situation.

**Insight**- "The clear (and often sudden) understanding of a complex situation" (wordnet.princeton.edu).

When children are suffering from unmet needs and an insecure parent-child attachment, they are enduring distress at a level that can be very traumatic. In order to understand the extent of our children's emotional and behavioral problems, it is important to take a brief look at how trauma affects children's brains and bodies. We will also learn why trauma doesn't seem to heal no matter how much we reassure children that they are safe and no matter how many years that children attend regular therapy.

## What is trauma?

Trauma is emotional damage from...

- A frightening event,
- An upsetting event or
- A chronic situation

...that causes a person severe distress and overwhelms the person with a sense of helplessness. Trauma develops according to the *individual's* perception and *ability* to cope. In other words, *what might be experienced as a minor event to you may be traumatic for your child.*

## Examples of trauma

- Difficult birth
- Infant left to scream in incubator after birth
- Circumcision
- Parents failing to respond to infant's cries immediately
- Crib sleeping
- Child left alone at night
- Having basic needs ignored or denied
- Physical abuse, *including* "spanking", "smacking", "paddling" or rough handling of a child
- Sexual abuse
- Emotional abuse
- Neglect of physical and emotional needs
- Abandonment
- Being left in day care
- Being forced to go to school
- Lack of support in upsetting situation, injury, illness or other trauma
- Out-of-home placement (foster care, group home, juvenile boot camp or detention center)
- Loss of parent or loved one
- Death of parent or loved one
- Witnessing domestic violence
- Witnessing any type of violence or attack on a person or animal
- Peer harassment
- Being the victim of racist or derogatory remarks about one's nationality, sex, gender, sexual orientation or appearance
- Pain or illness
- Hospitalization
- Homelessness
- Seeing frightening, violent or sexualized TV shows, movies, games or websites

## Why is "spanking" traumatic?

Physical punishment has no place in attachment parenting. Naturally, when a child is deliberately hurt by their parent, it severely harms the parent-child attachment.

Physical punishment, also known as *corporal punishment,* is any type of hitting or frightening rough handling of a child, including "spanking" and "smacking" or painful neglect of children's basic needs. Physical punishment is frightening, and often terrifying to children of all ages. It is a physical attack on a younger, smaller or weaker person by a larger, more powerful person, causing children to feel helpless. Even large adolescents are helpless to stop physical punishment for fear that they will be hit again. As we read in the previous pages, trauma is emotional damage that happens when a child feels severe distress, fear and a sense of helplessness.

Hitting children is also unfair. In all 50 US States, it is a crime for anyone to hit:

- Spouses
- Domestic partners
- Senior citizens
- Psychiatric patients
- Employees
- Servants
- Soldiers
- Prisoners
- Any other adult citizen
- In some cases, pets

It is even a crime for a child to hit an adult! However, none of the 50 states has a law that says it is a crime for parents to hit their own *children*! In fact, in almost half of our 50 states, mostly in the South, it is still legal for teachers, principals, coaches, day care providers and workers in youth residential and detention programs to hit children with paddles! Boys and African American children bear the worst brunt of physical punishment in "pro-paddling" schools, being the children who are hit the most often.

Although most women and men would never accept that it is okay for a child or another adult to "smack" them for wrong doing, many men and women still think it is okay for children to be "smacked". Unfortunately, there are consequences to hitting and rough handling children. There is over 60 years of research in the fields of psychology, science and child development that shows that physical punishment is emotionally harmful to children and increases their aggression.

Physical punishment puts children at risk for:

- Physical harm
  - Bruises are the most common injury from physical punishment. Children can also have bone, muscle and teeth injuries and injuries to delicate organs from physical punishment. Most cases of severe physical beatings start out with a "smack" that escalated with a parent's rage.
- Post Traumatic Stress Disorder
- Aggression and violence
  - Young children imitate what adults do. If we hit them, we model hitting and aggression.
- Acting out and other behavioral problems
  - Children's anger and hurt will often come out in their behavior because they are unable to hit back or hold the adult accountable for hurting them.
- Rage
  - Children will naturally feel the need to get revenge on

the adults who hurt them. However, the "revenge" is often taken out on someone they don't fear; someone they know won't hit back. "Revenge" is usually taken out in more subtle ways such as rude talk, "sassing" or vandalism.

- Anxiety
- Depression
- Withdrawal
- Poor self esteem or self hatred
- Suicidal thoughts
  - In some cases, children have actually attempted or committed suicide due to fearing "a spanking".
- Domestic violence in adulthood
  - Violence begets violence. People who are hit as children are more likely to hit their spouses or domestic partners.
- Using physical punishment in adulthood
  - Children who are hit in childhood are more likely to hit their own children someday.
- Sexual violation
  - Since most physical punishment involves hitting a child's buttocks, this can feel very emotionally uncomfortable and sexually violating to children.
- Sexual problems
  - There is a nerve that runs from a child's buttocks into the genital area, sometimes causing sexual excitement during a "spanking". Some people who have been "spanked", "smacked" or "paddled" grow up to feel sexually excited by pain and need someone to hurt them in order for them to feel sexually excited. *No one could ever know who this will happen to* and most parents never have any idea that their child is developing this fetish.

Physical punishment is a violent and harmful act against a child, even if it is "mild". If you were hit as a child, you probably can remember the fear and the anger you felt when the adult who was supposed to protect you, hurt you. You probably grew up believing that you deserved to be hurt for some childish thing that you did.

If you use or have used physical punishments on your children, it is critical that you never do it again. The guilt we feel as parents when we realize that we have hurt our children can be immense. It may help to know that our culture is responsible for passing this violence down through the generations and causing loving parents to lose their natural instincts, but it is possible to heal our relationships with our children! It is important that we apologize to our children, even if we haven't hurt them in awhile, and let them know that we are learning better ways to teach and guide them. Allow them to express their feelings *without becoming defensive and without blaming them* for your actions. *Physical punishment is never justified,* even if your children speak rudely to you, swear at you or act deliberately defiant.

Also, show some empathy for yourself. Realize that if you were raised in harmony with nature you would have never hurt your child. The last part of this book will help you learn to parent in a way that is natural and helpful to your children.

## Child abuse and neglect

Child abuse and neglect is severely traumatizing to children and severely damaging to the parent-child attachment. Child abuse and neglect is any action that a parent (or other adult) takes that

intentionally causes a child...
- Pain or physical discomfort,
- Non-accidental physical injury,
- Non-accidental emotional injury,
- Physical deprivation or
- Sexual violation

...for the purposes of...
- Punishment,
- Keeping a child contained for the adult's convenience,
- Restraining a child out of anger,
- Due to lack of developmentally appropriate supervision, or
- Adult sexual gratification.

Child abuse is not...
- When a child is accidentally hurt,
- Necessary medical care, or
- Short periods of restraint for safety purposes (such as using car seats or preventing children from harming themselves or others).

## Examples of physical abuse

- Physical punishment: Hitting, spanking, smacking or striking any part of a child's body with the hand or with an object

- Whipping, beating or paddling a child

- Punching a child

- Attacking a child

- Pinching or clawing a child

- Pulling a child's hair

- Not allowing a child to use the toilet when they need to
- Shaking a child
- Grabbing or yanking a child
- Shoving or dragging a child
- Strangling, chocking or suffocating a child
- Electroshocking, tazing or other types of shocking a child
- Forcing a child to do labor that is unsafe
- Cutting or stabbing a child
- Burning or scalding a child
- Putting a child in a closet
- Restraining or tying a child to a tree, bed, chair, etc.
- Disfiguring a child's body part
- Torturing a child
- Attempted murder of a child
- Committing any other form of deliberate pain infliction on a child

## Examples of sexual abuse

- Sexualized kissing of a child
- Sexualized groping or embracing a child for the adult's sexual gratification
- Sexualized voyeurism (watching) of a child nude
- Deliberate exposure of the adult's genitals to a child for adult's sexual gratification
- Sexualized fondling of a child's body
- Touching a child's genitals for the adult's sexual gratification

- An adult asking a child to fondle the adult's genitals or body

- Forcing a child to masturbate in front of the adult or an adult forcing a child to view the adult masturbating

- Penetration of a child's mouth, anus, vagina or penis with fingers or objects

- Rape of a child

- Taking sexualized photos or videos of a child

- An adult forcing child victims to perform sex acts on one another

- Prostitution of a child

Sexual abuse happens to girls and boys, young children and adolescents. Sexual abuse and rape are perpetrated by both men and women. Sometimes, traumatized older youth sexually act out against younger children.

Unfortunately, society often overlooks or shows less concern about the sexual abuse of boys and the fact that women and older girls do sexually assault and rape children in numbers higher than once believed. Sexual assaults by females can be both as subtle and brutal as assaults carried out by males.

*Note: In cases of children who act out sexually, they are almost always victims of sexual abuse and are in need of specialized help and treatment, not criminal punishment.*

### Examples of emotional abuse

Parents and teachers who yell, scream and swear at children can be just as terrifying to children as parents and teachers who hit or rough handle children. These emotional attacks often include put downs, insults, sarcastic remarks, verbal harassment, threats of physical harm or abandonment, humiliation, comparisons with others, degrading a child's personality, body parts or appearance or cruel name calling. This abuse leaves emotional, rather than physical scars, and can result in severe emotional problems, including suicidal thoughts, depression, anxiety, self-mutilation, self-hatred, regressive behavior, apathy and rage.

## **Examples of physical neglect**

- Lack of adequate, healthy food and nutrition
- Lack of hydration
- Denial of elimination needs
- Denial of medical care
- Lack of adequate sleep
- Lack of a safe, clean environment
- Lack of appropriate clothing for the temperature
- Lack of properly fitting, clean clothing
- Denial of hygiene needs
- Leaving children to care for themselves
- Leaving children in the company of inappropriate or dangerous people
- Engaging in dangerous, reckless and illegal practices around child (drug use, prostitution)

## **Examples of emotional neglect**

- Emotional and physical abandonment
- Lack of physical affection
- Lack of love or withdrawal of love
- Lack of nurturance or care
- Emotional coldness

- Lack of empathy, understanding and patience
- Denial of social interaction with people who may nurture or love the child

## Trauma's affect on children's brain development

*Children's brains are not wired to naturally expect or cope with trauma.* When trauma occurs, it affects every aspect of a child's brain and development in a very damaging way. When a child has been traumatized...

- The child's brain re-wires itself for hypervigilance and a fear reaction to anything unexpected;
- The child's brain learns to dissociate;
- Symptoms of Post Traumatic Stress Disorder are likely to develop;
- Anxiety, fear, depression, rage, restlessness or inattention are likely to develop;
- A compulsion to repeat the trauma may develop;
- The trauma is stored improperly;
- The traumatic memory becomes stuck at the age and emotional condition of the child at the time of the trauma;
- Reminders of the trauma may constantly trigger the child;
- The child's immune system functioning decreases;
- The child's cognitive/learning functioning decreases;
- Functioning decreases in all of the child's body systems; and
- Functioning decreases in all areas of a child's development.

# Post Traumatic Stress Disorder

Post Traumatic Stress Disorder, or PTSD, is a serious anxiety disorder that often develops after people suffer a trauma. PTSD can develop whether children suffer one traumatic incident or several years of traumatic situations. Children may have PTSD and only show mild symptoms or their symptoms may be severe. Many of the symptoms may be misdiagnosed as behavioral problems, "ADHD" or bipolar disorder.

### Symptoms of PTSD include:

- Being preoccupied with upsetting images, thoughts or memories
- Aggressive or upsetting play themes that occur over and over
- Hallucinations
- Nightmares
- Flashbacks
- Dissociation
- Trying to reenact the trauma
- Distress when reminded of the trauma
- Avoidance of reminders of the trauma
- Amnesia of parts of or all of the trauma
- Hypervigilance, restlessness or hyperactivity
- Irritability
- Rage outbursts
- Inability to concentrate or focus
- Sleep difficulties
- Lack of interest in doing things

- Expressing only a few emotions such as anger or depression
- Negativity
- Being easily startled

# A theory of how trauma is stored in the brain

A traumatic memory is like a huge box of old objects that sits in the middle of the "floor" of the brain. The brain continually "trips over" the box, but yet it can't find a better place to store it. Rather than being stored in a way that allows learning experiences to heal it, the traumatic memory sits alone, isolated from the parts of the brain that could heal it. If there are many traumatic memories, they all sit isolated, improperly stored.

Traumatic memories may store in the *creative right brain* and in the impulsive *temporal lobe* where our instinctual "fight-or-flight-or-freeze" reaction is triggered. Childhood traumatic memories store vividly, in their original emotional form. Whenever something reminds children of the trauma, the "fight-or-flight-or-freeze" panic reflex may be triggered, no matter how many years have passed! This will continue into a child's adulthood if trauma is not healed. These factors cause traumatic memories to be isolated from:

- Maturity
- Adaptation
- Learning
- Insight
- Therapy
- Self help
- Spirituality

No matter how many years people attend regular therapy, read about, learn about or rationalize about their trauma, it continues to haunt them because it is stored in the *right brain, temporal lobe*, where traditional therapy, reassurances of safety, learning, understanding and maturity can't reach. Why can't these things reach the trauma?

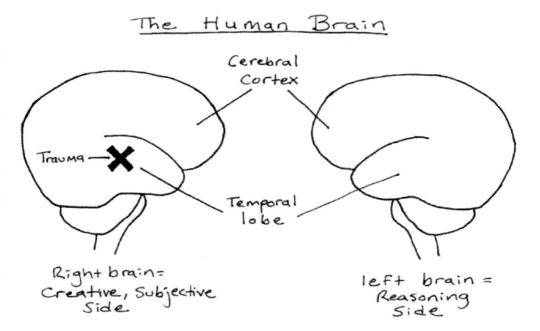

Maturity, growth, reassurances of safety, learning and under-standing from therapy are stored in the *left, rational brain*, towards the front of the brain in the *cerebral cortex*. The cere-bral cortex is the thinking, insightful and rational part of the brain. Unfortunately, it is believed that the traumatic memory can't reach the rational parts of the brain because it was stored improperly. Regular therapy cannot heal the traumatic memory because regular therapy uses discussion, insight and under-standing, which store in the left brain and cerebral cortex—no where near the traumatic memory!

In Chapter 11, Part I, we will learn about a type of trauma therapy, Eye Movement Desensitization and Reprocessing (EMDR) that is able to bring traumatic memories to the parts of the brain that can make sense of and heal them.

# Chapter 9
# Extreme Breaks in Attachment: Foster Care, Institutional Facilities and Adoption

*"To many people, children are not important enough to be placed first. To the politician, for example, a child may not be critical because a child does not vote, does not contribute funds to political campaigns, wields no real power in any political sense. Children are the easiest segment of our population to ignore. Any politician will tell you, children do not bite, so worry not about how they are treated."*
   *-Bob Keeshan, "Captain Kangaroo"*

*Definitions*
   **Failure-to-Thrive**- A condition in which a child fails to physically grow and develop in a way expected for her/his age due to medical conditions or psychological conditions such as physical and emotional neglect, abuse or distressing life circumstances. The child is often very small, thin or short for her/his age.

   **Residential program**- A program that houses a group of children with moderate to severe behavioral problems. Residential programs are often run in a very strict, regimented manner requiring children to do chores and earn higher levels of privileges based on obedience. Often these programs are referred to as "therapeutic", but the direct-care staff are generally very young and do not have any formal mental health training or a degree. Unfortunately, most residential child care staff relate to children based on reward and punishment, having full control over them and offering very little opportunity for attachment. Restraint is used in most of these programs.

# The world's worst tragedy

The worst tragedy that humankind has ever suffered was when our ancestors began to turn away from natural, instinctual parenting and instead began to neglect, hurt, brutalize, orphan and murder their children. All of history's worst acts of hatred and violence are the consequences of that tragedy, and today's most severely wounded children who find little or no connection to a parent figure will be tomorrow's warlords and criminals. Although laws are in place in modern times to show a little less tolerance for the neglect and abuse of children, most industrialized cultures hide ugly secrets behind closed doors and office buildings:

- Even though children are the future of their societies and nations, governments do not ever put children's needs and rights as *the* national priority...

- Over a half million children in the United States, and millions more worldwide, are wasting away in foster homes, orphanages, residential "treatment" programs, youth detention centers, youth boot camps and other institutions...

- These numbers do not include the numbers of boys and girls of all ages who are runaways, street dwellers or who survive by living as prostitutes because of severe abuse, neglect or abandonment at home.

When we in industrialized societies go about our busy routines, satisfy our wants with buying gadgets and toys and drown ourselves in unreality TV at night, children in our own countries are waiting, languishing, dreaming and begging for permanent, loving parents and homes. Even more tragically...

- The more severe the abuse,

- The more severe the neglect,

- The earlier the abandonment,

- The more placements or different caretakers that the child has had,

- The more attachments that have been broken and

- The longer the child has waited for a permanent attachment figure

... The more severe the damage to the child physically, neurologically, emotionally, mentally, behaviorally, spiritually and morally.

Brain scans of children who grew up in the extremely emotionally neglectful conditions of orphanages show that the part of the brain where the ability to feel attachment, love, empathy and remorse would be, *is not developed at all*...To clarify what that means, *children's brains do not have the ability to wire themselves without attachment, love and affection!* Children who have suffered severe abuse, neglect and abandonment *cannot be expected* to love, attach, focus, learn, "behave", or feel empathy or remorse for even actions as severe as murder *if those parts of their brain do not exist!*

## Children living in institutions and programs

Children who live in residential facilities, orphanages and the brutal, inhumane conditions of prisons, youth detention and youth "boot camp" programs are generally suffering extreme neglect of their basic physical, emotional, social, spiritual and attachment needs. Many of these programs are extremely physically and emotionally abusive.

Institutions and programs for severely troubled children generally operate under the philosophy that aggressive, "delinquent" children must be dominated, terrified and treated harshly to "reform" them. Staff persons in many of these programs and institutions regularly commit brutal, abusive and neglectful acts such as:

- Restraining children who are *not* in extreme danger of harming self or others;
- Using physical force— *not* to prevent imminent danger of harm to self or others but to intimidate, break, scare or to prove "who's boss";
- Forcing children to sit for long periods of time (from one hour to several hours);
- Tying or chaining children;
- Caging and imprisoning children;
- Hitting, punching, kicking and tazing children;
- Forcing labor and exercise; and
- Denying or rationing food, hydration, elimination, sleep, medical care, play and other basic needs.

It is no surprise that many children have died in institutions and programs by homicide, suicide or neglect. Despite that these programs claim to "treat", "reform" or "care" for children, most of them are causing severe trauma, anxiety, rage, depression and a level of emotional and spiritual distress and damage that is likely to haunt children for their entire lives. It is unthinkable to me that adults entrusted with the care of society's neediest, most hurt children callously give these children *more torment and pain rather than the love, care and understanding they need and deserve.*

The president of The Coalition Against Institutionalized Child Abuse states on her website that she "has read many letters from children to their parents and has seen a pattern where children appear to be completely broken, begging for "Mommy", pleading to come home" from youth detention, boot camp or residential facilities. One 15 year-old boy, who died of medical neglect in a "wilderness" boot-camp program, wrote to his mother, "I want to wear Sponge Bob PJs and Teddy Bear slippers and cuddle with my Mommy. I used to think I was too hard of a gangster that nobody could break me, but they found my weakness and I want to go home... PS - I want my Mommy." These heart-wrenching words from a child are testimony to the pain and suffering our children are feeling when their basic attachment needs are left unmet.

Harsh, tough, "scared straight" behavioral modification programs do not meet children's unmet needs! Parents must retrieve their children from these nightmarish programs and repair and heal the attachment relationship! Find a person who is willing and able to help you heal your child *or, find someone who is willing and able to take that responsibility themselves.*

## Children living in foster care

Children who live in foster care are often living in a family situation and *ideally* are receiving nurturance and overall excellent care. In one study, young children who were suffering from severe "failure-to-thrive" in orphanages began to show major developmental improvements when moved to a caring foster home. However, the very purpose and nature of foster care is to be a temporary relationship; its very existence implies more loss for a child, and another shattered attachment relationship.

There are many wonderful foster parents who provide a loving, nurturing, playful environment where abused and neglected children can experience a sense of family, safety and attachment that they may have never known. Unfortunately, not all foster parents are ideal and far too many of them provide only "acceptable" or mediocre care to the children in their homes. These foster parents tend to see foster parenting as a job, and may be motivated by pay rates, may have minimal investment in bonding with the children, may treat the children as borders, may care little about keeping the relationship once the child leaves or they may covey that the foster children are not part of the family. There are also a dangerous number of foster parents who are neglectful or physically, sexually or emotionally abusive to foster children— Ironically, the foster children were placed in their homes to be *protected* from the abuse and neglect in the biological home!

Obviously, mediocre, neglectful and abusive foster parents are only slamming deeper layers of trauma, detachment and emotional and behavioral instability into children's hearts and minds. What about an ideal foster home?

Foster parents, by their job description, are *temporary* caring figures, offering a safe place for individual children to live until:

- Children return home to the biological parents,
- Children find a permanent home with adoptive parents,
- Children find a legal guardian, or
- Children age-out of the foster care system.

Children in foster homes are naturally trying to attach to the adults, even if they try to indicate by extreme acting out behavior that they are not. It is natural and biological for children of all ages to attach to caretakers for survival. Even the most severely detached children, such as those living on the street, or in prisons, will gravitate towards older youth or an adult for survival.

Temporary attachments are not what nature intended for children. Just like the body is not designed to eat once per week and still function, *children's brains are not designed to function on temporary attachment relationships.*

The most ideal situations for children who must be in foster care would be:

- To have the biological family in a foster home *with* the child while attachment behaviors are intensively taught to the biological parents;

- To have the biological family move into a staffed, group foster program so that the parents and children receive the nurturing they need;

- If biological parents are unable or unwilling to meet their children's needs or are unwilling to parent nonviolently after receiving education and interventions, parental rights should be terminated and an adoptive parent found as soon as possible for the children;

- If the biological parents have committed any acts of torture or extreme abuse, they should have parental rights relinquished immediately;

- To keep siblings together when they are adopted;

- To require that all foster parents who do longer term care be willing to adopt foster children who form attachments to them...

- ...Or, at least, require ethically that foster parents stay actively involved with children who have formed attachments to them;

- To focus state funds into *aggressively and immediately recruiting adoptive families for every single child under 21 who will not be returning to the biological home,* rather than focusing resources on "independent living" or "guardianship"; and

- To place children in foster care for only a few weeks until one of the above placements is found.

Of course, in order for any of these bold options to be possible, children and their needs must be viewed as *the highest priority* in every single state and federal government or the lack of necessary funding and training will make these options impossible. Considering the cost of prisons, substance abuse and social service programs for the human beings that societies and governments leave behind, efforts such as these should be well worth it!

Unfortunately, though, some of the most damaged children in our societies are children living in foster care, acting out in extreme ways the rage, pain, suffering, grief, anxiety, longing and detachment they feel towards their biological families and any other lost caretakers they dared to trust. Children know that their foster parents will eventually let them go; the lack of attachment, the lack of permanency, the lack of someone to call their own, the lack of someone to cherish and treasure them forever, is excruciating for children of all ages. Like children in orphanages, residential placements and other institutions, foster children show this excruciating pain to us through their behavioral and psychological instability, taking it to the extremes.

Behavioral and emotional states may include:

- Relentless oppositionality and defiance
- Mood swings
- Aggression
- Depression
- PTSD symptoms
- Rage
- Anxiety
- Extreme fears
- Withdrawal
- Delusions, hallucinations, paranoia
- Obsessions and compulsions
- Poor social relationships
- Poor boundaries
- Clinginess
- Regression
- Constant relapse from newly learned, positive behaviors
- Charming personality, but not genuine
- Indiscriminately friendly to strangers
- Tactile defensiveness (pushes away any affection or touch)
- Reacts hysterically to tiny bumps or cuts
- Barely reacts to a more serious injury
- Running away
- Sexualized acting out
- Poor hygiene

- Gorges self with food
- Refusal to eat or will only eat one food
- Day or nighttime wetting or soiling self
- Eliminates in inappropriate places (not due to accident or no other option), such as around toilet, on toilet seat, on walls
- Steals and hordes
- "Crazy" lying
- Makes up elaborate stories or exaggerates situations
- Can't tolerate being wrong yet will contradict most of what other people say
- Shows lack of remorse or shows pleasure in harming others
- Self mutilation
- Self harming
- Harming others
- Destructive to property
- Fire setting
- Suicidal feelings and attempts
- Homicidal feelings and attempts

I cannot stress this enough: *These behaviors and emotional states are natural reactions to trauma, attachment disruption and unnatural and extremely distressing situations for the child.* Unfortunately, rather than the community making it a priority to repair the biological family or to find a permanent adoptive parent for the child, "experts" and helpers find it much easier and more convenient to:

- "Medicate" the child with multiple mind-altering drugs,
- Keep children for months or years in ineffective one-to-one counseling,
- Expect children to function intellectually and educationally in yet another institution (school), and
- Punish and threaten these children.

## Foster children who return to the biological family

Children who return from foster care to the biological family will exhibit many of the same types of attachment-disrupted behaviors that they show in foster care. When children are removed from biological parents due to abuse and neglect, they are suffering from serious trauma, anger, grief and pain. The added wounds of being placed in foster care, an institution or program will intensify the trauma, attachment disruption and pain, leading to a long list of emotional and behavioral problems.

## Children who are adopted

Adopting a child who cannot be safely and optimally parented by the biological parents is a beautiful, loving gift for both the child and the family. When a child and his or her "forever family" finally find one another, the joy and hope they ideally feel is as rapturous as the birth of a child. Although attaching and attached adoptive parents and children deeply love one another, it is important to understand that *adoption always means loss for the adoptive child.*

236 Instead of Medicating and Punishing

The nine months that children spend in the womb are physically and emotionally critical to a secure parent-child attachment. Children and biological mothers are forming their cellular attachment in the womb. The body sounds, voice, smell, feel, essence and heart beat of the birthmother all become a part of the developing fetus' cellular and emotional memory. Often, children who are not told that they were adopted at birth *know* instinctually that their adoptive mother wasn't their first mother.

Whether adopted at birth or adopted later from foster care or from an orphanage, all adoptive children suffer a severe break from the natural attachment relationship with the birth mother. The emotional and behavioral difference between children adopted at birth and children who waited for adoption lies in:

- The age at adoption and

- The *intensity and severity* of the trauma suffered by the child prior to adoption.

Most adoptive children, and probably *all* children who waited past birth for adoption, suffer moderate to severe attachment disruption or some degree of Reactive Attachment Disorder (RAD). RAD is a mental illness diagnosis that describes a collection of symptoms of the most severe degrees of attachment disruption. Behavioral and emotional states may include:

- Relentless oppositionality and defiance

- Mood swings

- Aggression

- Depression

- PTSD symptoms

- Rage

- Anxiety

- Extreme fears

- Withdrawal

- Delusions, hallucinations, paranoia

- Obsessions and compulsions

- Poor social relationships

- Poor boundaries

- Clinginess

- Regression

- Constant relapse from newly learned, positive behaviors

- Charming personality, but not genuine

- Indiscriminately friendly to strangers

- Tactile defensiveness (pushes away any affection or touch)

- Reacts hysterically to tiny bumps or cuts

- Barely reacts to a more serious injury

- Running away

- Sexualized acting out

- Poor hygiene

- Gorges self with food

- Refusal to eat or will only eat one food

- Day or nighttime wetting or soiling self

- Eliminates in inappropriate places (not due to accident or no other option), such as around toilet, on toilet seat, on walls

- Steals and hordes

- "Crazy" lying

- Makes up elaborate stories or exaggerates situations
- Can't tolerate being wrong yet will contradict most of what other people say
- Shows lack of remorse or shows pleasure in harming others
- Self mutilation
- Self harming
- Harming others
- Destructive to property
- Fire setting
- Suicidal thoughts and attempts
- Homicidal thoughts and attempts

## Optimal infant adoptions vs. traumatic infant adoptions

If a birthmother nurtured her fetus during the nine months and the adoptive mother was present at the birth, immediately putting her adoptive infant on her bare skin (and constantly for 12 months) as birthmother said goodbye and gave emotional permission to the child to attach to the new mother, the child may appear to suffer very mild emotional damage from adoption.

However:

- If the fetus was unwanted,
- If the birthmother did not care well for the fetus,
- If the birthmother was not present when the adoptive mother first arrived,
- If the adoptive mother did not meet her new infant immediately upon the child's birth,

- If the birthmother did not say a loving goodbye, emotionally conveying permission to the infant to attach to the adoptive mother,

- If the birthmother abused and neglected the child before the adoptive mother became involved,

- If the adoptive mother did not begin to show attachment behaviors to her new infant immediately (skin-to-skin contact, constant holding, cosleeping, etc),

- If the adoptive mother did not breastfeed her infant (yes, *adoptive* mothers can and optimally should breastfeed),

- If the adoptive mother did not feel bonded to her infant, or

- If the adoptive mother suffered depression...

... Then it is likely that the adoptive child could suffer moderate to severe emotional damage, manifesting immediately, later in childhood or at some point in her adult life.

## Older child adoptions: Traumatized children who waited

The most extreme cases of damage to adoptive children are children who were adopted as toddlers, young children, older children or as adolescents. The older the child is when he joins his adoptive family,

- The more severe his attachment disruption will have been,

- The more severe the symptoms of Reactive Attachment Disorder (RAD) will be,

- The more losses she has endured,

- The more severe his trauma history,

- The more severe the soul damage will be,

- The more severe the mental and emotional damage will be, and

- The more severe her behavioral problems will be...

All adoptive children, whether adopted from birth or from foster care, suffer a profound and mortal wound to their soul. The child's loss of his or her primary attachment relationship with the birth mother is a wound that adoptive parents will spend the rest of their son or daughter's childhood helping to heal... Delving into this healing process with your daughter or son will often have the behavioral and emotional intensity of being involved in a highway car accident—almost daily, for children with the most severe attachment disruptions. In addition to the soul wound of losing the birthmother, children adopted from foster care or orphanages have almost always suffered severe, and in some cases extreme and repetitive, physical and emotional neglect and/or physical, sexual and emotional abuse.

We will discuss re-parenting our adoptive children, healing their trauma and further resources for repairing extreme breaks in attachment in Chapter 11, Part II.

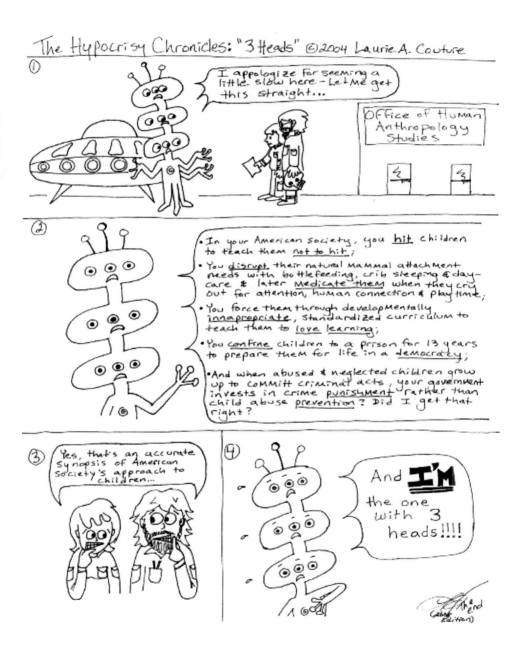

# Chapter 10
# Does Your Child Have a Brain Disorder or Is *Our Culture* Disordered?

*"Human ignorance is unbounded, mostly because the intellect can so easily get carried away with itself and ignore the data of commonsense experience... This over attachment to belief as a substitute for awareness of commonsense experience is a kind of insanity. The healing of our commonly shared insanity will come from re-grounding ourselves in our senses..."*
*–Brad Blanton, psychotherapist and author*

## Children need something deeper than a pill

The mental health, psychiatric and pharmaceutical industries have capitalized on human suffering for years, marketing everything from macabre experiments in gothic "asylums" in centuries past, to the simplistic self-help books, charismatic "inner child" workshops, trendy therapies and mood-numbing chemicals of modern times. It should be of no surprise that the mental health and pharmaceutical institutions eventually turned from a focus on adult "pathology" to the financial goldmine of the suffering of society's most vulnerable and most captive subjects... *children.*

Are our children really as brain disordered as the experts wish for us to believe or are their behaviors and extreme emotions *natural reactions* to a toxic cultural environment? Do our children really require powerful mind-altering chemicals every day just to function or are our children screaming out for something deeper than a pill? Does it *really* make us feel better as parents when the "experts" and authors assure us that "it's not our fault", the child has a "chemical imbalance" or "the child's brain doesn't have any brakes"? Do we believe that deep down? The multi-billion dollar pharmaceutical industry hopes that we do!

What did we learn from the last nine chapters about what children need in order to function optimally physically, emotionally, intellectually, socially, sexually, morally and spiritually? To sum up briefly, we leaned *that for children to develop optimally in all areas*:

- Children require a *secure* parent-child attachment;

- Children's basic physical and emotional needs must be *consistently met as soon as possible*, especially in infancy, but also all throughout childhood;

- Children require that mothers hold or "wear" them continuously on the skin for the first 12 months of life;

- Children require that their mothers breastfeed them as often as needed, for no less than two and a half years and optimally more;

- Children need a physically and emotionally safe, stable, loving and nurturing home environment;

- Children need to be loved, treasured, cherished and respected for who they are as individuals;

- Children need continuous physical affection at all ages;

- Young children naturally feel safest, most attached and most comforted by cosleeping with their parents;

- Children need guidance and discipline that is physically and emotionally *nonviolent* and based on strong family and community modeling;

- Children need to be with their parents, friends and communities during the day;

- Children do best in mixed-age groups of peers;

- Children need freedom, exploration and play in order to learn and keep the desire to learn;

- Children ideally need to be able to imitate and join parents and adults in their community doing work that children find interesting;

- Children need constant, regular, high-energy physical activity all through out the day;

- Children need to direct their play, learning and exploration;

- Children need their developmental pace and abilities respected;

- Children need to learn according to their learning styles;

- Children need to learn primarily through the unique intelligences that they possess and need to have their intelligences treated as valid;

- Children need to have their parent's time, affection and playfulness— Substitutes won't do!

- Children need entertainment and cultural modeling that is developmentally appropriate, fun, enriching, fulfilling and active.

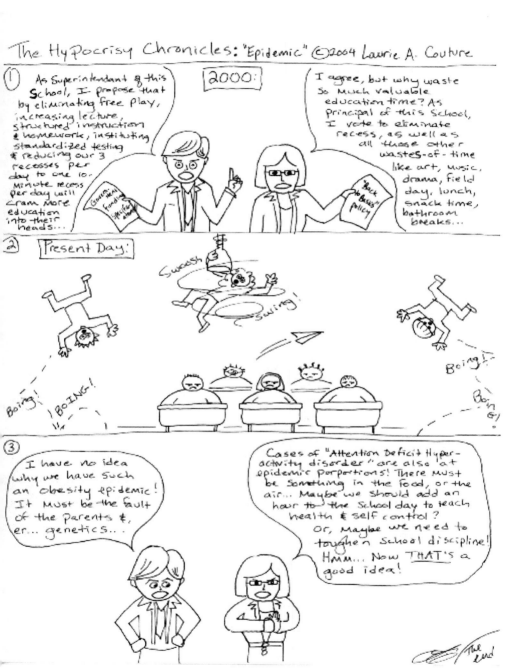

We learned that if children have most of the conditions met on the list, that they are most likely to be happy and emotionally and behaviorally stable people. However, we also learned that if children do *not* have most of the conditions met on the list, they *very naturally* will exhibit emotional and behavioral alarm signals as well as emotional and behavioral instability. Tragically, most of the children in our culture aren't living with more than *three* of the conditions and needs on the list!

If we as parents feel guilt or defensiveness about not meeting our children's needs, we are likely to justify our actions or deny how we have contributed to our children's behavioral and emotional acting out. We are likely to blame other people such as an ex-spouse, an ex-partner, a doting grandparent or a "bad crowd". We are also likely to put the blame for our children's *entire* set of symptoms on other circumstances such as, "the divorce", "the move", "the accident", "the injury", "the seizure", "the diagnosis", "the illness", "the surgery" or "the loss".

Any one of those situations certainly is likely to cause emotional distress, and in some cases, even neurological damage. However, if we use these situations to excuse *all* of our children's signals, emotional and behavioral instability, we are making ourselves feel good but our children are still suffering from unmet needs (sometimes, children won't act out until a serious incident in their lives triggers anger and grief that couldn't be expressed prior to the trigger). When we are quick to try to blame other people and other reasons for our children's alarm signals, we are not meeting our children's needs. More problematic, we become vulnerable to "experts" *who are financially invested in making us believe that our children's brains are at fault* for their emotional and behavioral instability!

A pill won't fill unmet needs

We can *expect* natural alarm signals from children whose needs are not being met. We can *expect* natural emotional and behavioral instability to result when children's needs aren't met. That being the case, when children give us alarm signals and emotionally and behaviorally show us their distress, are they telling us that there is something wrong with their *brains*? Or are they telling us that they are *suffering distress* from disrupted attachment, unmet physical and emotional needs, trauma or unnatural learning conditions?

Let's look at the following charts to view symptoms of insecure attachment, Post Traumatic Stress Disorder and a developmentally inappropriate learning environment and compare them with the impressive-sounding diagnoses that children commonly receive from...

- Mental health counselors,
- School psychologists,
- Psychiatrists and
- Pediatricians...

## *IS IT A BRAIN DISORDER OR DISRUPTED ATTACHMENT?*

| Disrupted Attachment Symptoms | Common Misdiagnosis |
| --- | --- |
| Lack of focus or concentration | Attention Deficit Hyperactivity Disorder (ADHD), Bipolar Disorder |
| Lack of impulse control | ADHD, Bipolar Disorder |
| Sadness, depression or helplessness | Major Depressive Disorder, Dysthymia, Bipolar Disorder |
| Anger or rage | ADHD, Oppositional Defiant Disorder (ODD), Bipolar Disorder |
| Anxiety or restlessness | ADHD |
| Hyperactivity | ADHD |
| Verbally or physically aggressive | ODD, Bipolar Disorder |
| Self-harming or self-destructive | ODD, Bipolar Disorder, a psychotic disorder |
| Antagonistic | ADHD, ODD, Bipolar Disorder |
| Irresponsible with age appropriate expectations | ADHD, Learning Disabilities (LD) |
| Oppositional and defiant | Oppositional Defiant Disorder (ODD), Conduct Disorder, Bipolar Disorder, ADHD |
| Bossy or manipulative | ODD, Bipolar Disorder |
| Unstable peer relationships | Pervasive Developmental Disorder (PDD), Bipolar |
| Indiscriminately friendly | ADHD, Bipolar Disorder |
| Cannot tolerate limits | ODD, ADHD, Bipolar Disorder |
| Exaggerated emotional responses | Bipolar Disorder, a psychotic disorder |
| Difficulty with change | PDD, Obsessive Compulsive Disorder (OCD), ODD |
| Tactile defensiveness | PDD, OCD |
| Needy or clingy | Separation Anxiety Disorder |
| Not mutually affectionate | PDD, ODD |
| Destruction of property | ODD, Bipolar Disorder |
| Stealing | ODD, Bipolar Disorder |
| Lying | ODD, Bipolar Disorder |
| Grandiosity/exaggerated sense of strength or ability | Bipolar Disorder, a psychotic disorder |
| Incessant chatter but little serious talk | ADHD |
| Lack of remorse | ODD, Conduct Disorder, Bipolar Disorder |
| Preoccupation with "evil", fire, gore | ODD, Bipolar, Conduct Disorder, a psychotic disorder |

## IS IT A DISABILITY OR A DEVELOPMENTALLY INNAPROPRIATE LEARNING ENVIRONMENT?

| Symptom | Common Misdiagnosis |
| --- | --- |
| Crying, clinging to parent, school refusal | Separation Anxiety Disorder |
| Protesting school, skipping class, truancy | Oppositional Defiant Disorder, Conduct Disorder |
| Difficulty learning to read, write or understand math the school's way and on the school's timetable | Attention Deficit Hyperactivity Disorder (ADHD), Learning Disability (LD) |
| Difficulty learning or processing verbal or auditory information | ADHD, LD, Pervasive Developmental Disorder |
| Dislike of writing, reading, math, etc. | LD, ADHD, ODD |
| Talented at art, music, sports or other craft but difficulty with "academics" | LD, ADHD, PDD |
| Preoccupation with one subject or hobby | LD, ADHD, PDD |
| Inability to focus or concentrate | ADHD |
| Hyperactivity | ADHD |
| Restlessness and fidgeting | ADHD |
| Boredom, being "off task", daydreaming | ADHD, LD |
| Refusal to do school work and homework | LD, ADHD, ODD, Conduct Disorder |

## *IS IT A BRAIN DISORDER OR POST TRAUMATIC STRESS DISORDER?*

| PTSD Symptom | Common Misdiagnosis |
|---|---|
| Rage outbursts | Bipolar Disorder, Pervasive Developmental Disorder, Oppositional Defiant Disorder |
| Hypervigilance | Attention Deficit Hyperactivity Disorder, Learning Disabilities |
| Anxiety | ADHD, LD, Bipolar Disorder |
| Dissociation | ADHD, LD, PDD |
| Traumatic acting out | ODD, Bipolar Disorder, ADHD, a psychotic disorder, PDD, Conduct Disorder |
| Distress at reminders of trauma or triggers | ADHD, ODD, Bipolar Disorder, a psychotic disorder, PDD, Conduct Disorder |
| Self-protective acts | ODD, Conduct Disorder |
| Inability to concentrate | ADHD, LD |
| Hyperactivity | ADHD |
| Restriction of range of emotions | PDD |
| Startle response | ADHD, Bipolar Disorder, ODD |
| Illusions/Hallucinations | A psychotic disorder, Bipolar Disorder |
| Avoidance behaviors | ODD, ADHD, LD, Conduct Disorder |

## Some words about neurological impairments, mental illness and medical issues

Tragically, neurological impairments and developmental disabilities due to genetics, injuries, illness and exposure to toxins do exist. However, they are rare occurrences and must be diagnosed by a neurologist using a thorough series of conclusive examinations.

However, most professionals who diagnose children with questionable disorders such as "ADHD" will give this diagnosis and others based on parent and teacher questionnaires and subjective reports of "hyperactivity", "out of control energy", "explosive mood swings" and "lack of focus". Some families report that their children received the ADHD diagnosis *and a stimulant drug* after meeting only once with a psychiatrist or pediatrician and reporting to them that their children are "hyper" and "can't concentrate" in school! Psychiatrist Dr. Peter Breggin disputes that ADHD even exists. He believes that it is simply a set of *natural childhood reactions to intolerable conditions.*

In adults, emotional instability or "mental illness" is often:

- A set of deeply ingrained patterns of coping behaviors,
- Extremes of natural emotions, and
- Extremes of unexpressed grief...
- ...Combined with a person's temperament and genetic makeup...

That is the result of...

- An insecure parent-child attachment in childhood,
- Having unmet physical and emotional needs in childhood,

- Childhood trauma such as neglect, abandonment or physical, emotional or sexual abuse,
- Developmentally inappropriate or traumatic school experiences,
- Childhood losses, or
- Traumatic religious experiences.

Professionals must use extreme caution in diagnosing children and young adults with mental illnesses— *What professionals are really diagnosing is human suffering from unnatural childhood conditions!*

Diagnosing and "treating" a child while leaving the child's basic attachment needs unaddressed and unmet *is like treating the symptoms of a starvation victim while never actually feeding the person.*

If we as professionals choose to diagnose children for insurance purposes, we must make sure the true purpose of diagnosing is *to help parents meet children's real needs*— not so we "can put a name to the behavior", set up behavioral plans, make children cooperate at school or medicate them!

Although it appears that there may be some genetic tendencies, or predispositions, to extreme emotional patterns passed on to other generations, it is scientifically uncertain if mental illness is genetic. My theory is that individuals are expressing their traumatic distress in patterns that are temperamentally similar to their biological family members. If it *is* the case that specific mental illnesses are genetic, punishing children's behavior to extinguish it "young" will not *prevent* mental illness! In fact, it will be likely to *onset* or *exacerbate* mental illness! Any possible predispositions to mental instability are more likely to manifest in children if there are insecure parent-child attachments, if early needs are not met and if children experience trauma.

It is uncertain if the apparent genetic predispositions are actually genetic or cultural... People in peaceful tribal cultures and many primates reportedly rarely exhibit mental illness symptoms unless they are exposed to outside cultural conditions that are...

- Traumatic,
- Violent, or
- Exploitive of their land or way of life.

Likewise, the current popular medical theory is that mental illness is the result of "chemical imbalances" in the brain. However, this impressive-sounding hypothesis cannot conclusively answer some very important questions:

- Do chemical imbalances in the brain *cause* mental illness? Or, does chronic emotional distress from unmet needs and from intolerable environments *result in* chemical imbalances?
- Are chemical imbalances genetic *disorders?* Or, are chemical imbalances a result of chronic emotional distress paired with a person's (genetically-influenced) *temperament and personality patterns?*

Other stressors that may affect behavior, emotions and brain chemistry are:

- Vitamin, mineral or amino acid deficiencies
- Poor hydration
- Low or unstable blood sugar
- Toxins, chemicals and additives in foods

- Eating food (even fruits and vegetables) that is processed and not grown organically
- Toxins and chemicals in household cleaning and hygiene products
- Toxins in vaccines
- Lead poisoning
- Food allergies
- Environmental allergies
- Environmental pollution
- Candida yeast overgrowth
- Acidic vs. alkaline pH level in the body
- An undiagnosed medical condition
- Sensory Integration and sensory-motor problems (which may be due to our lack of carrying infants in the first 12 months of life)
- Head and brain trauma

Directing attention to these very real and serious stressors is vital, yet is beyond the scope of this book. Please see the resource list in Chapter 12 for more information.

## Diagnosing and manipulating doesn't meet needs

As parents, it is vital for us to put our conveniences and wishes aside and attune ourselves to our children's needs and alarm signals. Professionals must help parents heal from their own unmet needs in order for them to help their children.

Diagnosing children with the "alphabet soup" of serious sound-ing categories of human suffering does not alleviate children's suffering, nor does it focus on where the suffering began. Most mental health professionals, even if they are trauma-oriented, are not trained to even ask questions about birth trauma, whether the child was left to cry alone in infancy, whether there was a lack of skin-to-skin contact in infancy, whether the child was breastfed, whether or not parents are hitting or yelling at children, or whether or not school is a good place for the child. A shocking number of psychiatrists and other professionals will even *overlook* circumstances such as undiagnosed medical con-ditions, loss, foster care, adoption and physical, sexual or emo-tional abuse in childhood when they diagnose brain disorders!

As professionals, we are trained to focus on symptoms and sometimes, specific traumas such as sexual abuse. Overall, we are trained to play with or talk one-to-one with children about their feelings with the goal of therapeutically manipulating our clients into cooperating with parents and teachers. We measure "progress" by how well a child is cooperating with parents and teachers, rather than how well parents and schools are meeting children's attachment and learning needs.

Rarely do we have the training, time or professional backing to put our entire focus on educating parents (beyond "charts, tools and rewards") about how to heal, repair and secure a deep par-ent-child attachment with children of all ages. Rarely do we as professionals dare advocate for children to NOT sit still in school, to NOT do their school work and homework; we are bound by professional alliances and partnerships...

What if we focused on finding our young clients natural learning environments that are within the means of the parents? State

Departments of Education and local school boards need to feel pressure from parents, mental health professionals and child development experts to cease their developmentally inappropriate practices!

As professionals, we also need to move beyond seeing trauma or "mental illness" as an individual's problem. If we truly wish to help people, it would be in children's best interests if we come to the realization that *our entire culture is traumatized by the unnatural ways of parenting that have been passed down for thousands of years*. Nature calls upon us to work creatively towards *challenging our culture to accommodate the needs of human beings* (especially children). Otherwise, by failing to see our culture's expectations and practices as *the* problem, our job (however well-intentioned) will continue to focus on coercing individual children and adults into accommodating our culture's pathology.

## When angst becomes a youth sub-culture

Sometimes the warning signals that children give us to let us know that they are in emotional pain are so gigantic that they become large pop-cultural "scenes" or sub-cultures. In my view, youth sub-cultures are the manifestation of millions of adolescents and young adults raising their voices in a collective rage, sadness and despair. These youth differentiate themselves into separatist groups, cliques and sub-sub-cultures, often based on music and styles, but the message is the same: A signal of pain. Let's take a brief look at two of the most popular youth sub-cultures of today and the warning signals that children in these sub-cultures are conveying to us:

### Emo "Scene Kids"

If the punk scene of the 1970's and the heavy metal scene of the 1980's reflected the rage and anger of Caucasian youth, the emo scene of the first decade of the 2000's reflects the *pain, angst and depression* of today's unconnected Caucasian youth. The rock genres, hairstyles and "outcast" clothing styles morph and evolve over time. However, fast-paced, intense forms of rock have reflected the alienation, rage, longing, despair and deep sadness of lower and middle class Caucasian youth for decades. Instead of the adult world taking a hint at the severity of the deep pain industrialized children are feeling, emo "scene kids" (like the punks and "headbangers" of the previous youth generations) are dismissed as being caught up in a fad that will pass. In reality, *these music-based "fads" are actual sub-cultures that revolve around the shared pain and alienation of unmet emotional needs, unhealed trauma and insecure parent-child attachment.*

### "Gangstas"

Since the 1970's, the poetic, raw, street-based sounds of rap and hip-hop have reflected the rage, despair and righteous indignation of impoverished African-American and Latino youth who have been worn down by the hopelessness of their violence and drug-infested communities, by the disrespect and racial prejudice they endue and by the harsh treatment they receive at the hands of their fractured families, schools and law enforcement agencies.

Rap began as a mode of cathartic expression; a lyrical and musical art form used as a tool to express the problems of impoverished African-American and Latino youth. However, in the early 1990's, part of the sub-culture around rap and hip-hop devolved into a commercialistic "gangsta rap" scene heavily focused on

258 Instead of Medicating and Punishing

drugs, promiscuous sex and gaining "respect" through fear, violence and money. The commercialistic "gangsta" scene has become so mainstreamed since the late 90's that many culturally disconnected lower and middle class Caucasian youth have assumed it as their "scene" as well. Again, the adult world overlooks the "gangsta" scene as simply a cultural fad and *fails to see the signs and heed the cries of children for emotional connection, secure attachment, safety, security and stability.*

## Congratulations! Your children are behaving naturally, our culture *isn't!*

If you are like I was when I first began to question our culture and my professional training, than you are probably feeling very overwhelmed at this point. Over the past two decades, I have watched, observed, talked with, listened to, researched, played with, cared for, learned from, educated, counseled, mentored, advocated for and hopefully helped, youth of all ages. I have been fortunate enough to have worked with children in a number of different capacities, including as a child care provider, early childhood teacher, school photographer, art teacher, child advocate, researcher, consultant, mentor, social worker, mental health counselor and parenting educator. I am also a proud Mom and Auntie, the most wonderful roles I have ever had in my life!

Through all of the conversations that I have had with children, through all of my cultural observations and research on child development and trauma, and after all of the reflections on my own childhood experiences, too many things weren't making logical and moral sense to me about the way our children are treated in our culture. It didn't make sense to me that children are treated from day one in a way that seems to go against all of their natural needs, wishes, dreams and drives— yet when they grow to be resentful, angry, depressed and unhappy, our culture comes down on them mercilessly for their own suffering. It didn't make sense to me why parents repeat the same practices that caused them to feel terror, rage, sadness and pain in their own childhoods. It didn't make sense to me that out of all of the organisms on the planet, that the human being was born flawed, violent, hateful and apathetic and would deliberately act in ways that would put its children, its species and the entire planet in jeopardy.

I came to understand that human beings are born pro-social and wired for love and attachment. Violence, hatred, selfishness and destructiveness are learned behaviors. I also came to understand that human beings are born to expect the natural conditions that they need in order to develop, attach, learn and thrive. When they don't receive those conditions, they suffer. When a human being suffers, watch out... Humankind, the animal kingdom, the natural environment or the planet will end up paying the price.

I began to question our culture's parenting practices, the entire institution of schooling, our lack of child protection laws, our lack of children's rights, our discrimination and disrespect of children, our disregard for the needs of children, our move away from natural attachment parenting, our move away from freedom and play in learning and our desire to have teachers, TV sets, electronics and other children raise our children. Finally, I began to question the culture itself and its toxicity to parents and children.

Understanding, accepting and integrating all of this new information will take time and more reading. I hope you will read the books and visit the websites that I have recommended in Chapter 12 so that you can increase your knowledge of your children's needs and of further ways to repair and heal your relationship with them.

*"...And these children*
*that you spit on*
*as they try to change their worlds*
*are immune to your consultations.*
*They are quite aware*
*of what they're going through."*
    *–David Bowie, quoted from* <u>*The Breakfast Club*</u>

# Chapter 11 Part I
# Repairing Attachment and Healing Trauma for Children of All Ages

*"All the little boys and girls,*
*Living in this crazy world,*
*All they really needed from you*
*Is maybe some love..."*
*-John Lennon, Real Love*

## Looking beyond "services," "programs", punishments and "techniques": Healing children's deepest voids

When our children become angry, rageful, depressed, aggressive, addicted, withdrawn, hyperactive, anxious, unfocused, learning "disabled" and oppositional, in desperation we turn to "experts" and programs. Unfortunately, because our culture is sick and so far away from nature's intent for raising young humans, *our society can only offer advice, diagnoses and interventions that reflect the culture's ignorance to children's real needs.*

Children do not need behavioral charts, therapeutic techniques, service plans, five different medications, tougher punishments, tutoring, school programs or tricks from the latest parenting "tool" books... *Children need their most basic emotional and physical needs met, a secure attachment to the most important people in their lives and a deep, affectionate connection to those loved ones.* Parents are not told this emphatically, as they should be, nor are they guided in that direction; the well-meaning helpers and "experts" are all products of the conditioning of this culture!

The experts and helpers believe what they are taught in college and grad school and in trainings, text books, journals, the media and from their savvy senior colleagues. Unfortunately, although many experienced helpers and professionals instinctually *know* what children truly need, they don't have the time, resources, professional support, backing, diagnostic code numbers and insurance authorization to make secure attachment and meeting basic needs *the* primary and *only* treatment plan...

The common "services" in the mental health, social service and educational fields:

- A bi-monthly, 15- minute appointment for drug refills with a psychiatrist,
- A monthly meeting with a social worker,
- A twice-monthly fun time with a mentor,
- A weekly visit from a parenting aid or short term social service program worker,
- Three-fourths of an hour of weekly "play therapy", one-to-one with a therapist,
- A once-per-day "check in" with a school adjustment counselor, or

- An "as needed" cool-down time in the "time-out room" of the school

*...do not meet the requirements of nature's intent for child development...*

While these are commendable attempts at temporarily alleviating human suffering, *none of these interventions fills children's natural requirement for a secure parent-child attachment, nor do they fill years and years of voids and empty holes in children's development from unmet basic needs and a disrupted attachment cycle.*

As a mental health therapist, I have worked with children who have literally worked with 10 or more therapists in their young lifetimes— That's more than one for every year of their lives in some cases! Exhausted parents, in desperate situations, try to do everything they are able to do, to the best of their understanding, to try to find relief from the struggles their families are facing, yet nothing seems to help. Program after program, expert after expert, helper after helper, offers suggestions, treatment plans, programs, drugs, support groups, services and more resources, yet children become angrier, more depressed, more defiant and more lost while families become more fractured and deeper and deeper into an abyss of despair and punitive reactions.

Compare our culture's interventions and services to the natural ways that peaceful tribal cultures grow children: Could the experts and helpers ever begin to make up for what our culture's children lack? Is it possible for parents and helpers to make up for what children have been missing? Is repair, healing and respite from our culture's emotional malnourishment possible?

Although we cannot re-live our own childhoods and our children's childhoods by joining a peaceful tribal culture (we would only taint the tribes that are still in existence), there *are* some critical ways that we as parents can begin the slow process of healing our children's trauma and the damage done to the parent-child attachment.

Regardless of what any books or experts tell you, there is NO magical cure, no single, simple technique; no quick, rushed fix. If we want our children to be truly happy, if we want to repair our parent-child attachment to the best of our children's abilities to heal, then medication, charts, programs, punishment, yelling, tricks and threats will not help. We must be willing to put in double the amount of connection, double the amount of affection, double the amount of commitment and double the amount of substitute for whatever our children needed and didn't receive. We must be willing to accept and listen to our children's rage and grief, fully, with as minimal judgment or defensiveness as possible. We need to take responsibility for our children's pain.

Does that sound like a lot of intense work? *Yes, it is intense work.* Are our children hurting? Most of them are *intensely* hurting; *healing must be equally as intense.* Are our precious children; our fetuses, infants, toddlers, young children, older children, adolescents and young adults, worth it? Is their happiness and joy worth it? Are their lives worth it? *Absolutely!* Can every parent do this? Yes, but not without their own mentors and healing.

## Healing ourselves to heal our children

Most of us who grew up in our culture are deeply wounded children in full-grown bodies. We may find it impossible to give something we didn't receive. For the sake of our children, because they only have one childhood, we have *an obligation and responsibility to them* to heal ourselves enough to meet their needs whether they are toddlers or older adolescents. If we, as their parents, are unable or unwilling to undertake this task, we are responsible for finding someone who *will* be able to nurture our children in the way that *our children need*.

*No child should ever have to reach adulthood feeling as lost, abandoned and needy as most young adults feel in our culture.*

## Getting a breath of air in desperate situations

If you are feeling desperate in your relationship with your children right now and feel you must have a quick, temporary fix, please consider these options:

- Work out an arrangement with a friend to provide respite for you for a few days and on a regular basis;
- Set up a sleep-over for your children at one of their friend's homes;
- If you are fortunate enough to have family members who will help you out, send your children for a visit with one of them;
- If your children are adopted, contact your state's post-adoption services division of the health and human services department and ask about respite services; and
- Contact your state's department of health and human services and ask for parenting support resources in your area.

If you are feeling like you are in danger of hurting your child, please separate yourself from your child and contact:

- Parents Anonymous, free USA Hotline: 1-800-352-0528 www.parentsanonymous.org;
- Girls and Boys Town National (USA) Hotline 1-800-448-3000 www.parenting.org;
- Many community mental health clinics have crisis services, call the information operator to locate one in your area; and
- Contact your state's department of health and human services and ask about voluntary services for you and your child.

## Basic principles for repairing and healing attachment for children of all ages

- Physical Affection
- *Physical Affection*
- PHYSICAL AFFECTION!
- Stop all forms of physical and emotional abuse and neglect (including "spanking", yelling, threatening and ignoring basic physical and emotional needs).
- Stop all punishments.
- Protect your child from abuse and neglect by others and advocate fiercely for your child.
- Empathize, empathize, *empathize*!
- Re-parent earlier developmental needs, no matter what age.
- Hold, rock and cuddle your child regularly.
- Eye gaze with your child when you cuddle.
- Caress your child's face, arms and hands.

- Turn off the TV, video games and computer— Better yet, rarely turn them on!
- Play with your child 1:1.
- Allow a great deal of physical activity and join in with your child.
- Get into one of your child's interests.
- Give each of your children at least 1/2 hour of 1:1 time and your full attention <u>daily</u>.
- Allow your child to develop, progress and grow at your child's own pace.
- Nurture and love your child as your child is.
- Treasure and cherish your child and your child's unique qualities.
- Listen to your child and learn about your child's passions, concerns, views, interests, dreams and soul longings.
- Prevent conflicts before they start.
- Avoid situations that emotionally dysregulate (upset) your child.
- Model, guide and discuss important Family Principles that <u>*all*</u> family members must follow.
- Be a strong, safe, firm and gentle authority.
- When your children break a Family Principle, discuss the reasons why and decode the unmet needs.
- Listen to and validate your child's feelings.
- Empathize, empathize, <u>*empathize*</u>!
- Ask for restitution instead of using punishment.
- Heal the <u>causes</u> of your child's symptoms.
- Get help for yourself if you are angry, aloof, depressed, sarcastic, irritable or anxious.

- Allow your children to direct their own play and learning interests without structure or "educational materials".

- Find a child-centered educational environment such as unschooling, homeschooling, Montessori, Waldorf, other non-traditional private school or charter school.

- Do not allow homework to infringe upon your family time and peace.

- Help heal physical, sexual and emotional trauma by finding EMDR treatment for your child.

- Find alternatives to giving your child psychiatric drugs, such as holistic, body-centered treatments and brain-based Neurofeedback.

- Find an ethical attachment specialist if you believe that you need family therapy.

- Take responsibility for your mistakes and make restitution to your child!

## Attachment parenting

The foundation of attachment parenting is making sure our children's basic physical and emotional needs are being met daily so that the parent-child attachment is secure and not disrupted. Most well-meaning parents in our culture assume they are already meeting their children's needs, *but their children's behavior shows us otherwise.*

In this book, I outlined the many ways that industrialized culture causes the majority of its parents to parent in ways that disrupt or break the parent-child attachment cycle. The majority of the children in our culture, including our own, are not getting their basic physical and emotional needs and higher level needs met.

If you have not practiced attachment parenting from the beginning, then it is possible to repair parent-child attachment and work towards a secure attachment, no matter what your child's age! Whether your child is a toddler or stepping out of adolescence into adulthood, it is never too late to heal parent-child attachment and meet some of your child's unmet needs. Of course, the younger that this process begins, the more unmet needs you will be able to meet and the more likely it is that you and your child will heal your attachment to the point of it becoming secure.

## The Connection-Cooperation Principle

Pam Leo, author of *Connection Parenting*, lists two specific points that I believe are crucial for all of us as parents to understand if we wish to heal our attachment relationships with our children:

1. "All behaviors are need-driven. We do what we do to get our needs met."

2. "The level of cooperation parents get from their children is usually equal to the level of *connection* children feel with their parents."

Most of us grew up being taught that children are born with "bad", lazy, aggressive or selfish tendencies and it is the job of adults to "discipline" and "educate" those tendencies out of children. This belief is responsible for much of the suffering that we endured as children and then passed onto our own children. This suffering is caused by emotional coldness, apathy, punishments, coercion, physical, emotional and sexual abuse, traditional schooling and treating children like property, prisoners or sub-human beings.

The destructive and false belief that children are born flawed and wayward had its roots in various religions that were very punitive, fear-based and rigid. Unfortunately, this belief runs contrary to what is natural for human children and to what nature's intent is for how children should be parented.

Pam Leo's two points...
- "All behaviors are need-driven. We do what we do to get our needs met";

And:
- "The level of cooperation parents get from their children is usually equal to the level of connection children feel with their parents"...

...are contrary to the old way that we have been raised by and taught.

Remember, the foundation of attachment parenting is making sure our children's basic physical and emotional needs are being met daily so that the parent-child attachment is secure and not disrupted. When children's needs are met physically, emotionally, socially, intellectually and so on, they do not have a need to act out and they have no desire to be "lazy learners". If children are suffering from unmet needs, any alarm signals they give us (in the form of crying, refusing to do schoolwork and countless other upsetting behaviors) means *just that:* That they are suffering from unmet needs and they are doing what they are doing in attempts to bring attention to that fact. *We cannot expect children to feel close to us, care about learning and cooperate with us or with society's expectations when they are distracted by the distress of unmet needs.*

I love Leo's second point above, "The level of cooperation parents get from their children is usually equal to the level of connection children feel with their parents". This is in line with basic logic, commonsense, and the nature of human beings. It also strikes down the "expert advice" of our time which states that children who aren't cooperating are probably suffering from a brain disorder and must be offered treatment, a program or medication. If we see our children's acting-out as a "disorder" in their brains, then we absolve ourselves of the responsibility to discover their unmet needs and meet those needs.

I have found the "Connection-Cooperation Principle" to be true time and time again with my own son and nephews and also with the young people I have worked with over the years. I also know that it rang true for me in my own childhood: The adults that showed *me* the most respect and connection in my child-hood were the adults that *I* respected and felt the most connect-ed to! It sounds so obvious... Yet daily, parents, teachers, and people who work with children in the myriads of programs in our society still believe that they can threaten, scare, bully and punish children into cooperating and feeling respect and con-nection to them!

I adopted my 14-year old son from the foster care system. Many times when my son becomes oppositional, I can usually trace it to somewhere I was lax in meeting his emotional needs. When I ask myself, "have I been less affectionate lately? Have I found myself forcing him lately to do homeschooling "work" (instead of trusting his direction) because I fear we won't have enough to put in his homeschooling portfolio? Have I been spending a lot of time making excuses for being too tired or too busy to play with him or listen to him? Have I been snappy lately? Have I been apathetic to his feelings? Have I been dictating most of the "fun" activities and games we'll play lately instead of honoring his ideas? Have I been shooing him out to play with friends rather than taking that bike ride with him? Have I been rushing him when we do spend time cuddling, talking or playing?

I usually find that the answer to one or many of those questions is a guilty "yes, yes, yes". When I realize the pattern, I try to immediately reconnect to my son and discuss with him my thoughts about why he's been having such a tough time. He always agrees that he was missing something from me. After expressing his feelings about it and receiving empathy from me, he then grabs onto me with a relieved and soul-filling hug. After that, he is more likely to honor *my* requests for cooperation. Within a few hours or days, we fully reconnect, as I am mindful of meeting his needs, and his behavior becomes stable again, as it usually is. *I need to emphasize that this works even if serious life tragedies are occurring at the same time, such as the death of a loved one..*

*Our children will become emotionally and behaviorally unstable when they feel unconnected*, not only because of grief from tragedy. My son demonstrated this strongly when he experienced several emotional and upsetting situations all within a period of a few months and he destabilized emotionally and behaviorally: He lost his pet chinchilla. Some of our core family members were not spending time with us. Our homeschool group temporarily joined with another homeschool group, and temporarily moved from a beautiful ocean-side location to a concrete building. When my son's voice began to change with puberty, he lost his confidence and wouldn't sing for nearly a year; singing is his passion. His great-grandmother became critically ill and was in the hospital for nearly four months, and then she passed away after making it home and celebrating her 80th birthday. One of his close friends moved away. On top of this, my son received contact from a biological family member which led to an emotional visit and a mixture of happiness, grief and rage.

When my son began to destabilize, I attributed it to all of the tumultuous situations above. When his behavior and emotional distress increased, I realized that during this time, my son and I were slowly spending less and less time connecting and more time rushing. When my grandmother died, I became consumed with grief and I didn't spend as much time *as my son needed* with *his* grief. Once I figured this out and immediately met his needs, my son and I reconnected, and he became more emotionally and behaviorally stable over time, despite the grief he was still obviously experiencing.

## Children need us to empathize with their feelings and needs before they can cooperate with ours

Attachment parenting is anything parents do that promotes a secure parent-child attachment through meeting children's basic physical and emotional needs and then higher level needs. It starts in the womb and continues until young adulthood. However, since most parents in industrialized cultures have not been taught to parent naturally, they will be starting with children who are wrapped in layers of unmet needs, expressing rivers of anger, hurt and sadness, keeping a thick barrier of alarm signals and defenses barricading these layers of unmet needs.

You cannot heal your children and develop an attachment with them without physical affection, nurturance and frequent one-to-one play with your children. This is true whether your children are babies or in late adolescence! Although physical affection with adolescents should be at their pace, it is essential that parents prioritize affection: In fact, it must be as important as meals and sleep... Even if children resist initially, keep it light and non-invasive and gradually build their comfort level.

If your children are generally cooperative and are showing mild forms of attachment disruption through mild tantruming, sarcasm, rudeness, pulling away, social anxiety, shyness, clinginess, moodiness or materialism, you may notice that you can reconnect to your child very quickly once you discover their unmet needs and meet them.

If your children are showing moderate to severe emotional and behavioral instability, or are using substances, it will take a strong commitment by you as the parent...

- To meet your children's basic needs over and over; and
- To slowly replace your old parenting habits with showing respect and empathy to your children

...before you notice longer lasting cooperation and stability. We parents cannot do this without attending to our own unmet needs at the same time, through self care, proper trauma treatment, attachment treatment, finding mentors and enriching our lives by engaging in our own passions.

Our industrialized children have many, many years of rage, sadness, grief and hurt to express to us and *they need us to empathize with their feelings and needs before they can cooperate with ours.* It will take the oldest and most hurt of them awhile to trust that we are serious about their needs and about our connection to them.

# Instilling principles, self-discipline and responsibility

## Family principles rather than rules

Ideally, before your children come into your life, you should have a solid set of Family Principles firmly in place. Introducing our children very young to a strong set of Family Principles is as necessary as physical affection in helping them to develop an internalized set of moral principles.

Principles are *the way you live*; they are *not a list of rules that you enforce just to be in control*. People, children included, naturally resist rules, as rules tend to apply only to the people in a relationship with less power. Principles, however, are followed by everyone in a relationship and are based upon a way of living in harmony with everyone's needs.

Family principles ideally are necessities for having a happy, healthy family life. Below is a sample list of Family Principles that would work with children *who show mild to moderate attachment disruption*. For a sample list of Family Principles that would work best for children with severe attachment disruption or Reactive Attachment Disorder (RAD), including adoptive children, please read Part II of Chapter 11.

The following principles are simple and specific for promoting attachment, healthy self-care habits, responsibility, give and take, cause and effect and moral development for children. They can be updated as needed. Feel free to copy them down and use them with your family:

## Our Family Principles

- Mom and Dad's job is to take care of (list children's names here), keep them safe and make decisions about what is best for them physically, emotionally, education- ally and spiritually. (Children)'s job is to share closeness with our family.

- (Children) will have the freedom to direct their own inter- ests. Dad and Mom will set some limits to ensure safety and physical and emotional health, as well as respectful- ness and fairness for everyone. (Children) will earn more freedoms as they demonstrate the good judgment and responsibility to handle those freedoms. Freedom may be reduced if it is infringing upon someone else or on our Family Principles.

- We treat one another with love and respect in our family. We express emotions with words. We do not hit, scream at or say hurtful or sarcastic things to one another. We take space if we are too angry to talk.

- We treat all people, pets and living things with respect.

- We treat property and our home with respect.

- We cleanup after ourselves. Dad and Mom take care of most of the family responsibilities and (children) are responsible for helping out by each completing a daily chore.

- (Children)'s room time is _____ p.m.

- We treat ourselves with respect. We eat healthy, practice good hygiene and dress presentably.

- We use restitution in our family. If a Family Principle is broken, whether by child or adult, we must discuss it and make restitution. *We will all decide as a family* the ways we can make restitution for breaking a Family Principle.

---

Stating at the onset of the list that it is our job as parents to take care of our children and that it is their job as our children to work on sharing closeness to and with us is sacred: It puts in writing the most important purpose of family. The principles relating to natural authority and how we treat others also help children to build a foundation and skeleton of how families work, as well as pro-social and nonviolent behavior. These principles help children develop attachment, empathy, responsibility and moral values.

Assigning your children a daily chore will help them develop a sense of responsibility. Even toddlers can pick up a toy and place it in a toy box each day. Explain how each family member does their part and how it helps the whole family unit. In the case of children with mild to moderate attachment disruption, if chores are ignored or refused, discuss the situation with your children and make sure that your children understand how much their contribution matters to the functioning of the whole family. Do your children have unmet needs that they are expressing to you by refusing their responsibilities? Are chores presented as demands or as ways all family members cooperate with one another?

If your children have moderate to severe attachment disruptions *and their basic needs have been met,* refer to Part II of Chapter 11.

### Consequences and restitution

Clearly model and explain to your children that restitution is used by all family members (including parents) to make amends for broken family principles and broken responsibilities. *Whenever a Family Principle is broken, first find out if your children are really signaling unmet needs.* Once the needs are met, discuss how your children could let you know about their unmet needs next time, in a way that you can understand.

If your children have suffered mild to moderate attachment disruption, discuss *as a family* what consequences and restitution are fair for everyone. *Make sure that you are not justifying punishments and calling them "restitution"— Children immediately will notice your hypocrisy and will challenge you about it!* Restitution should be directly related to principles broken and to what family members say they need in order for restitution to be made.

Some examples:

- If your child is disrespectful to you, request that she "rewind" and repeat what she wanted to say to you in a way you can hear it.

- If your child deliberately breaks something, help him to earn money to replace the property.

- If your homeschooling child repeatedly refuses to cooperate with the state requirements for homeschooling, take her on a tour of the local public school so she can see the contrast in her freedoms,

- If your child came home 1/2 hour later than agreed upon, ask him to come home 1/2 hour earlier the next time he goes out.

- If your child is treating others with disrespect, ask that the other person tell your child how they are feeling about how they are being treated.

- If your child repeatedly interrupts you during your own quiet time, request that she pay the time back by agreeing to an earlier "in your room time" before bed.

- If your child hits a sibling or friend, ask that your child do something nice for the sibling or friend once feelings have been expressed.

Remember, hitting, grabbing, yelling, threatening, neglecting and punishing have no place in healing attachment:

- Never hit your child... Yes, "spanking" and "smacking" are hitting. All types of hitting are damaging to children.

- Never use any type of rough handling or scare tactics such as grabbing, shaking or pain infliction on your children.

- Punishments are not discipline, restitution or "consequences"— They are punishments and they cause resentment.

- Never neglect any of your children's basic physical or emotional needs as "consequences". Punishing children by making them suffer with unmet needs is neglect, not a "consequence".

- Although there are times when raising our voices may be appropriate in serious situations, yelling, name calling, threatening and sarcasm have no place in attachment parenting.

When your children break a Family Principle, here are a set of steps to help you both understand and learn from the incident. This process will help instill emotional regulation, cause and effect and teaching appropriate expression of emotions in your children. If you skip this process with children who are acting-out and let acting-out behaviors slide, your child's acting-out behaviors are likely to worsen.

1. Ask your child to discuss what he needed and why the incident occurred.
2. Ask your child what feeling she was trying to express by acting out.
3. Validate and empathize with his need and feelings and let him express them fully.
4. Express your feelings about the incident and express what you need.
5. Explain why the Family Principle exists and why break-ing it is not acceptable.
6. Discuss the alternatives your child has for expressing her feelings.
7. Allow your child to discuss ways to make restitution if restitution is necessary.
8. Once restitution is made, drop the incident, let your child resume his day and do not hold a grudge.
9. You may need to repeat this process countless times for the same or different incidents.

As with the other steps, if your child suffers from moderate to severe attachment disruption, refer to Part II of Chapter 11.

### Some words about "time-out"

In the 1990's, this overused form of punishment became the vogue "alternative" to hitting children. "Experts" everywhere began to instruct parents about the most "effective" uses of time-out, including counting before banishing children to a time-out, setting a timer for "one minute for each year of a child's age" or designating a special "time-out chair". I, myself, jumped on the bandwagon, recommending on my website and to parents of the children I worked with in the past that they use short, open-ended 30-second time-outs to "interrupt" the misbehavior of children. Although I certainly would prefer to hear a parent threaten to "time-out" a child rather than to hit a child, time-outs can be used abusively, can be neglectful of a child's needs and are generally very punitive.

After more research and insight into the subject, I have come to realize a few facts about time-outs:

- They don't work well over time;
- They don't work with most older children;
- They are a form of punishment;
- They can harm the parent-child attachment;
- They give too much power and control to the adult over a child;
- They are usually disrespectful of children and their needs;
- They banish children for having difficulty expressing their feelings and needs appropriately;
- They cover over the true needs of a child and the reason the child is acting out in the first place;
- They are often an excuse for not child-proofing an area or a room for young children;
- They are often a way for adults to avoid changing the arbitrary and nonsense rules that they enforce;
- They are often an excuse for parents who do not want to give children the one-to-one time and attention that the children need in a situation; and

- They are usually one-sided—Children can't "time-out" adults who act out.

I recall one of the first times that I began to realize the hypocrisy of "time-outs". In the 1990's when I was working as a preschool teacher, I did my share of giving short, 30-second "time-outs" to very young children who threw their toys across the room. One day, I was rushing while leading a "clean up time" in the class-room. In the interests of saving time, I took a handful of large Duplo blocks and threw them far across the room into their con-tainer, impressed with my accuracy! Suddenly, I heard a shocked, indignant admonishment by one of my fellow little "cleaners": She left her "job", marched up to me (her face set with justice), stood to her full three-year old height, shook her finger at me and bellowed, "Miss Laurie, TIME OUT!"

I had all I could do not to laugh, both at her cute, exaggerated reaction *and* my red-faced hypocrisy. Suddenly she and a group of tiny boys and girls took me by the arms and all giggled or called out loudly, "Time out, Miss Laurie!" I humorously pretend-ed to protest, giving them the pleasure of feeling empowered to execute justice while I good-naturedly allowed them to lead me to the "time-out area"... I sat on a toddler-sized couch, pretend-ing to sulk for several minutes as a class full of little people hopped up and down and giggled at "Miss Laurie's time-out"!

How many of us allow children to "time us out" when we have "misbehaved"? Do you need a testimony to the fact that "time-outs" don't meet the need behind the "misbehavior"? Not too long later when I was working in another preschool, a similar incident occurred: Again, in the interest of time, I was caught throwing toys across the room, into their containers! This time, a whole group of little ones ran over to decry my hypocrisy, ending up with me in the "time-out area" yet again! Many other children in my life, including the adolescents I worked with in the past who lived in residential facilities, as well as my oldest nephew and my son, have taught me that time-out is punitive and ignores or covers up the need behind the acting out behavior. These children slowly helped me *realize* what my research on attachment parenting was trying to teach me!

Can time-out ever be a good thing? I have found that time-out can be a very much needed way for parents and older children to calm down when they have *both* agreed to use it *ahead of time.* For example, you and your child might come to an agreement to yell out a word such as "break!" or "space!" when both of you become heated—then you can both go into a separate room. Your older children may also agree, ahead of time, to give you permission to ask them to "take space" in another room when they are becoming emotionally out of control and unable to talk with you. (If you are in a small living space, these strategies can be especially helpful). If time-out is used in these ways by older children *and parents together,* as a strategy for calming down, getting centered and thinking before speaking, it can be a valuable tool for modeling emotional stability.

## Tools for nonviolent emotional expression

Children cannot be expected to be able to express their emotions and needs acceptably if they are not taught and allowed to practice the necessary tools for regulating emotions. For most of our children who have suffered disrupted attachment and unmet needs, irritability, anger, depression and sadness are the primary emotions that they may express. Daily, over and over, model and teach your children the following tools when they are calm, and then guide them in using these tools when they are showing signs of needing them.

Here is a list of tools for children to use to help them develop emotional stability:

---

**Tools for Emotional Stability for Parents and Children**

- Express your feelings and needs honestly, fully, calmly and respectfully;
- Ask yourself, what do our Family Principles say about this?
- Check in with yourself and figure out what you are feeling;
- Feel your feelings and needs, letting the intensity sink in;
- Take five to ten *slow, deep* breaths *from the stomach*
  - It is important to stretch or inflate the stomach on the deep breath *in* and deflate the stomach with the breath *out*.
  - Do not breathe shallowly from the upper chest or rapidly or you may become light headed. This is one of the single most important tools for getting anger and anxiety under control.
- Can you change your negative thoughts to more rational statements?
  - For example, instead of "I hate doing these dishes", say, "I dislike these dishes, but I know I am doing my part to help out. After I am done, I am free to do something I want to do."
- FREEZE MOUTH AND BODY!
- Do a physical activity such as biking, running, push ups, etc.;
- Take space alone;
- Express your feelings with art, music or a project;

- Do a "grounding" exercise:
  - Starting with the feet, focus completely on how your skin feels in your shoes and sock. Work up slowly to the top of your head, feeling every texture against your skin.
  - Gently push firmly on all of your major muscles, such as your upper and lower arms and legs, your back, chest, thighs, etc.
- Tell yourself, "I may not act out my feelings."
- Remind yourself that it is ok to feel feelings, but feeling them is NOT acting them out in harmful ways.
- Think of the possible consequences of your actions;
- Think of the last time you lost control. Ask yourself what you do want and what you don't want to happen;
- Think of the stone in the water metaphor:
  - When you throw a stone, it creates widening circles of ripples around the spot of impact. These ripples represent the consequences of the action. The action is represented by the stone thrown.
- Do an audio tape to whoever you are angry at;
- Think out loud in private;
- Remind yourself that you are a role model for the younger children in your life. What would you tell them to do in your situation?
- Don't judge others until you look at your own actions.

---

Here is an example of a plan that my son and I have been using since he first joined our family through adoption. Parents and children can use this plan together to help them regain emotional stability if they begin to lose control of their emotions or if they enter into a power struggle:

## Sample Plan to Reverse Power-Struggles

- Parent or child yells out a signal word that both of you agree on such as "RESPITE!" or "FREEZE!" Both parties must freeze their voices and bodies once someone yells it out.

- Parent asks child, "What do you need right now?"

- Child expresses his need— He may need something as simple as a hug to ground himself back in reality. Suggest a need if she does not come up with an answer.

- Both parent and child take deep breaths and use any other tools to calm down.

- Child expresses his feelings first; parent empathizes and validates.

- Parent express her feelings next, parent empathizes with herself (in her head).

- Child expresses his need, parent responds.

- Parent expresses her need (for example, the need for child to be safe or the need for some time alone), asks child to respond.

- Both come up with a mutual agreement or compromise. Parent has final say if there is no mutual agreement on safety and health issues, but parent must do her best to work towards a compromise.

---

Memorize the tools in this section that work for you and your child, carry a list of them in your pocket or purse, remind yourself and your child to use them and practice them! They really do work when they are used! *If you are meeting your children's basic needs* and any of these tools or principles still do not seem to help your child stabilize, your child's attachment disruption may be moderate to severe. In the case of children adopted from orphanages or from the foster care system, they may suffer from Reactive Attachment Disorder, which is an extreme form of attachment disruption. For moderate to more severe forms of attachment disruption, please read Part II of Chapter 11.

## Nonviolent Communication and S.A.L.V.E.

Here are two exceptional, empowering and spiritual models for respectful, nonviolent ways of responding to human conflicts in addition to the ideas I suggested. The S.A.L.V.E. model by Naomi Aldort and the Nonviolent Communication (NVC) model by Marshall B. Rosenberg help us to:

- Rise out of our own hurt feelings and defensiveness,
- Empathize with ourselves and our children,
- Focus on the needs and feelings of our children,
- Validate our children's feelings and our own, and
- Respond in a way or come to a solution that is respectful to both child and parent.

### NVC

The Nonviolent Communication model, or NVC, was designed to be used with all types of human relationships and conflicts. The basic principles of NVC involve trying to understand and empathize with the view points, wants or needs of the other person and opening up a dialogue to balance their needs with our own.

NVC has been successfully used between parents and children, couples, friends, coworkers, teachers and students, as well as supervisors and employees. It has even been used successfully in life threatening conflicts, such as between street gang rivals, between victims and perpetrators of attempted rapes or assaults and even between two ethnic groups of people suffering and retaliating with attacks and war.

I strongly encourage parents to read *Nonviolent Communication: A Language of Life* by Marshall Rosenberg in order to obtain an understanding of the life-changing steps and principles involved with the NVC process.

## S.A.L.V.E.

Naomi Aldort specifically designed the S.A.L.V.E. model to be used by parents of children of all ages, from toddlers to adolescents. She explains that her model "offers a way to relieve ourselves from the unwanted reactions we have to our children, which we often regret later. It allows us to be able to respond to our children in the kind and connecting way we always wish we did. When we do, our children act well not out of fear and not because of seeking approval, but because they want to, out of feeling connected, capable and content".

Aldort's model, outlined in her book, *Raising Our Children, Raising Ourselves,* helps us as parents to:

- "Transform parent-child relationships from reaction and struggle to freedom, power and joy";
- Heal the blocks inside of ourselves that prevent us from responding to our children in the way they need;
- Allow our children the safety to express what they need;
- Allow our children the emotional freedom they need in order to thrive physically, emotionally, behaviorally and spiritually; and
- Allow children the freedom to make choices and direct their lives.

*Raising Our Children, Raising Ourselves* outlines the S.A.L.V.E. model in step-by-step detail and I highly encourage parents to read it.

Since most of us were not taught by our parents to express our feelings honestly, openly and respectfully, we strongly need to seek out the guidance and help that positive communication models such as NVC and S.A.L.V.E. can provide us.

## Alternatives to traditional school

*"I try never to let my schooling get in the way of my education." -Mark Twain, author*

*"It is a fact nothing short of a miracle that the modern methods of instruction have not yet entirely strangled the holy curiosity of inquiry; for this delicate little plant, aside from stimulation, stands mainly in need of freedom; without this it goes to wrack and ruin without fail." -Albert Einstein, scientist*

*"Working on the kindergarten and first-grade programs, I observed something that I thought was truly remarkable. In these grades, children spend most of their time learning things that no one growing up in our culture could possibly avoid learning. For example, they learn the names of the primary colors. Wow, just imagine missing school on the day when they were learning blue. You'd spend the rest of your life wondering what color the sky is." -Daniel Quinn, author*

*"I see public school as a burning building, and I'm going to save every child I can." - John Holt, author and educator*

It is impossible for children's development to meet natural, optimal levels if children spend 14 years in an institution that treats them like prisoners. As parents, it is our responsibility to provide the best learning environment possible for our children, within our means and circumstances.

For children in our culture, one of the biggest disrupters of secure parent-child attachment is traditional school. Not only are children away from their most important relationships for most of the day, their basic needs and their higher level learning needs *are not being met*. This is one of the most difficult concepts for today's parents to grasp; some parents defend traditional school aggressively! We have been so ingrained for decades to believe that forced schooling is a good and necessary thing for children that many parents think that removing their children from school is akin to sentencing them to death!

In reality, most of the children who manage to drag themselves through school are not at all happy and joyful about being there, nor do they keep the same craving for learning that they showed as toddlers. Parents watch with disbelief when they see their children worked harder and harder at younger and younger ages. Parents deny their instincts when they watch their children's outdoor time, play time and time for expressive arts melt away. Parents watch their children slowly disconnect from them more and more as they climb the grades of school, replacing parents with peers, fads, material objects, TV shows, video games, homework and school sports.

Parents find that their family lives are dictated by school schedules, homework, "extracurricular" activities and school projects. Over the years, parents watch their once upbeat children become emotionally sullen, distant, anxious and sarcastic.

Parents feel helpless as their children become bullied or bullies in school. Parents try to deny their hurt when their children (at younger and younger ages) try to pretend they "don't know" their parents when their peers are around. Parents tell themselves that "it's normal" when their children ask them to stand apart from them, drop them off a block from school, not to kiss or hug them, not to hold their hands or not to act "uncool" or "weird" in front of their peers.

Parents try to justify a number of unnatural symptoms of disrupted attachment and unmet needs as "normal" just to keep themselves believing that school is good for children. How much worse does it have to get?

Most parents in our culture do not realize that there are wonderful, joyful alternatives to public school and religious private school that will help their children excel to learning and social potentials that most traditionally schooled children could only dream about. *The closer the learning environment is to natural learning, the more likely it will be that our children will keep their joy and love for learning and meet their learning potentials.* I have included a list of alternatives to traditional schooling and a description of each. I have listed books and resources about alternatives to traditional school in Chapter 12.

## Unschooling

> *"My grandmother wanted me to have an education,*
> *so she kept me out of school."*
> -Margaret Mead, anthropologist and writer

> *"Comparing me to those who are conventionally schooled is like comparing the freedoms of a wild stallion to those of cattle in a feedlot."*
> -Colin Roch, 12 year old unschooler, 1998, from The Unschooling Handbook by Mary Griffith

The most natural form of education is based on a child's needs and interests. "Unschooling" is the term for homeschoolers who allow their children to live their lives naturally through play, exploration, curiosity and through designing their own "curriculum". Unschooling is based on self-directed learning, play, creativity and children following their own interests, passions and directions. The freedom that unschooling parents and children enjoy cannot be believed or understood until people actually break free from the confines of traditional schooling and live it! Unschooling focuses on parent-child and family relationships, healthy friendships, community involvement, joy in learning and children living their dreams and lives *now*, not when they reach adulthood.

Unschoolers, like all homeschoolers, must follow their state's homeschool requirements for information covered each year. Children must take a yearly exam or put together a portfolio of work at the end of the year. An evaluator from the public school, a private school or a paid independent licensed educator reviews the portfolio and makes suggestions if areas are not being covered. Generally, unschoolers do not use grade levels, grading, tests, curriculums, work books and specific study times unless children themselves request these as tools in their learning. Progress is determined by conversations with children and by observing children and the products of their learning. Often, unschooled children function at advanced or adult levels in one or many "subjects" of learning because they have the freedom and time to develop their creativity, skills and talents beyond traditional textbooks, curriculums, grade levels and time tables.

Unschoolers are some of the busiest, most active families in our society, but not in the rushed, stressful, routine way of traditional schooled families. Unschoolers are generally involved in several homeschool and non-homeschool community groups, events and courses, spending time with mixed age groups of children. There is no "typical day" of an unschooler, and there is no distinction between living and learning... Everything in their lives is learning!

There is also no limit to what unschoolers can do with the time that they have, including taking early college courses, starting businesses, exploring and studying nature outdoors and history in their surrounding communities, devouring books, researching any subject that interests them, taking community classes on art, music, theater, electronics, gaming, literature, writing and any other subject imaginable; learning in museums, getting involved with public speaking and political activism, job shadowing and traveling... Many unschoolers are involved with several activities in the homeschooling and non-homeschooling communities and do a mixture of self-directed learning with some specific "academic" work to satisfy state homeschooling requirements in areas that children may not be practicing on their own.

How can parents accommodate unschooling? Sacrifice! I am a single parent, and I have managed to make unschooling possible for my son. I am fortunate enough in my work that I can schedule many of my son's activities around my work schedule, work partially from home and do some of my work at night. Work flexibility is the key to unschooling children who are not yet old enough to be left alone at home. Older adolescents with driver's licenses can be much more independent with unschooling. Since unschooling is living life, there are no timetables; learning happens every day, at all times, not five days a week between the hours of 8 and 3.

Unschooling is doing everything and anything that children find interesting and enjoyable about life, especially play and socialize! It means exploring, developing and following interests, meeting people and becoming active in the community. It means parents supporting children's interests with materials, books, trips, classes and community contacts. Parents must be active in helping children discover their interests, not only connecting them to materials, books, trips, classes and resources they might find interesting but also *abandoning* materials, books, trips and classes that aren't inspiring their children. Unschooling is about trying out new interests, even switching several times. Firm commitments aren't necessary unless your children have made contracts to be part of something which others relay on them for, such as theater or musical performances.

I strongly recommend that parents distract children from TV and video games, restrict TV and video games to the weekends *or turn them off totally*, especially if you are new to unschooling. This will allow your children time to develop their interests and not just sit around and numb themselves. Boredom is a tool to motivate children to discover interests, but TV and video games actually put children's brains into a state similar to a trance. This defeats the purpose of boredom. Sometimes hours can melt by before children decide to turn off the TV or game and actively go do something. The only exception to the restriction would be for mature children who are able to regulate their TV and video gaming time on their own and balance it with active pursuits.

Unschooling is not allowing children to "do nothing". It is not allowing children to "do whatever they want" all the time. It means balancing state requirements for homeschooling with your child's needs, interests and passions.

## Homeschooling

Homeschooling is a broad term that describes families with children who learn at home. The term covers everyone from conservative curriculum-based families who "do school at home" to very freedom-based unschooling families who do everything opposite from school, as well as everyone in between. Most homeschoolers fit somewhere in the middle. The most important point to consider is that the most natural form of education *is based on the child's needs and interests*. The more natural the child's learning environment, the deeper, more enjoyable and life long the child's "education" will be. The more freedom children are allowed in their learning, the more passionate children will stay about learning.

Like unschoolers, most homeschoolers focus on family relationships, healthy friendships and community involvement. Homeschoolers tend to put more focus on curriculum, work books, right and wrong answers, tests, grading and specific study times than unschoolers. Many homeschooling families report that although they started out as curriculum-based, they gradually became more and more relaxed, sometimes abandoning work books and curriculum all together, especially as their children became more involved in the community. Children who do highly structured "school-at home" homeschooling tend to be more socially isolated than their peers who do less curriculum learning and more community-based learning.

All homeschoolers must follow their state's homeschool requirements for information covered each year. Children must take a yearly exam or put together a portfolio of work at the end of the year. An evaluator from the public school, a private school or a paid independent licensed educator reviews the portfolio and makes suggestions if areas are not being covered. As a whole, homeschooled children surpass their public schooled peers in almost all areas, and many function at college level years before they are college age. Many homeschoolers begin taking college courses in early adolescence, exploring careers or apprenticing.

All types of homeschoolers can get into college, and more and more universities have admissions requirements that accommodate the diverse experiences of homeschoolers. In cases when an actual diploma or transcript is required at a certain college, parents can legally create a diploma and transcript for their children: A homeschool that follows state homeschooling requirements is legally recognized as a school.

## Democratic schools

Democratic, or free schools, are schools that function like unschooling families. These hard to find gems ideally are wonderful, utopian environments that, like unschooling, are play-based and allow children to direct their own interests. Most democratic schools do not use grades, tests or any curriculum that children have not designed themselves. Like unschoolers, children who attend democratic/free schools tend to be passionate about learning and function at advanced or adult levels in one or many "subjects" of learning because they have the freedom and time to develop their creativity, skills and talents beyond traditional textbooks, curriculums, grade levels and time tables.

Children in democratic schools truly live democracy: Most of these schools allow children of all ages, including the youngest students, equal power in making decisions for the school, including financial matters, school rules and hiring and even firing of teachers. In democratic schools, teachers function as facilitators, mentors and guides, helping children in any way that children need to meet their individual potentials and pursue their interests. Teachers may offer classes, but they must work hard to keep children engaged and interested or children will not attend their classes!

There is generally a set of principles or ground rules that all children and adults in the school agree to follow that help the school function as a respectful, caring, safe atmosphere for all learners and mentors. Teachers who repeatedly show disrespect to children, their needs and their ways of learning may be fired by the consensus of children and other teachers. Likewise, children who repeatedly show disrespect to fellow teachers, students or property may be asked to leave the school as well.

Democratic schools allow children as much time as they need for play, socialization, gaming, building, exploring, creating and working alone, with their peers or with their teachers. Relationships tend to be strong, caring and solid, not surface, professional and distant like in traditional schools. Parents and families are often welcomed into the school to volunteer, teach classes or work with their children. Parental involvement is usually integral to the success of the school.

The drawback of democratic schools seems to be their scarcity; there are few true democratic schools around compared to the thousands of public and religious private schools. The other drawbacks are that children are separated from their parents during the school day and children are usually expected to attend school when school is in session. However, since parents are often allowed to be at the school at anytime and children are usually free to design their own curriculum, democratic schools, as a whole, surpass traditional schools in every area of excellence in natural learning!

## Waldorf schools

Based on the philosophies of Rudolf Steiner, who founded Waldorf education in 1919, Waldorf schools ideally place a strong focus on sensory experience, imagination, play, fantasy, art, creativity, and in the later years, also social responsibility and mastery of complex abstract and analytical specialties. Art, music, fantasy, social responsibility and hands-on projects are integrated into all areas of challenging academics. Waldorf education's philosophy, "head, heart and hands", is *holistic*, educating the whole child. Waldorf teachers follow the same class of children from kindergarten through 12th grade. Tuition at Waldorf schools can be high. Check with individual schools for information on possible scholarships and financial aid.

## Montessori schools

*"One test of the correctness of educational procedure is the happiness of the child." -Maria Montessori*

Dr. Maria Montessori, a strong supporter of children's rights, founded the Montessori teaching method in the early 1900's based on her observations of children's development. Montessori schools focus on the development of the individual child, rather than on the entire group. Children are free to explore and move freely around the classroom, which is divided into centers where children can complete a series of step-by-step tasks. Individual teachers work with individual children to complete the tasks according to the child's interests and abilities.

Freedom and choice are important to the Montessori philosophy, including how individual children pace their day. There is less focus on fantasy and imagination and more focus on sensory experience, practical life skills (fine and gross motor), language and math in Montessori schools. There is also more emphasis on individual work and less emphasis on group work.

Unfortunately, the name "Montessori" was not copyright protected, so any school can use the name in their title or description. Be sure that the school is truly an authentic Montessori school by asking if they have accreditation by the American Montessori Society. Check with individual schools for information on possible scholarships and financial aid.

## Other non-traditional private schools

Schools that allow children to develop at their own pace, that emphasize play, physical activity, joy in learning, multiple intelligences, multiple learning styles and hands-on exploration are other optimal alternatives to traditional schooling. While many of these schools have teacher-led curriculums, the emphasis on play, joy, outdoor exploration, multiple intelligences and a relaxed learning atmosphere (tables, couches and bean bags, children working on the floor or curled up in a window sill) allow most children to thrive and excel in learning. However, these schools do not meet the needs of children who need a self-directed curriculum or who are not ready to explore a subject that the class is learning.

Child-centered, non-traditional schools tend to focus on strong school principles of mutual respect, positive, nonviolent relationships, helpfulness, compassion and mutual responsibility for doing one's part in protecting the peace and caring for the trees, wildlife and grounds of the school. For example, in one non-traditional school I visited, a public schooled child who was visiting the school grabbed a bucket of caterpillars from a student, dumped them out and began to stomp on them. Several students of various ages, horrified, intervened nonviolently and demanded that he stop and then they informed the teachers. Like in democratic schools, children in cohesive, caring non-traditional schools model for one another appropriate, caring behavior and keep one another in check when someone acts in hurtful ways.

Again, private schools require tuitions. Parents would need to check with individual schools for information on possible scholarships and financial aid.

## Charter schools

Charter schools are public schools "of choice" that operate independently of their community's traditional public school. If your city or town has a charter school, you have a choice to send your child to that school free of charge. Some charter schools have a lottery in which names are randomly draw from a list of children waiting to attend. Others run on a first come, first serve basis. If you are interested in your local charter school, put your child's name on the list as soon as possible.

Charter schools usually have more freedom to develop a style of education, and may use principles from Montessori, Waldorf, schools of the arts or other philosophies in their mission. Although they are not required to follow all of the same state regulations as the main public schools, they must follow some regulations, including standardized testing in many states. Many charter schools are contracted for only a few years and can close if they cannot demonstrate academic success in their students.

Charter schools that truly offer children a more natural environment from the main public school are certainly a better choice than traditional school. However, many charter schools are staffed with public school teachers who are only familiar with the traditional power and control, paperwork, homework, teacher-led curriculum model of schooling. Children may find that they receive just as much sit down busywork and homework as their public schooled peers, with not much more free time than they had before. Some teachers may be just as punitive as many public school teachers. Charter schools also keep children away from their families during the school day and expect children to attend daily, all school day.

## Early college

Adolescents can take college courses and even enroll part or full time as college students in many states. Many homeschoolers take college courses, some as young as 14! Not only does this allow children to pursue their career interests sooner, it allows them a more advanced level of study in subjects of which they have deep interest. Youth have more freedom in their schedules when they attend college rather than high school. Although the work load will often be as high or higher than public school, the work is often more relevant to the "real world" and introduces a greater depth to the subject being studied.

Parents need to be careful of negative influences on their children by young adult students; an open communication with your adolescents about their socialization on the college campus is important. Financial aid, scholarships and grants may be available for students who qualify.

There is also a movement of "Early College High Schools" that are grant-funded by corporations, allowing adolescents to earn both a high school diploma and a two year college Associates degree. Search online for more information.

## Internet correspondence schools

It is possible to attend school online from grades kindergarten through 12th grade, in the comfort of a child's own home. Although this certainly is not as natural as more relaxed forms of homeschooling, some online schools offer individualized curriculum, attention and independent study. Other online schools are more rigid, and run their programs similar to "school-at-home" homeschoolers.

Online schools allow families to plan their own schedules, maximizing family time, play time, social time and time to pursue interests. They also cut out the negative peer influences of tra-ditional schools. Socialization could be an issue with online schools for older children. I strongly recommend connecting with your local homeschool groups if your older child's is not involved in community activities.

Online schools, like private schools, require tuitions. Parents would need to check with individual schools for information on possible scholarships and financial aid.

### Independent study at a traditional school

Some public schools and private schools allow an independent study option, sometimes referred to as "homestudy". Individual school districts or private schools determine how much freedom a child can have with independent study, what subjects will be "counted" as "legitimate" and how much contact the child must have with the school. Independent study allows children to par-ticipate in school activities, teams and events. You would need to contact your local school district or individual private schools to find out if they would allow this option.

### Part-time attendance at a traditional school

Some public and private schools may offer the option of your child attending school *part* time. You would need to contact your local school district or individual private schools to find out if they would allow this option. Generally, most schools would expect students to be able to "keep up" with classes and assign-ments on the days and times when they do not attend.

### The options are out there!

Most parents do not realize that there are alternatives to public school and religious private school! There are growing numbers of children and families who are exercising their freedom every year to choose lifestyles and ways of learning that are more in line with human happiness, joy and freedom. Children and families do have other options, but they require research, trust and sacrifice to make them work. Our children are worth it!

## Trauma therapy: Eye Movement Desensitization and Reprocessing (EMDR)

Eye Movement Desensitization and Reprocessing, or EMDR, is one of the few treatments in the mental health establishment that has been shown to have high success for healing trauma. EMDR therapy consists of:

- Several sets of side-to-side eye movements,
- Intense focus on a traumatic memory,
- Intense focus on body sensations, and
- Frequent "interruptions" by the therapist of the client's focus on the traumatic memory.

These features are part of an eight-phase process that:

- Reaches traumatic memories in the improper area of the brain where it is believed that they are stored and
- Brings the traumatic memories to the part of the brain that can make sense of and heal them.

EMDR therapists may also use sound or tapping to access traumatic memories, either with eye movements or instead of eye movements, depending on an individual client's preference. EMDR should only be practiced by a licensed mental health therapist who has completed a two-part EMDR training.

## The theory of how EMDR heals trauma

Remember, it is believed that traumatic memories store in the creative, less rational right brain and in the impulsive temporal lobe. Childhood traumatic memories store in their original emotional form, *from the perspective of a child*, no matter how many years go by. Both of these factors may cause traumatic memories to be isolated from:

- Maturity
- Adaptation
- Learning
- Insight
- Therapy
- Self help
- Spirituality

No matter how many years people attend therapy, read about, learn about or rationalize about their trauma, it usually continues to haunt them (often without their being aware that the trauma still bothers them) because it is stored in the *right brain, temporal lobe*, where traditional therapies, books, insight and rationalization can't reach.

EMDR allows the brain to access and spread traumatic memories to the *left brain and cerebral cortex*. These are the parts of the brain that allow adaptation, maturity, learning and insight from therapy, self help and spirituality to finally reach the traumatic memories and process them. In other words, *EMDR brings traumatic memories to the parts of the brain that can make sense of and heal traumatic memories!*

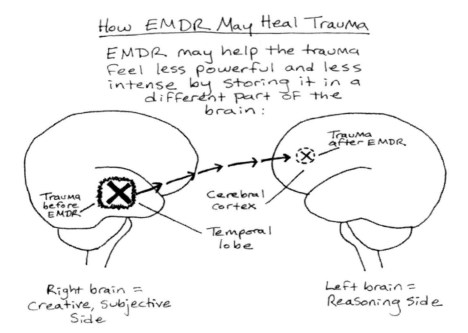

EMDR is different from other therapies because:

- It uses *dual stimulation*, which is a focus on both the past and the present at the exact same time;

- It uses *bilateral stimulation*, which means that both halves of the brain and body are stimulated in a continuous back-and-forth pattern; and

- EMDR helps traumatic memories spread to the rational left brain and the thinking, conscious cerebral cortex.

## <u>Finding the right EMDR specialist</u>

EMDR is one of the most effective of the therapies for healing traumatic memories. I strongly recommend that parents find an EMDR therapist who:

- Is a licensed mental health counselor,

- Has received "EMDR Two" training,
- Has experience and a high success rate, and
- Works well with children.

You can locate an EMDR therapist in your area on the EMDR Institute's website, www.EMDR.org

## Natural attachment-based therapy

If you are seeking therapy for your child and your child has suffered moderate, severe or extreme attachment disruption, *finding a licensed mental health therapist that is either attachment focused or an attachment specialist is critical.*

Most traditional therapists focus on building an individual relationship with your child through play and discussion. This does little to help you and your child repair and heal disrupted attachment and can actually worsen the problem. *Individual therapy cannot meet your child's unmet needs*, nor can a child form a secure attachment to a therapist. If your child "bonds" to her individual therapist, she may be less likely to view you as the person she must attach to, play with and discuss important issues with. It is critical that *you*, as your child's parent, be the person that provides the warm, affectionate, playful, loving connection he needs. If you are unable or unwilling to fulfill those needs in your child, please find a permanent caretaker, not a therapist, who can provide your child with the love, attention and attachment relationship that he needs.

Traditional family therapy often focuses on family dynamics and patterns and on how to force or manipulate children into complying with their parents. Behavioral charts, reward systems and contracts are usually the "tools" of choice for "getting children under control". Children are sometimes given a say about surface issues that annoy or upset them such as chores or curfews, but their early unmet needs are not a focus. Traditional family therapy rarely focuses on parent-child attachment or on helping parents meet children's needs.

Unfortunately, many traditional individual and family therapists do harm to children by:

- Failing to prioritize attachment;
- Failing to prioritize helping parents to meet their children's basic physical and emotional needs;
- Sometimes supporting parents who use punishments and violent ways of parenting such as "spanking", yelling, threatening or sarcasm; and
- Routinely referring children for psychiatric medication.

Licensed therapists who are truly attachment focused or who are attachment specialists are ideally trained in:

- Helping parents discover the unmet needs behind children's emotional and behavioral instability,
- Helping parents meet their children's needs,
- Helping children heal from trauma,
- Helping parents and children repair and heal attachment disruptions, and
- Helping children develop the tools for emotional stability and social skills they are lacking because of trauma and unmet needs.

Good attachment specialists are very difficult to find because there are few of them and the few are in high demand. The best referral sources for finding attachment specialists are:

- Casey Family Services
- The adoption or post-adoption division of your state's department of health and human services
- Private adoption agencies
- Adoptive families

*What to look for* in an attachment-based therapist or attachment specialist:

- Find someone who practices ethically and follows their professional ethical codes on respectful treatment of clients;
- Find someone who treats your child and you with respect;
- Find someone, if possible, who practices attachment-based Dyadic Developmental Psychotherapy;
- Find someone who is trained in EMDR or someone who is accepting of you seeing someone else for EMDR as an adjunct to the attachment therapy;
- Find someone, if possible, who practices Neurofeedback, a form of treatment that trains the brain to manage emotions and regulate itself;
- Find someone, if possible, who practices Theraplay, a fun, nurturing form of attachment treatment that actually teaches parents how to connect with and re-parent their children;
- Find someone who is well skilled in treating attachment disruption;
- Find someone who has expertise on the developmental affects of child trauma;

- Find someone who is attachment-focused;
- Find someone who primarily meets with both you and your child together, and focuses the treatment on the parent-child relationship, not one-to-one therapy with your child;
- Find someone who will use a lot of fun and engaging techniques for promoting closeness, cooperation and attachment;
- Find someone who is comfortable with children age-regressing *on the children's own terms;*
- Find someone who respects your position as your child's parent, and sees you as a partner in your child's treatment;
- Find someone who recommends physical affection between you and your child during sessions, including having your child on *your* lap, but never against your child's will;
- Find someone who recommends intensive physical affection "homework" and parent-child nurturing play at home, but never against the child's will;
- Find someone who recommends optimal parenting with a goal of your child and you developing a secure parent-child attachment;
- Find someone who will take your child's oppositionality and defiance very seriously and not belittle it;
- Find someone who will both support your natural authority as your child's parent and respect your child's need for a democratic say in the family;
- Find someone who will tell you respectfully, privately when you are doing or saying something that is harmful or not helpful to your child's healing process; and

- Find someone who will support you when you are struggling with your child's misplaced rage and defiance.

Be sure to call therapists and ask if they meet these criteria before you set up a session. For information on types of "attachment therapy" to avoid, please read Part II of this chapter.

## Retraining the brain: Neurofeedback

As an adjunct and supplement to EMDR and attachment treatment, Neurofeedback (also known as EEG biofeedback) is a safe, fun and life changing, symptom-healing alternative to psychiatric drugs.

Children who are suffering from...
- Anxiety
- Depression
- Rage outbursts
- Hyperactivity
- Poor focus
- Learning challenges and "disabilities"
- Autism spectrum symptoms
- Enuresis and encopresis
- And many other distressing symptoms of trauma and insecure attachment

...May benefit from Neurofeedback.

Neurofeedback involves training the brain to improve focus, calm itself, control impulsiveness and improve mood. Gains made with Neurofeedback are safe and are usually permanent, unlike symptom reduction with psychiatric drugs. When psychiatric drugs are given to children, symptoms are being masked and there is a risk of drug side effects. Children's distressing symptoms usually return when psychiatric drugs are stopped, because the brain has not been trained to change or make any new connections. Neurofeedback actually trains the brain:

- To "wire" new and healthier connections between brain cells;

- To allow parts of the brain to communicate that weren't communicating properly between themselves before;

- To function more fluidly and efficiently; and

- To switch more quickly to healthy brain patterns when children are showing distressing symptoms...

...So that many of the most distressing symptoms can be "healed" permanently.

Neurofeedback involves a practitioner placing small electrodes on the child's scalp using a conductor gel. The child is connected to one or two computers:

1. A computer that allows the practitioner to track the child's brain waves and brain patterns to monitor problem areas as well as  to track progress; and

2. A computer that displays a game or movie that the child controls with her brain waves by practicing focus, calmness, self control and a positive mood.

3. Newer technology even allows children to relax and work on tasks that do not involve looking at the computer. The brain is being positively reinforced and rewarded with special sounds whenever it produces healthy brainwaves.

The practitioner can control the child's game or movie to allow positive feedback for progress and to alter the difficulty level if the child is finding a task too difficult or too easy. Neurofeedback treatment can target specific areas of the brain. For example, focusing the electrodes on a specific spot by the right eye, called "FP02", is helpful for relaxation and healing trauma.

Neurofeedback is completely safe; your child controls his own brain waves as well as the signals going to the computer. There is nothing going "into" the child's brain. Instead, children have fun controlling the video game or movie by exercising parts of the brain that help them control their distressing symptoms. Gains are usually noticed within 20 to 40 sessions.

### Biofeedback

Some practitioners may also supplement Neurofeedback with biofeedback. Biofeedback may involve using an engaging computer program that requires children to practice relaxation breathing and monitor their heart rate while playing games that require calmness. Their breathing and heart rates are monitored through sensors placed on the finger tips.

### Cranial electrostimulation devices

Cranial electrostimulation devices may also be used by some practitioners to help support the progress of Neurofeedback. These small devices look similar to a large MP3 player with earphones that clip onto the earlobes. This device is different from Neurofeedback because it stimulates the brain from the outside. The device passes low intensity "micro" currents through the ear lobes to:

- Stimulate calming alpha brain waves,
- Decrease the stress hormone, cortisol, and to

- Increase the chemicals in the brain that help stabilize mood, such as serotonin, norepinephrine and dopamine.

People may notice a calming effect after using these devices that may help deescalate panic attacks or rage outbursts. Please talk to your practitioner to learn more about cranial electrostimulation devices.

You can locate a Neurofeedback practitioner in your area on the EEG Info website at http://directory.eeginfo.com. Please visit Chapter 12 for more information about Neurofeedback.

## "Just say no" to psychiatric medication?

*Is psychiatric medication ever ok for children?*

Dr. Peter Breggin, psychiatrist and author of several books on the detriments of psychiatric drugs, says "no". Although psychiatric drugs are certainly a way to subdue and calm the severe behaviors of traumatized children, Dr. Breggin's research states the following:

- There is no hard, scientific proof that ADHD exists.
- Psychiatric drugs are being used on children in epidemic levels.
- Many children who start out on one psychiatric drug have another drug added to "fix" the side effects of the first drug.
- Sometimes children are put on four or more drugs to "fix" the side effects caused by each drug that was added!
- A common drug scenario = stimulant > anti-

depressant/anti-anxiety> mood stabilizer> anti-psychot-ic> sleeping aid.

- Sometimes two types of anti-depressant/anti-anxiety drugs may be added that reportedly affect two different types of brain chemicals.

- Children who suffer from urinary incontinence may have another drug added.

- Psychiatric drugs are dangerous to children's brains. Some, such as stimulants, affect every system of the brain in a *negative* way.

- Psychiatric drugs can be dangerous to *every system* of a child's body, including to their growth and adolescent development.

- Psychiatric drugs can cause the brain to stop producing necessary and natural neurotransmitters (brain chemicals).

- Psychiatric drugs can cause severe psychological distress and symptoms of mental illness, including panic, akathesia (a severe inner restlessness), anxiety, insomnia, rage, aggression, psychosis (hallucinations, paranoia, etc.), nervous tics, obsessions and compulsions.

- Antipsychotic drugs can cause a permanent neurological movement, spasm and tic disorder called tardive dyskinesia.

- Psychiatric drugs mask symptoms, but do not treat or heal the *causes* of children's behavioral and emotional instability.

- Psychiatric drugs may cause violence, suicidal and homicidal tendencies in some children.

- The American Psychiatric Association, psychiatrists and pro-diagnosis organizations such as CHADD (for ADHD) and NAMI receive large sums of money from the pharma-ceutical companies that produce psychiatric drugs.

- Many psychiatric drugs prescribed to children are not even approved by the FDA for use with children.

- Withdrawal from psychiatric drugs can be very difficult, painful and dangerous.

- Psychiatric drugs are used to keep children under control in intolerable situations such as in traditional school and in dysfunctional, unhealthy and even abusive homes.

- Helping repair parent-child attachments and helping parents find active, energetic hands-on learning environ-ments for their children are not the priorities of most psychiatrists.

- Many children do not like the medication, nor do they want to be on it. Many parents, psychiatrists or pediatri-cians ignore children's complaints and requests.

Recently I engaged in a discussion with a parent whose son suf-fers from severe depression and suicide attempts. Despite his regiment of psychiatric drugs, her son is still disabled by depres-sion and suicidal thoughts. She defended her efforts of "helping him", stating, "I'm giving him his medication and taking him to his therapist and psychiatrist— That's all I can do!" I have heard this defense far too many times by social work professionals, mental health professionals and parents who have no idea that alternative treatment options are available.

Parents are usually not told much about the severe dangers to their children of introducing powerful chemicals into children's developing brains. Drugs such as stimulants, anti-depressants, mood stabilizers and anti-psychotics are given so frequently to children, sometimes as a first response, that most parents believe that these drugs are safe! These drugs affect *every system of the brain and body* and may include the following side effects:

<u>Physical side effects:</u>
- Abdominal (GI) pain
- Constipation
- Diarrhea
- Urinary frequency
- Nausea
- Skin rash
- Poor appetite
- Weight loss or gain
- Insomnia
- Fatigue and drowsiness
- Stunted or slowed growth
- Drug dependence
- Trembling
- Headaches
- High blood pressure
- Cardiac symptoms
- Chest pain
- Joint pain
- Blurred vision
- Sudden death

<u>Emotional and mental side effects:</u>
- Anxiety
- Agitation
- Rage and anger
- Aggression and hostility
- Affect (emotional) flatness
- "Zombie" effect
- Passivity
- Restlessness

- Depression
- Obsessions and compulsions
- Inflexible thinking
- Hyper-focus
- Lack of spontaneity
- Psychosis (hallucinations and delusions)
- Increased risk of suicidal thoughts and gestures
- Increased risk of homicidal thoughts and gestures

Neurological side effects:
- Motor and vocal tics (involuntary movements)
- Tardive dyskinesia (a permanent disorder of involuntary movements usually caused by long term use of anti-psychotic drugs)
- Neuroleptic Malignant Syndrome (a life threatening adverse reaction to anti-psychotic drugs)
- Psychosis (hallucinations and delusions)
- Nightmares
- Hyperactivity
- Hyper-focus
- Akathesia (a severe sensation of inner restlessness and panic)
- Dizziness
- Seizures
- Tremors
- Severe withdrawal symptoms

Desperate parents, looking for a way to ease the turmoil in their families, will often accept the doctor's apparently "easy fix". Although psychiatrists often recommend that children and parents see a therapist, *rarely is parent-child attachment, a child's unmet needs or finding children a developmentally appropriate learning environment ever on the treatment plan of either the psychiatrist or therapist. Brain-based treatments such as EMDR and Neurofeedback or holistic alternatives are rarely mentioned to parents as alternatives to drugs.*

Sometimes parents become so dependent upon their belief in the drugs that they will insist that their children need them even if the drugs aren't helping, even if the drugs are making symptoms worse and even if the parents are informed that the drugs are potentially dangerous to their children.

Although most professionals find Dr. Breggin's advice to be extreme, it is imperative to children that parents as well as professionals in the fields of mental health and psychiatry come to the conviction that psychiatric drugs should be considered *only as a very last resort for children.* In cases of children who present a persistent and escalating danger to themselves or others or who are showing serious symptoms of breaks with reality, psychiatric drugs may need to be considered as a temporary stabilizing tool in order for attachment-based treatment, developmentally appropriate educational environment and brain-based treatments such as EMDR and Neurofeedback to take effect. It is imperative for parents to educate themselves about the potential dangers to their children of using psychiatric drugs.

*Important note: NEVER stop your child's medications without discussing it first with your child's doctor or psychiatrist!* Many psychiatric drugs have very powerful effects on brain chemistry and abrupt withdrawal can be *dangerous or even fatal!* Children must be properly weaned from their psychiatric drugs, one at a time, with professional assistance. If your child's doctor or psychiatrist refuses to help, do not withdraw your child from the drugs on your own— Ask for a referral to a doctor or naturopathic health care provider who will assist you. *Never attempt any alterations to the drugs your child is taking on your own!*

The dangers of psychiatric drugs, ADHD diagnosis fraud and the relationships between the pharmaceutical companies, psychiatrists, public schools, mental health field, medical field and citizen-run support organizations are topics that are too broad to cover in this book. For further information about alternatives to psychiatric drugs, the dangers of psychiatric drugs, ADHD diagnosis fraud and the influence of the pharmaceutical companies on society, please visit Chapter 12.

> *"The psychiatric diagnosing and drugging of children should be viewed as a form of technological child abuse – conformity enforced by physical suppression of the brain... I hold my colleagues responsible for this national catastrophe." –Peter R. Breggin, M.D.*

## Holistic and body-centered treatments

The deepest, most spiritual, emotional, physical and holistic way that parents can nourish, nurture and heal their children is through repairing the parent-child attachment, healing trauma, meeting physical and emotional needs and through allowing children to learn in an educational environment that is developmentally appropriate. The wisdom of natural healers can assist parents in helping children become physically, nutritionally, emotionally and spiritually balanced using natural remedies, body-centered therapies and ancient energy healing techniques.

These treatments listed below are tailored to the individual child and to your child's specific needs. These therapies are natural and safe alternatives to psychiatric drugs and support natural, attachment-based healing. These are some of the many holistic and body-centered treatments that parents can research and seek out for their children:

- Homeopathic treatment:
  - Any naturally occurring substance can be used as medicine in micro doses;
  - Practitioners consider the animal, plant and mineral "personality types" of individuals and medicines;
  - Heals from the inside out;
  - Homeopathic medicine is safe, without side effects.
- Herbal remedies:
  - Involve the use of plants and plant extracts;
  - Sometimes includes the use of minerals and animals parts such as shells, honey and fungi;
  - Herbs come from several different cultures and countries:
    - Chinese herbs
    - Indian Ayurvedic herbs
    - European herbs
    - Western herbal combinations
- Nutritional and naturopathic treatment:
  - Practitioners identify the causes of physical and emotional imbalances;
  - Practitioners help remove toxins from the body;
  - Practitioners set up a plan to fuel the body with healthy organic food, vitamins, minerals and other supplements;
  - Holistic practitioners may recommend body cleanses:
    - Candida yeast cleanse
    - Colon cleanse
    - Heavy metal cleanse
    - Kidney and bladder cleanse
    - Liver cleanse

- Lymphatic cleanse
- Parasite cleanse
- Body-centered therapies:
  - Acupuncture
    - Very thin needles are inserted into specific points on the body to unblock life force energy, called Qi (pronounced "chee"), allowing the Qi to flow through the body in a healthy manner.
  - Craniosacral therapy
    - Practitioners massage the spine, skull, fascia, nerves and tissues to unblock cerebrospinal fluid and allow it to flow properly.
  - Emotional Freedom Technique
    - Children are taught to tap on 12 specific energy points on the body while focusing on a negative emotion.
    - Tapping these points releases and balances Qi, similarly to acupuncture.
  - Massage therapy
    - Releases toxins from the muscles and tissues;
    - Relaxes muscles and eases muscle tension.
  - Qigong
    Specific movements based on three principles:
    - Lengthen the spine with proper posture;
    - Deep breathing from the abdomen;
    - Clearing the mind of negativity and replacing negativity with healing intentions.
  - Reflexology
    - Practitioners apply pressure to the feet and hands at specific points;
    - Specific body systems correspond to the pressure points on the hands and feet;
    - This ancient technique uses the body's reflex

responses in the hands and feet to heal imbalances in the body.

- Reiki
    - Practitioners place their hands on or above a person to help move Qi, or life force energy, from the practitioner to the individual, with the intent to heal.
- Rolfing
    - Deep muscle, ligament and joint massage;
    - May realign the body's posture;
    - May reduce chronic stress.
- Tai chi
    - A series of slow, graceful martial arts movements with the intent of improving the flow of Qi through the body;
    - Improves focus, a calm state of mind and emotional centering.
- Yoga
    - An ancient art of balancing the body, mind, emotion and spirit using body postures, meditation and relaxation breathing;
    - Yoga's body postures are said to increase circulation and stimulate organs to function optimally.
- Martial arts that focus on centering
- Sensory integration physical and occupational therapy
    - Strengthens muscles and improves fine (small) and gross (large) motor coordination;
    - May help a child's visual, auditory and vestibular systems work together;
    - May improve and balance sensory perception and focus.
- Energy healing:
  - Energy healers offer spiritual guidance and spiritual healing;

- Work is done on the seven energy centers of the body, called chakras;
- Energy healers help ground and center children;
- They may help children to unblock pent up, disconnected emotions;
- They help children repair spiritual wounds that affect how energy flows through the body;
- Practitioners may incorporate energy healing methods such as Reiki and Qigong.

## Healing on a society-wide level

Here are the three priorities parents, mental health professionals, social workers, doctors, scientists and law makers must work on to heal children and to prevent the upcoming generation from suffering the damage sustained by the rest of us:

### Priority one: Meeting children's needs now

It is the *moral obligation and responsibility* of all parents, professionals and governments *to make secure parent-child attachment and meeting children's basic physical, emotional and developmental needs our top priority.*

### Priority two: Healing damage done to children

The second priority of parents, professionals, governments and their citizens must be *to stop, heal and repair the damage already done to our children* at home and in schools and to the children languishing in orphanages, foster care, residential facilities, detention centers and youth "boot camp" programs.

### Priority three: Helping young adults; preventing damage to the next generation

The third priority of parents, professionals, governments and their citizens must be for mature, compassionate, emotionally stable adults to informally or formally *offer mentoring to young adults and to young parents who are coming out of abusive and neglectful childhoods.*

Sue Gerhardt, author of *Why Love Matters: How Affection Shapes a Baby's Brain* states, "The paradox is that people need to have a satisfying experience of dependency before they can become truly independent and largely self-regulating. Yet this feels counter-intuitive to many adults, who respond to the insecure [adult] with a punitive attitude, as if becoming more mature and self regulating were a matter of will-power."

Mature, older mentors can offer caring maternal or paternal relationships to young adults and young parents who have survived abusive and neglectful childhoods. *By helping to meet some of the unmet childhood emotional needs of young adults, mentors prevent further spread of child abuse and violence to the upcoming generation.*

# Chapter 11 Part II

# Re-parenting Adoptive Children with RAD and Biological Children with Severe Attachment Disruption

*"Each of us is the hero some young person needs. But those youth who most deeply hunger for love often back away. They need adults who can conquer fear and rejection with love."*
- Muhammad Ali, human rights advocate and former boxing champion

**Definition:**
<u>Reactive Attachment Disorder (RAD)</u>: A mental illness diagnosis that describes a collection of symptoms of the most severe degrees of attachment disruption.

This section is for the following parents:

- Any parents who have biological children with moderate to severe behavioral problems and emotional instability,
- Parents who have biological children who spent time in foster care and then returned home,

- Grandparents and relatives who are raising children related to them,
- Parents who adopted children at birth,
- Parents who adopted children from the foster care system, from an orphanage or from a program or institution,
- Foster or guardianship parents who intend to adopt their foster children, and
- Any biological or adoptive parents who have a child who has been diagnosed with Reactive Attachment Disorder (RAD).
- Although the information in this section can be helpful for foster parents and residential staff, most of it is intended for parents who are able and willing to offer permanency to their children.
- Although I will be speaking mostly about adoptive children in this section, most of the information will apply to biological parents of children with moderate to severe attachment disruption.

Parenting adoptive children and children with severe attachment disruption and Reactive Attachment Disorder requires an *extreme and intense form* of everything listed in Part I of this chapter (please read Part I before reading Part II; I went into depth about many vital ways to help your children heal that are not repeated in Part II).

If any professional attempts to tell you that raising an adoptive child is the same as raising a biological child, run in the other direction! Whether adopted at birth or adopted later in childhood from foster care, *all* adoptive children suffer a severe break from the natural attachment relationship with the birth mother.

# First step: Secure respite, post-adoption services and resources!

Hopefully, ideally, all adoptive parents grow to cherish their children with the intensity and deep love that causes them to sometimes "forget" that they did not give birth to their children! As an adoptive mother myself, I can testify to the deep physical, psychological, spiritual and soul love that I feel for my child, as if I birthed him. I am thankful that he and I have been able to nurture such a deep, connected attachment. However, his periodic cycles of emotional turmoil remind me regularly that I didn't give birth to him. Although the depth of the *love* you feel for your adoptive children will ideally be the same as for biological children, *parenting* your adoptive children will always be different from parenting biological children: Depending upon the severity of your children's trauma, you will *always* be *re*-creating the early attachment relationship, *repairing* it, *healing* it... never creating it perfectly from the womb forward.

I cannot stress this strongly enough: If you have an adoptive child, especially a child adopted from the foster care system, *make certain that you build up a strong, reliable, stable network of resources for support, breaks and respite.* If you are considering adopting a child, this is *crucial!* If you are a *single* parent who has adopted a child from foster care or if you are considering adopting, it is an *absolute necessity!*

When we adopt children, we are accepting them along with all of their raging pain. We are making a *permanent, lifetime commitment* to be our children's parents and primary source of support. If we as parents do not have readily available support and respite resources in place, we could be pushed to a point where we lose control and emotionally or even physically hurt our children... Hurting our children would strike a severe blow at the fragile attachment relationship and confirm to our children that all adults *will* hurt them and cannot be trusted. We must build a safety net ahead of time to prevent ourselves from losing control!

Without firm support and respite in place, we may be eventually worn down to the point where we are completely used up and unable to tolerate any more of the relentless defiance, oppositionality, grief and rage misdirected at us by our children who suffer from severe attachment disruption or Reactive Attachment Disorder. It is a tragedy when adoptions disrupt; the already shattered attachment and trust of adoptive children receives another mortal wound, with deleterious affects to children's ability to trust, attach and love again in their lifetime. It is critical to have post-adoption services and respite in place *before* you need them... This includes having a list of available psychiatric hospitals and live-in programs for our children with moderate to severe RAD incase they ever become a danger to themselves or others and cannot live at home. Certainly not all children with RAD become dangerous, but some do.

*Adoption is forever; "divorcing" our children should never feel like an option.* If our children become dangerous and cannot live at home, we have a responsibility to continue to support, visit and provide love and nurturance to them. Make sure you know the post-adoption services ahead of time in case of the worst!

## Find an attachment specialist

Do not waste your time and your child's time by placing your child in traditional therapy. In fact, doing so can actually worsen the symptoms if your child suffers from Reactive Attachment

Disorder. Most psychologists, psychiatrists and mental health counselors know little to nothing about RAD and are not qualified to do any type of attachment work. Once during a mental health crisis with my son, I took him to the hospital emergency room. The mental health counselor on duty had never even *heard* of RAD!

Adoptive and foster parents know the unique frustration of trying to explain to a professional the major differences between children with RAD and children who are "simply testing" their parents. Adoptive families also know the annoyance and confusion that results when well-meaning counselors refer to a child's biological mother as "the mother" or "your mother", confusing the child and conveying (however unintentionally) that the adoptive mother isn't the "real" mother. Experienced attachment specialists understand RAD behaviors and don't belittle what regular counselors miss. Experienced attachment specialists also use attachment-promoting and family-validating language, referring to biological parents as "your birthparents" and adoptive parents as "your parents".

Good attachment specialists are very difficult to find because there are few of them and the few are in high demand. The best referral sources for finding attachment specialists are:

- Casey Family Services
- The adoption or post-adoption division of your state's department of health and human services
- Private adoption agencies
- Other adoptive families

**<u>A strong word of caution about attachment therapy!</u>**
Children with severe cases of RAD are the most difficult children in the field of mental health to heal. The psychological damage

that these children have sustained and suffer is extreme; the lack of brain development in critical emotional areas of the brain is profound. Some mental health professionals have broken away from ethical practice in attempts to find extreme "techniques" for bullying and traumatizing children "out of" their rageful patterns. Of course this only worsens children's trauma and rage and certainly doesn't meet any of their unmet needs! This group of unethical professionals, mostly trained in Colorado and Ohio, claim to practice "attachment therapy", but actually advocate for abusive treatment of children! Some of these practitioners actually killed a child, and some have reportedly instructed parents to use punishments on their children that were unhealthy, dangerous and fatal. Protect your child from this type of abusive treatment!

Recently, ATTACh, The Association for Treatment and Training in the Attachment of Children, released a position statement referred to as *The White Paper on Coercion in Treatment* that calls for all professionals and parents to cease the use of these overpowering, forceful and domineering practices.

## <u>STAY AWAY from these types of "attachment specialists"!</u>

- Stay away from therapists who forcibly hold child clients on their laps or force eye contact as part of the treatment!
- Stay away from therapists who advise use of "Basic German Shepherd" obedience approaches!
- Stay away from therapists who are hostile, threatening or often confrontational towards children!
- Stay away from therapists who forcibly touch and caress children against children's will!
- Stay away from therapists who use any form of physical pressure, pain or antagonism on children!

- Stay away from therapists who try to control or direct the actions of parents!
- Stay away from therapists who make inappropriate demands and unnecessary comments about children's appearance and personal choices!
- Stay away from therapists who force age-regression!
- Stay away from therapists who tell parents to forcibly hold their children against their children's wills!
- Stay away from therapists who tell parents to deny or restrict children's movement, nutritious food, hydration, elimination, sleep or *any* other basic need!
- Stay away from any therapist who tells parents to make children ask permission to meet any basic need such as movement, food, hydration, elimination, sleep, affection or any other basic need!
- Stay away from therapists who tell parents to deny children physical affection or attention!
- Stay away from therapists who tell parents to use "strong sitting", a punishment of forcing a child to sit in a fixed position, motionless, for a certain amount of time!
- Stay away from therapists who tell parents to do any-thing painful, physically uncomfortable or dangerous to a child, including hitting!
- Stay away from therapists who tell parents to cage or tie up a child, lock a child in a room or alarm the child's bed-room door!
- Stay away from therapists who restrain a child for "rage expression" and recommend that parents also do the same!
- Stay away from therapists who tell parents to make children sit on the floor and "earn" sitting on chairs!
- Stay away from therapists who tell parents to gorge children with sweets and candy!
- Stay away from therapists who tell parents to force food or water down children's throats!

- Stay away from therapists who tell parents to give children several chores, forced exercise, or repetitive tasks as punishments!
- Stay away from therapists who tell parents to force children to give "respect"!
- Stay away from therapists who tell parents to put children in "no-win" situations in which children's needs and wishes are disrespected!
- Stay away from therapists who tell parents to force children to "attach" to parents!
- Stay away from therapists who tell parents to isolate children from other adults or other children!
- Stay away from therapists who tell parents to put children in "solitary confinement" as punishment!
- Stay away from therapists who tell parents to do any type of "rebirthing" technique involving wrapping children up with blankets and pillows against their will and forcing them to struggle out!
- Stay away from therapists who disrespectfully refer to children with the RAD diagnosis as "RAD Kids", "RADishes" or similar dehumanizing terms!
- Stay away from therapists who use or tell you to use *any type of technique that YOU wouldn't want done to YOU!*

*These are NOT attachment treatment techniques; they are forms of child abuse and are not supported by any scientific research!* Stay away from any books and websites that recommend any of the above techniques.

<u>*What to look for* in an attachment specialist</u>:

- Find someone who practices ethically and follows their professional ethical codes on respectful treatment of clients;
- Find someone who treats your child and you with respect;

- Try to find someone who practices Dyadic Developmental Psychotherapy;
- Find someone who is trained in EMDR or someone who is accepting of you seeing someone else for EMDR as an adjunct to the attachment therapy;
- Find someone, if possible, who practices Neurofeedback, a form of treatment that trains the brain to manage emotions and regulate itself;
- Find someone, if possible, who practices Theraplay, a fun, nurturing form of attachment treatment that actually teaches parents how to connect with and re-parent their children;
- Find someone who is well skilled in treating RAD;
- Find someone who has expertise on the developmental affects of child trauma;
- Find someone who is attachment focused;
- Find someone who primarily meets with both you and your child together, and focuses the treatment on the parent-child relationship, not one-to-one therapy with your child;
- Find someone who will use a lot of fun and engaging techniques for promoting closeness, cooperation and attachment;
- Find someone who is comfortable with children age-regressing *on the children's own terms;*
- Find someone who respects your position as the parent, and sees you as a partner in your child's treatment;
- Find someone who recommends physical affection between you and your child during sessions, including having your child on *your* lap, but never against your child's will;
- Find someone who recommends intensive physical affection "homework" and parent-child nurturing play at home, but never against the child's will;
- Find someone who recommends optimal parenting with a

goal of your child and you developing a secure parent-child attachment;

- Find someone who will not undermine you in front of your child;
- Find someone who will take your child's oppositionality and defiance very seriously and not belittle it;
- Find someone who will support your natural authority as your child's parent;
- Find someone who will tell you respectfully, privately when you are doing or saying something that is harmful or not helpful to your child's healing process; and
- Find someone who will support you when you are struggling with your child's misplaced rage and defiance.

*Be sure to call the therapist and ask if they meet these criteria before you set up a session. If they are a member of ATTACh, ask them if they support ATTACh's White Paper on Coercion.*

## Physical affection and one-to-one play

You cannot heal your children and develop an attachment with them without physical affection, nurturance and frequent one-to-one play with them. This is true whether you are a biological parent or whether you adopted your children at birth or in late adolescence! Although physical affection with older children should be at their pace, *it is essential that parents prioritize affection*: In fact, it must be as important as meals and sleep! Even if children resist initially, keep it light and non-invasive and gradually build their comfort level. Your attachment specialist should be assisting both of you in this process.

Adolescents often resist intense physical affection because they feel embarrassed; let them know that they have unmet needs that have not gone away just because they grew. Let them know that "baby" needs need to be met for them to mature into adults and assure them that it is acceptable and natural. Respect their privacy and comfort level and *cherish when they trust you enough to act infantile around you* — They are coming to you with their vulnerable unmet needs, trusting that you will nurture that "baby" part of them...

I cannot stress this point enough: *Children cannot thrive without physical affection. Children who have suffered trauma and extreme breaks in attachment desperately require intense and frequent physical affection in order to develop, repair and wire vital parts of the brain that make emotional regulation, love, empathy and attachment possible!* Without physical affection, your child's emotional, behavioral, and attachment problems will not improve and are likely to worsen in severity.

Adoptive children of all ages need physical expressions of affection such as:

- To be cradled in your arms and cuddled daily,
- To be caressed,
- To engage in eye-gazing,
- To be rocked,
- To be held on your lap or to sit leaning up against you,
- To be hugged and kissed,
- To hold your hand,
- To be carried if physically possible,
- To be "babied" in the privacy of your home,
- To be gently wrapped up in blankets by you (at their will) if they initially resist direct affection,
- To play with baby toys (yes, adolescents can wire important parts of the brain by engaging in infant and toddler play), and

- To have active fun with you daily, playing outside, rough-housing, wrestling, riding bikes, hiking, doing crafts, puzzles and games together.

All of these expressions should be at your children's will. If you are unable or unwilling to work towards providing this intensive level of physical affection for your young, older and adolescent children, please get assistance from your child's attachment specialist so that you can overcome this boundary, or find someone who is willing to provide this to your children. It will be detrimental to your children if you are unable or unwilling to meet this basic need of theirs.

## Re-parenting

Linked with the need for intensive physical affection is the basic need of attachment disrupted and older adoptive children to be re-parented at earlier stages of development. *The rule of thumb: You usually can't go wrong if you let your child convey to you what he or she needs.* Re-parenting experiences should always be at the child's direction, with you showing openness to what they need. As long as it is within appropriate physical boundaries, it will begin to fill voids in their development.

When your child begins to show signs of attaching to you, he is likely to begin to crave the kind of nurturing and physical affection that he didn't receive in infancy. Untrained parents can become frightened or shocked by older children, especially adolescents, suddenly acting like babies, talking in baby talk, wanting to cling and cuddle up, crawl or even be bottle-fed. *Please be assured that this is completely natural and a sign of healing!*

To facilitate attachment, make sure regressive behaviors are done with you as the parent, not by the child alone in isolation. The purpose is for you to respond to the behavior with nurturance and meeting the needs as they should have been met in infancy. Be sure to discuss any uncomfortable feelings with your attachment specialist so that you do not hurt your child by shaming or discouraging his regression. This is especially when having an attachment specialist is vital: Regular mental health professionals, untrained in attachment, are likely to try to force children to "act their age" and may even convey that the regressive need to cuddle, drink from a bottle or be rocked is "inappropriate".

Remember, your child's chronological age is not what is important; her emotional age is where the work and the healing will be done. You should notice over time that when your child's early developmental needs are met, he will start to "grow up" on two levels: His emotional age will eventually grow up along with his chronological age! Children adopted older, especially in adolescence, will require many more years at home, in dependency, than their non-adoptive peers. *Please do not focus on chronological age: Parent your children at whatever age and stage they present to you!*

### Infants

If you have adopted an infant, here are some important ways you can promote a secure parent-child attachment:

- Infants can and should be breastfed by adoptive mothers! Contact The Le Leche League at www.lalecheleague.org for information on how. Make sure eye-gazing and face caressing are part of breastfeeding.
- Carry your infant in a sling, against your bare skin, for at least a year from the time of adoption.

- Cosleep with your infant— Never leave your infant in a crib!
- Constant skin-to-skin contact and caressing is vital...

## Young children, older children and adolescents

If you have adopted or are repairing a biological relationship with a young child, older child or adolescent, here is what you can do together, *at their will*, to promote attachment:

- Cuddle your child every day, with your child cradled in your lap. If your son or daughter is physically too big, prop their head and back on pillows in your lap, their legs over the arm of the chair or on the bed and your arm behind their shoulders.
- Make sure that you work up to a few minutes of eye-gazing. This can be intensely difficult for children at first, so start with a few seconds.
- Caress your child's face and hair while you cradle and cuddle him.
- Rock her in a chair or in your lap.
- Toddlers can be breastfed by adoptive mothers! Contact the Le Leche League at www.lalecheleague.org for information on how. Make sure eye-gazing and face caressing are part of breastfeeding.
- Bottle-feed young children while you hold them on your lap— Of course you should always hold the bottle— "Babies" should never feed themselves! Young children may request the bottle for a few years.
- Your attachment specialist may suggest that you offer juice to your older child or adolescent child in a sports bottle, which is less embarrassing than a "baby bottle". If your child requests a "baby bottle", respond supportively and use one. As with young children, cuddle your older

child or teen and eye gaze while offering the sports bottle... As long as they wish for you to do so, always hold the bottle to send the message to your child that you want to provide the nurturing *for* them! Older children will usually stop requesting the bottle within a few months to two years once their need is filled.

- Cosleep with younger children.

- Camp out and share a tent in the living room or outside with an older child. This will help older children experience the benefit of cosleeping while respecting their physical boundaries. Let older children and adolescents pile into bed with you in the morning; or, lay in bed with your child to cuddle or while talking. *Be very careful of physical boundaries with older children and adolescents, especially those youth who have been sexually abused. Be especially mindful of physical boundaries with older children of the opposite sex.*

- Let children crawl, talk in "baby talk", toddle and show infantile behaviors around you. Respond in the way you would respond to an infant or toddler, using nurturing, accepting tones and words.

- Buy children infant or toddler toys and set up a play area. You will be surprised at how older children and adolescents light up and explore these toys for long periods of time! Children are meeting earlier, unmet developmental needs by using these toys.

- Expect to see your child act various ages throughout the day, and respond to your child according to whatever developmental age you are seeing. For example, your 15-year old may talk in baby talk one minute and act and talk as an adolescent a few minutes later.

*Do not be pressured by well meaning friends and relatives who show distaste for you "babying" your older child. You must do what is best for your child.* If you wish, attempt to briefly explain to them what you are doing, and why, but if you alter your re-parenting, your child may get the idea that he should feel ashamed of his early unmet needs.

Again, if you are unable or unwilling to work towards providing this intensive level of re-parenting for your young, older and adolescent children, please get assistance from your child's attachment specialist so that you can overcome this boundary or find a person who is willing to help you re-parent your child. It will be detrimental to your children if you are unable or unwilling to meet this basic need of theirs.

## Put in place a sacred, solid set of Family Principles

Ideally, as soon as your older adoptive child comes into your life, you should have a solid set of Family Principles firmly in place. Most adoptive children with trauma histories lack development in the parts of the brain that allow them the natural tendency to want to cooperate with and please their parents.

Remember the attachment disruption cycle from Chapter 3? Children adopted after infancy have developed a deep mistrust that their needs will be met. They have learned to cope with trauma and unmet needs by developing the survival skills of resisting natural authority and resisting any responsibilities expected of them. The most wounded of these children will often resist attachment, or will relentlessly challenge family principles, routines and even positive experiences, sometimes years after routines and principles have been set in place.

## Wiring the under-developed parts of the traumatized brain

Children who suffer with severe attachment disruption and RAD are thought to be under-developed in the parts of their brains that understand the concepts of good judgment, safety, body awareness, cause and effect, right and wrong and remorse. These parts of the brain must be *wired* through a developing attachment to a permanent adoptive parent. Remember, this lack of moral and emotional development is a *natural response to unnatural early life experiences* and should not be viewed as "badness".

In order for us to build up a wounded child's internal sense of stability, and a sense of what family "give and take", responsibility and restitution-sharing are all about, we must help them develop the wiring for understanding cause and effect. Introducing them as soon as possible to a strong set of Family Principles is as necessary as physical affection in helping them to stabilize and develop an internalized set of moral principles.

Principles are *the way you live*; they *are not a list of rules that you enforce just to be in control.* Remember, exerting power and control over children are not part of attachment parenting. The goal is always to meet needs and guide children into directing their own interests as they heal.

In the beginning, children with severe attachment disruption and RAD can be extremely oppositional and defiant and may not show interest in cooperating or sharing. Moral development must be built in these children in a way that would not be appropriate for children with a secure attachment or with mild to moderate attachment disruption.

Following is a sample list of the Family Principles specifically for children with severe attachment disruption and RAD. We will also discuss the reasons why this list is different from the list in Part I of this chapter.

Update these principles as needed. Again, please, do not use punishments and justify them as restitution. The goal is to connect with your child and repair or initiate parent-child attachment— Punishments and illogical control only infuriate children and force them to resist you more intensely.

---

## Our Family Principles

- (Parent/s) job is to take care of (child's name here), keep him/her safe and make decisions about what is best for him/her physically, emotionally, educationally and spiritually. (Child)'s job is to work on showing and sharing closeness with her/his new family and learning healthy ways of expressing emotions.

- (Parent/s) is the person/people in charge of taking care of the family and the home. (Parent/s) will set limits to ensure safety and physical and emotional health, as well as respectfulness and fairness for everyone. (Child) will earn freedom as she/he demonstrates the responsibility to show safe judgment. Freedom will be reduced if it is infringing upon someone else or on our Family Principles.

- We treat one another with love and respect in our family. We express emotions with words. We do not hit, scream at or say hurtful or sarcastic things to one another. We take space if we are too angry to talk.

- We treat all people, pets and living things with respect. We spend time with our guests. We are gentle and caring to animals, trees, insects and plants. We are respectful to people and to any living creatures and things that we encounter daily.

- We treat property and our home with respect. We do not throw things, break, ruin or destroy things.

- We cleanup after ourselves. (Parent/s) do most of the household chores and (child) will be asked to help out with a daily chore as well. (Child) is asked to keep his/her room clean and pick up after her/himself.

- (Child)'s room time is ____ p.m. and bedtime is ____ p.m. on weeknights. (Child) will have an earlier room time for not cooperating with the morning or evening routine.

- We treat ourselves with respect. We eat healthy, practice good hygiene and dress presentably. Daily, we brush our teeth and hair, wash hands after using the bathroom (etc.) and wear clean clothes. We shower properly every morning. We will not treat ourselves with disrespect or harm.

- We use restitution in our family. If a family principle is broken, we must discuss it and then make restitution. For the first six months to two years, (parent/s) show the ways that (child) can make restitution for breaking a Family Principle. After that, (child) will have a say in deciding upon restitution.

## Why is this version of Our Family Principles different for children with severe attachment disruption and RAD?

- Children who have suffered neglect and trauma or no attachment at all often do not know the purpose of family or of relationships. They need those concepts to be stated literally for them. They do not understand how love and healthy attachment sharing feels.
- Some children with severe trauma and neglect histories suffered brain damage. They also have suffered a severe lack of brain development in the areas of the brain that allow good judgment and cause and effect thinking to develop as well as the ability to attach, feel empathy, feel remorse and understand emotions.
- Similarly, these children often feel the extreme need to be in control of the household in order to avoid abuse and harm. They need us to show them safe, healthy, natural authority.
- Many children adopted from orphanages and from foster care were forced into parental roles with younger siblings or other children. In my work with children, I have heard of toddlers left alone  to care for infant siblings for hours at a time, adolescents abandoned to the streets alone or with siblings and older children left alone so long as to find a dead sibling. These children need to literally hear that their new parents are now taking the burden off of their children's backs by stating that they, the parents, are in charge of providing for the family's needs. This will be a hard role for children to give up.
- Freedom can literally be a life and death issue when older children with severe attachment disruption are allowed freedoms that would be completely appropriate for most other children—Due to severe neglect and abuse, these children may have a very poor sense of body awareness, very poor judgment and a very poor sense of safety.

- Remember- These areas of the brain are under-developed, regardless of how big your child looks and how "mature" your child presents. In the beginning of the relationship, assume your older adoptive child may require the safety monitoring of a toddler.

- Children with severe attachment disruption and RAD, from toddlers to teens, often display extremely explosive emotions, dangerous behaviors and aggression. Some children with severe attachment disruption and RAD can be physically, verbally and sexually violent towards others, towards themselves and towards animals. A small percentage of children with RAD are fire setters and have engaged in severe criminal acts. A small percentage of children with RAD, even children as young as three, are homicidal or have actually attempted or succeeded at homicide.

- Children who are physically and sexually violent and involved with other criminal acts are in need of strong guidance about how to safely express anger and rage as well as guidance about what is and what isn't an acceptable form of emotional expression. They need to be taught through modeling and restitution that any type of violence towards the self and towards others is not acceptable. In addition to intense amounts of nurturance and attachment parenting, they require intense supervision and very tight limits for safety purposes. In some cases, an out-of-home placement may be necessary for the safety of the family or community.

- The room time for children at night is especially critical for parents (especially single parents) of extremely challenging children. This is the time when parents can recharge and meet some of their own needs. Parents of very challenging adoptive children who are unable to recharge from the intensity of each difficult day are more likely to consider disrupting ("divorcing") the adoption. This of course, is severely detrimental to the children.

- It is imperative to keep a routine in the evening (including a nightly ritual of holding and rocking). Since children will often resist room time, I have found that in the case of children with RAD, it is necessary to give them an earlier room time the next night if they sabotage the room/bed time.

- Children with histories of severe neglect and abuse often have little or no concept of basic self-care and hygiene habits.

- Children with severe attachment disruption or RAD are often not aware of the give-and-take and cause and effect relationships of restitution and thus need it modeled for them.

- They often do not feel remorse for hurting someone or infringing upon someone's rights in the beginning, as those parts of the brain are under-developed by lack of parental nurturance and lack of secure attachment.

- In our punitive society, it is difficult for most people to understand that if a child's emotional and physical needs were severely neglected, the child, and later adult, *will not understand right and wrong, conscience and remorse*. These children may seem to intellectually understand "right and wrong" on the surface, but it is little more than a conditioned response to punishment.

- In the beginning, these children need parents to assume control of the restitution process and gradually allow children to learn it through first watching, then by participating in it, *all while their attachment needs are being intensely met*.

Older children adopted from foster care or orphanages often need very specific information about basic daily living skills that we take for granted, especially regarding health and self care habits. For example:

- Older children whose physical needs were neglected and ignored may be so out of tune with their bodies that they may need you to help them develop their natural internal signals. *They are likely to literally need you to remind them to eat, hydrate, use the toilet, put on a coat, sleep and avoid dangers.*

- Older children who have suffered neglect often need to be taught everything about self care, including *how* to shower, to use soap when showering, how to wash their hair, to use shampoo, when to shower, how to brush their teeth, how to dress, how to eat at the table, how to wash hands and when, to expel bodily waste *into the toilet*, and to change clothes daily.

- List in order all of the things your children need to do in the morning and evening, including very obvious tasks. A sense of structure and routine helps children with RAD feel stable, even if they test the routine.

- Day and bed time wetting or soiling is very common in traumatized children, especially boys. Most traumatized children outgrow bedtime enuresis by age 15, but it may last past 18.

- If your children suffer from nocturnal enuresis, they likely need to be told to change disposable underpants, throw them in the trash and to clean themselves.

- To rule out any medical problems such as fecal impaction or a urinary disorder, it is a wise to have your child evaluated by a specialist. Although daily medication for fecal impaction is usually necessary, *do not rush to use medication for bedwetting.* Do your research first— Drugs for bedwetting do not cure the problem; they interfere with normal urine production!

- Parents should be patient, gentle and supportive with wetting and soiling problems. Parents should purchase a plastic mattress covering, teach children to wear disposable underpants such as Pull Ups' Goodnights, teach them how to clean themselves, how to change their bed sheets and how to wipe down the plastic mattress lining (there are even swim diapers available online for older children).

- The more negative attention you draw to the wetting or soiling, the longer it will take for your child to naturally develop and emotionally heal.

Assigning your children a daily chore, immediately when they join your family, will help them develop a sense of responsibility. Explain how each family member does their part and how it helps the whole family unit. If chores are deliberately not completed well, ask your child to re-do the chore. Remember, this is not as a punishment, but a way to instill a sense of cause and effect and give and take. Start with just one chore, regardless of the age. It may be difficult for children in foster care to manage *one* chore; two will lead to unnecessary problems.

In the case of children who deliberately function like "chore machines", limit them to one very small chore to help them to develop an appreciation of contributing verses being forced to work.

## Consequences and restitution

Children who are adopted from orphanages and foster care usually find it very difficult to accept natural authority, family principles, responsibilities and expectations once they settle in to their new home. The best time to introduce children to Family Principles and family expectations is during your visitations, before they even move in. Older adoptive children are most receptive to agreeing to Family Principles and expectations *before* they begin to start forming an attachment to their parents! Remember, feelings of attachment are frightening and trigger the need to test, challenge and resist. This is why child care providers and parents of friends often report that our children are very well behaved and delightful when they take care of them— People who they are not attaching to do not threaten their sense of safety.

Clearly explain to your children that restitution is used by all family members (including parents) to make amends for broken family principles and broken responsibilities. *Whenever a family principle is broken, first find out if your children are really signaling unmet needs.* Once the needs are met, discuss how your children could let you know about their unmet needs next time in a way that you can understand.

Explain what consequences children may face when they deliberately act out in oppositional ways. Make sure that you are not justifying punishments and calling them consequences— Children immediately will notice your hypocrisy and will challenge you about it. Consequences should be directly related to principles broken and what family members need in order for restitution to be made.

Some examples:

- If your child refuses to cooperate with her morning routine, she will be asked to take an earlier room time later on;
- If your child is disrespectful, request that he "rewind" and repeat what he wanted to say to you in a way you can hear it. Do not fill her request as long as she is disrespectful;

- If your child runs off in stores, he must stand with you and hold onto the shopping cart;

- If your child deliberately destroys property or damages the walls, have her earn money to replace the property or inform the landlord of her deed, asking the landlord how she can make restitution for the damage!

- If your child is acting oppositional and generally uncooperative on the day he has a fun event planned, lie down on the couch and refuse to move until he expresses himself in a way you can understand;

- If your homeschooling child repeatedly refuses to cooperate with the state requirements for homeschooling, take him on a tour of the local public school so he can see the contrast in his freedoms;

- If you are a single parent and your child has a severe outburst and is verbally abusive most of the day and causes severe emotional distress to other family members, as restitution you may request that he pay you free time to help you recuperate. She could spend a few hours playing in her room (coming out for basic needs, of course), or doing a couple of outdoor chores for you. Of course this is not used as a way to banish, but as a way to meet a genuine need of yours for time alone to mend; and

- If your older child has a severe outburst and behaves in a threatening or violent manner towards anyone in the household, call 911 and ask the police to help you transport your child to the emergency room.

Remember, hitting, grabbing, yelling, neglect and punishment have no place in healing attachment:

- Never hit your child... Yes, "spanking" and "smacking" *are* hitting. *All* types of hitting *are damaging to children.*

- Never use any type of rough handling or scare tactics such as grabbing, shaking or pain infliction on your children.

- Punishments are not discipline, restitution or "consequences". They are punishments and they cause resentment.

- Never neglect any of your children's basic physical or emotional needs as "consequences". Punishing children by making them suffer with unmet needs is neglect, not a "consequence".

- Never discipline, shame or punish your child for enuresis or encopresis (wetting or soiling), even if you believe that an incident was deliberate. Day and night time wetting is very common in traumatized children and may last throughout adolescence. Simply purchase a plastic mattress covering, disposable underpants (such as Pull Ups' Goodnights) and ask your child to change the sheets if accidents leak.

- Although there are times when raising our voices may be appropriate in serious situations, yelling, name calling, threatening and sarcasm have no place in attachment parenting.

- Restraining a younger child should only be attempted if there is a serious threat to someone's safety. *Restraining a child to control a harmless tantrum or to prevent your child from coming out of "time-out" is not acceptable.* Do not attempt to restrain older children—Call 911 if there is a threat to someone's safety.

## Protocol for broken Family Principles

When your children break a Family Principle, follow this set of steps below every time. This process is vital to instilling emotional regulation, cause and effect and teaching appropriate expression of emotions. If you skip it and let acting out behaviors slide, your child's acting out behaviors and lack of emotional development are likely to worsen.

1. Ask your child to discuss what he needed and why the incident occurred.

2. Ask your child what feeling she was trying to express by acting out.

3. Validate and empathize with his need and feelings and let him express them fully.

4. Express your feelings about the incident and what you need.

5. Explain why the family principle exists and why breaking it is unacceptable.

6. Discuss the alternatives your child had for expressing feelings.

7. If your child has newly joined the family, explain the way your child can make restitution. If your child has been part of the family for six months to two years and is acting out less and less, allow her to discuss ways to make restitution.

8. Once restitution is made, drop the incident, let your child resume his day and do not hold a grudge.

9. You will need to repeat this process thousands and thousands of times, sometimes countless times *per day* for the *same* repeatedly broken principle.

### Cautions about the popular books for adoptive parents

- Some books recommend that adoptive parents should execute swift punishments for infractions and refuse to give explanations, allowing the child to become hysterical trying to figure out why. Doing this is not only disrespectful to your child, but is teaching that family is about power and control rather than love, safety, cooperation and mutual responsibility.

- Some books convey that your child's feelings or needs during an incident of acting out are irrelevant and should not be discussed. These same books generally instruct adoptive parents not to reveal their feelings so their children do not feel they "have won" or see parents as "affected by their behavior". This is dishonest, inauthentic and will not help children develop the parts of the brain that feel empathy and remorse. Denying feelings is also likely to cause resentment to fester in parents.

- Some books recommend that adoptive parents use extreme and crazy-making punishments such as forcing a child to get out on the side of the highway and walk home, to sit for long periods of time or to put alarms on bedroom doors so that children are unable to use the toilet until parents choose to get out of bed.

- These same authors tell parents to be deliberately unpredictable and treat children in bizarre ways to force children to "attach" by destroying their defenses. Again, our job is to teach our children that family is about love, safety, cooperation and mutual responsibility. *We cannot convey this message in a crazy-making, violating, abusive manner by asserting power, control and punishments! Our children's respect and attachment must be earned and cannot be forced!*

## Tools for nonviolent emotional expression

Traumatized, wounded children cannot be expected to be able to express their emotions and needs acceptably if they are not taught and allowed to practice the necessary tools for regulating emotions. For most of our children who have suffered disrupted attachment, abuse, neglect and profound losses, rage and grief are the primary emotions that they seem to express. Daily, over and over, hundreds and thousands of times, teach your children these tools when they are calm, and then guide them in using these tools when they are showing signs of needing them.

Here is a list of tools for children to use to help them develop emotional stability:

---

## Tools for Emotional Stability

- Check in with yourself and figure out what you are feeling;

- Feel your feelings and needs, letting the intensity sink in;

- Take five to ten *slow, deep* breaths *from the stomach*
  - It is important to stretch or inflate the stomach on the deep breath *in* and deflate the stomach with the breath *out*.
  - Do not breathe shallowly from the upper chest or rapidly or you may become light headed. This is one of the single most important tools for getting anger and anxiety under control.
- Express your feelings and needs honestly, fully, calmly and respectfully;

- Ask yourself, what do our Family Principles say about this? Why are the Principles in place?

- Can you change your negative thoughts to more rational statements?
  - For example, instead of "I hate doing these dishes", say, "I dislike these dishes, but I know I am doing my part to help out. After I am done, I am free to do something I want to do."
- FREEZE MOUTH AND BODY!

- Do a physical activity such as biking, running, push ups, etc.;
- Take space alone;
- Express your feelings with art, music or a project;
- Do a "grounding" exercise:
  - Starting with the feet, focus completely on how your skin feels in your shoes and socks. Work up slowly to the top of your head, feeling every texture against your skin.
  - Gently push firmly on all of your major muscles, such as your upper and lower arms and legs, your back, chest, thighs, etc.
  - During panic attacks, or during an urge to self-harm, hold an ice cube for several seconds.
- Tell yourself, "I may not act out my feelings."
  - Remind yourself that it is ok to feel feelings, but feeling them is NOT acting them out in harmful ways.
- Think of the possible consequences of your actions;
- Think of the last time you lost control. Ask yourself what you do want and what you don't want to happen;
- Think of the stone in the water metaphor:
  - When you throw a stone, it creates widening circles of ripples around the spot of impact. These ripples represent the consequences of the action. The action is represented by the stone thrown.
- Do an audio tape to whoever you are angry at;
- Think out loud in private;
- Remind yourself, "My past makes it hard for me to stay in control of my emotions once I get upset. My past makes it hard for me to be close to my parents sometimes. I know that my past is not my fault and that my parents are helping me to heal. I know I need to do my part and use these tools so that I can remain in control of my actions."

- Remind yourself, "My anger and rage belong to the people in the past who have hurt me. It is not ok to hurt Mom/Dad for what someone else did to me in the past."
- Remind yourself, "My job is to learn to show and share closeness with my family and to work on being emotionally healthy."
- Remind yourself that you are a role model for the younger children in your life. What would you tell them to do in your situation?
- Don't judge others until you look at your own actions.

---

Children can also be asked to visualize a part of themselves that can act as a compassionate, kind but firm "Sentry", to stand strong enough to bar the angry part of themselves from crossing a line of acting-out. Help your children to visualize the angry part of themselves as a hurt, innocent infant who is in need of help and guidance, not punishment. "Locating the Sentry" may take practice, but can be added to your children's tool list.

## Contracting

The above list of individual tools can be memorized, used and practiced regularly, in an a la carte manner, depending on the situation and circumstances. However, parents and emotionally unstable children may also need a specific plan in place to prevent incidents of minor upset from escalating to crises. Here is an example of a plan that my son and I use together. It can be turned into a contract, for those children who like to use contracts. Parents and children can use this contract together to help them regain emotional stability if they begin to lose control of their emotions or if they enter into a power struggle:

## Sample Plan to Reverse Power-Struggles

1. Parent or child yells out a signal word that both of you agree on such as "RESPITE!" or "FREEZE!" Both parties must freeze their voices and bodies once someone yells it out.

2. Parent asks child, "What do you need right now?"

3. Child expresses his need— He may need something as simple as a hug to ground himself back in reality. Suggest a need if she does not come up with an answer.

4. Both parent and child take deep breaths and use any other tools to calm down.

5. Child expresses his feelings first; parent empathizes and validates.

6. Parent express her feelings next, parent empathizes with herself (in her head).

7. Child expresses his need, parent responds

8. Parent expresses her need (for example, the need for child to be safe or for the family to be safe), asks child to respond.

9. Both come up with a mutual agreement or compromise. Parent has final say if there is no mutual agreement on safety and health issues, but parent must do her best to work towards a compromise.

Making a commitment to practicing and using the list of tools and the contract above is vital to helping children with severe behavioral problems learn self regulation. Without a commitment to these tools, it will be very chaotic for your child to navigate through his emotions and almost impossible to organize them and develop internal regulation. Memorize these tools, carry a list of them in your pocket or purse, remind yourself and your child to use them and practice them! They really do work when they are used!

### Don't forget what you learned in Part I

Remember to also incorporate all of the healing suggestions, including the Nonviolent Communication (NVC) model and the S.A.L.V.E. model, as discussed in Part I of Chapter 11.

## Expect severe testing, sabotaging and relapse

When children suffer trauma and severe breaks in attachment, pain, suffering and loss are familiar to them. When wounded children begin to attach to someone, they experience intense anxiety that the relationship will be lost, like in their past. Their defenses fly up like a protective shield. They are likely to push us, their new parents, to our limits in attempts to "reject" us before we "reject" them.

Likewise, wounded children also fear that we, their new parents, will be abusive and neglectful to them, like in their past. For these children, the suspense of not knowing is unbearable. As a way to "get it over with", our adoptive children may literally attempt to push us to limits where we fear we actually might lose control and verbally or physically lash out at them. Unfortunately, some parents give in to this pressure and actually hurt their children, damaging the budding attachment and confirming to their children that adults will hurt them and can't be trusted.

As our children are attaching more and more to us, this testing is likely to intensify for awhile, and then finally stabilize. Don't get too comfortable! As the attachment deepens and our children's needs begin to fill up, they are likely to have cyclic episodes of relapsing and re-testing us with old behaviors! Some theorists have written that there are actually seven or eight intense stages of attaching to severely traumatized and attachment disrupted children!

Sometimes children's relapse cycles correspond with "anniversary reactions", unconscious memories that cause relapse on the anniversaries of certain days or months that were traumatic. Although these relapse and testing cycles are intensely exhausting times for adoptive families, it is critical that we, as parents, remain *iron* in our resolve to love and remain committed to our children and to our growing attachment. We also must rely on our support systems, such as respite providers, to prevent us from lashing out at our children and to allow us to keep our Family Principles firm in the face of testing.

Discussion of the depth needed to address all of the patterns and cycles of re-parenting and attaching to traumatized children is beyond the scope of this book. I have included resources in Chapter 12 so parents can read deeper and educate themselves about healing the unique needs of adoptive children, children with severe attachment disruption and children with RAD.

## Tools just for parents (of volatile children)

In addition to the tools for nonviolent emotional expression listed above, exhausted, burnt out parents who are struggling with children who display chronic, relentless behavioral problems such as rage episodes, often need an additional list of tools to prevent themselves from reacting aggressively. The following tools are designed to *prevent* exasperated, severely tested parents from triggering or escalating a rage episode in their children when their children begin to show signs of defiance and upset.

---

### The "Help My Child Avoid an Episode" Tool List

- My irritability, anxiety and rage are just symptoms of triggers in my own past, not reflective of my child.
- Try to respond to my child the way I would if my child were physically hurt.
- Take herbs or seek out natural remedies for my anxiety, irritability and anger.
- Think positive thoughts...
- Remember he is a child; what would I have needed at his age?
- Empathize with myself and the good job I am doing despite her chronic testing behavior.
- Take a slow, deep stomach breath, then five more.
- WATCH MY SARCASTIC, impatient, ANGRY TONE- This triggers him!
- Ask her to locate her "Sentry", the internal keeper of stability, and then locate my own.
- Remember, his angry side is really a hurt, innocent infant.
- Tell my child I need to take five minutes to keep myself calm in order to respond best to her.
- Remember how fast this can escalate and that my child mirrors what I do!

- Do not negate my child's feelings *even if they seem irrational to me.*
- Empathize with his way of feeling things right now and listen to his perspective— His anger is more about his past, not about now. This doesn't mean I agree or am "giving in" to anything inappropriate.
- (If your child was adopted) Most of her severe problems are about her past, and aren't reflective of ME.
- However, have I been meeting all of his or her needs?
- I am not going to lose control of him by empathizing and validating his feelings; it will reverse the course of him plummeting out of control.
- When she is escalating, she cannot hear or reflect on my words... Consequences mean nothing to her.
- Suggest that he run laps and then do a physical activity myself.
- Try to avoid giving her a "time-out" and take one myself!
- Yell "Respite!" or "Freeze!" and use the Plan to Avoid Power Struggles.
- Ask myself how my response will affect our connection and attachment.
- Be the adult and model for my child how to handle frustration, conflict and disagreements.
- He has to disagree with me and be angry at me sometimes—It is normal!
- Be honest about my feelings after she tells hers.
- If I can, say yes and agree with some aspect of what he is saying— We can "process" later when he can hear me.
- Let her be free to direct her life and choices as often as possible.
- Smile and remind him that I love him. Don't add a negating 'but...' after it!
- Model that we can get through this— It doesn't have to

be a crisis.

- We can and WILL get through this- My child is a good person and I am the number one person in his life and his entire world. He will follow the right path. I must stay connected with him so he can get out of his pain.
- I must do everything I can to prevent her from having to live in an outside placement. Call a friend for help and respite!
- I need to help him keep his sense of joy because these episodes cause him pain, shame and depression.

---

I strongly suggest carrying a copy of this tool list in your pocket, purse or car glove compartment and add a copy to your bedroom nightstand or anywhere else you could find yourself needing it in the case that your child begins to challenge you.

## Friendships should *not* be the priority for newly adoptive children for the first year

In the first year of your older child's arrival, the most important relationship for him to have is with his new family. Although children should be allowed to play with other children, friendships should not be the priority for the first year, regardless of her age. It is very important to understand that social skills and friendships develop from the foundation and quality of the attachment between parent and child. Often during the first year, your child will have minimal or poor social skills.

As your new child develops his attachment to you and to his

extended family, he will naturally be able to (and should be allowed to) extend his circle to friends. If you allow friends to take up her time during the first year, she will be less likely to develop an attachment with you. Homeschooling is the best way to introduce your child to friends who are more likely to be patient with your child as he learns basic social skills. Homeschooled friends are less likely to expose her to influences that will support detachment.

## Safety boundary issues for your child's emotional age

Do not be guided by your child's physical size, chronological age, or other people's opinions and looks when determining what safe boundaries are for your child. Most older children adopted from orphanages or from foster care are not able to make safe judgments and choices when left alone. When your child first arrives, keep her boundaries tight and gradually let her widen them once she demonstrates a developing sense of good judgment and responsibility.

Especially in the first year that your child joins your family, have his friends come to *your* home so you can keep a close eye on his needs, social skills, emotional stability and sense of safety. If he is over someone else's house, his friend's parents are unlikely to understand his need for monitoring and safety. Over time, with increasing good judgment she can work towards visiting her friends.

For example, it is unsafe for a 12 year old with a history of extreme attachment disruption, trauma, foster or orphanage placement to be allowed to bike around town or even off of your street upon arrival. He may have little concept of the danger of cars. He may have poor judgment around strangers. Although he is 12, he may be emotionally two. *Do not be pressured by well meaning friends and relatives who show distaste for you "babying" your child. You must do what is best for your child.* Children can earn wider boundaries by showing good judgment over time.

## When our children cannot live safely at home

Some children are so severely damaged that in spite of our best efforts at providing an attachment-based, healing environment, their capacity to tolerate triggers and stressors in their lives overwhelm their ability to function in a family setting. If your child is:

- Chronically refusing to cooperate with Family Principles or accept parental authority in a way that puts the family's safety and health in jeopardy,
- Chronically refusing to abide by treatment contracts in a way that puts the family's safety and health in jeopardy,
- Displaying repeated physical aggression that could potentially injure someone or has injured someone at home,
- Displaying self-abusive behaviors that are serious enough that you cannot prevent your child from self-injury,
- Displaying acts of torturing animals,
- Displaying sexual violence,
- Displaying homicidal threats, tendencies or attempts,
- Displaying suicide attempts,
- Preoccupied with fire, threatening to set a fire or has set a fire,

- Moderately or seriously involved with drugs or drug culture,

- Involved in moderate to serious criminal behavior,

- Involved with a gang, or

- Involved with other organized crime

...Then serious action must be taken on the part of parents to protect all family members. This action may need to include:

- Parents seeking long-term respite with a state or private agency post adoption services provider;

- Parents bringing their children to the hospital emergency room for evaluation and possible hospital admission (this may need to occur several times before hospital staff take parents seriously— Many providers have never heard of RAD or negate RAD);

- Parents calling the police in an emergency to have an officer talk to their children about what the law says about aggressive acts such as posturing, threatening, lunging, grabbing, hitting, etc.;

- Parents calling 911 to have their child taken by ambulance or police escort to the emergency room;

- Parents filing a petition for voluntary services with their state social services department;

- Parents meeting with a psychiatrist as a last resort to discuss temporary psychiatric drugs for their children's severe mood swings or psychotic symptoms;

- Parents filing a CHINS (Child In Need of Services) petition with their local probate court in cases of escalating oppositionality and aggression (the state may assume legal custody of your child in this case, so research your rights first); or

- Parents locating residential placement for their children

(please see Chapter 12 for programs in the USA with an attachment focus).

These steps should be used as a last resort. *Before serious steps such as psychiatric drugs, out-of-home placement or involvement with the legal system are taken, parents have an obligation to take inventory to be sure that all avenues in trauma healing have been tried*, including attachment parenting, non-traditional schooling, attachment therapy, EMDR, Neurofeedback, holistic and natural remedies and respite with friends and family members.

For parents who have adopted their children, remember, *adoption is forever! "Divorcing" our children should never feel like an option!* If our children become dangerous and cannot live at home, they are still our children— We have a responsibility to continue to support, visit and provide love and nurturance to them, with the goal of them returning home.

## Healing on a society-wide level

Following are a list of changes that need to be made to the foster care and institutionalized care systems. These are changes that parents, social workers, mental health professionals and law makers *must* make to protect children who need to be removed from their homes due to abandonment, abuse and neglect:

- No child should have to live more than a few weeks of their most critical years as an inmate or border in a program, facility or foster home. Instead of foster care, programs and institutions, the ideal situation for abused and neglected children would be for the biological parents to be in model foster homes *with* their children.

- Every effort must be made to recruit foster parents who are willing to commit to adopting longer term foster children who form attachments to them. Or, at least, require ethically that foster parents remain active parts of the lives of children who have formed attachments with them.

- If biological families are unable or unwilling to safely parent after help, education and mentoring have been provided, optimal adoptive families must be immediately available for all waiting children. Any parent who has committed sexual abuse, severe physical abuse or torture against a child should have parental rights terminated immediately!

- Each and every child, whether a newborn or an 18-year old aging-out of the foster care system, needs a *permanent*, safe, nurturing parent to provide a solid attachment with the child.

- No youth should ever be allowed to age-out of the foster care or juvenile "justice" system at 18 (or 22 in some states), *without an attachment figure or an adoptive parent to go to for support.*

# Chapter 12
# Resources to Help Parents and Society Make Changes

*"Be the change you want to see in the world"*
*–Mahatma Gandhi*

*"We live in a world in which we need to share responsibility. It's easy to say 'It's not my child, not my community, not my world, not my problem.' Then there are those who see the need and respond. I consider those people my heroes."*
*-Fred Rogers*

## Summing it all up

### Our culture is toxic to parents and children

Our culture has moved far away from nature's intended way for us to parent and care for our children. Unfortunately, over many centuries, as the world has become increasingly more industrialized, people have lost touch with their natural parenting instincts. Each generation is parented in a way that causes distress, pain, depression and anger. This in turn causes each new generation to pass down harmful ways of parenting that reflect their hurt, distress and resentment.

## Alarms in nature

Nature has built alarm signals into every animal to alert parents, companions and predators that the animal is experiencing or sensing a need, a threat or a danger. In nature, animal parents instinctively respond immediately to the alarms of their young. A human infant's alarm signal is crying, which is intended to alert parents to a need. As children grow older, they may still use crying, but their alarm signals become more sophisticated when their needs aren't met and often include behaviors that parents find disturbing.

## Recipe for a happy child: Secure parent-child attachment through meeting our children's needs

Children require a secure parent-child attachment in order to thrive. A secure-parent child attachment is *vital* to a child's optimal functioning in all areas of their development. It is the blueprint and foundation of a child's life long physical, emotional, social, intellectual, sexual, spiritual and moral functioning. It is the blueprint and foundation of a child's lifelong happiness and ability to cope with life and relationships.

A secure parent-child attachment develops as the result of parents meeting children's basic physical and emotional needs (and then higher level needs) from infancy until young adulthood. This natural function of parenting is part of the human attachment cycle:

1. The child feels a physical or emotional need;
2. The child expresses the need using a signal such as crying, showing, asking or telling;
3. The parent meets the child's need as soon as possible;
4. Every time the child's needs are met, the child feels calm, satiated, homeostasis, joy and trust in the parent.

As a result of this unbroken cycle, secure attachment builds and develops.

If parents do not meet their child's needs or delay in doing so, their child will feel distress, rage, grief, anxiety and distrust in the parents. Every unmet need builds and builds and an insecure or disrupted attachment develops. When a child suffers a disrupted attachment, emotional and behavioral problems may show up immediately or may slowly begin to surface over a period of years.

## Parenting and educating the way nature intended

People in peaceful tribal cultures and non-human mammals are the natural models that can teach us how nature intended us to parent. In tribal cultures where violence is very low and mental illness is reportedly a rarity, people are found to parent in line with the rest of our mammal relatives. The most basic features of natural parenting are:

- Constant skin-to-skin contact and non-stop carrying of the infant for the first 12 months of life;
- Breastfeeding for *at least* two and a half years and optimally, longer;
- Responding to the needs of children all through childhood;
- High levels of physical affection and cuddling through out childhood;
- Nonviolent, gentle discipline and guidance;
- Strong family and community relationships and modeling;
- Natural education through play, imitation and being an active part of the community; and
- Allowing children the freedom to develop at their own pace.

Our mammal relatives, including the bonobo, show similar ways of parenting, especially mammals that are of the carrying species. Carrying species must carry their infants at all times or their infants will cry out. Carrying mammals are different than caching mammals. Caching mammals must put their babies down and leave them for awhile to keep them safe from predators. Babies of caching species must remain totally quiet and still when they are left alone. We can tell that humans are a carrying species, because human babies cry when they are put down, as do all mammal babies of the carrying species.

## Child development

As children grow through life, they face certain developmental tasks at each phase of their life. A secure parent-child attachment helps them resolve and complete their developmental tasks to an optimal level.

## School and day care harms children and secure parent-child attachment

One of the most life-changing disruptions to the parent-child relationship is when children are placed in day care, preschool and grade school. Traditional schools are based on controlling large groups of people so they all do the same thing. The conditions of traditional schools are detrimental:

- To the parent-child attachment relationship,
- To democracy,
- To a child's natural development,
- To intellectual development and creativity,
- To the child's body and health,
- To social development, and
- To emotional and behavioral stability.

Children are often unhappy, bored, frustrated and mentally exhausted in school. They have little time for the high-energy, physical activity and free-play that they need for optimal brain development. Homework further takes children's time away from their own interests and from family and friends. Additionally, children are negatively influenced by their peers and pull away from their parents at younger and younger ages.

## Our everyday life causes emotional and behavioral problems

Constantly, parents are conditioned to accept and live with so many beliefs, trends, habits, routines and practices that seem harmless but are actually harmful to children's natural development. These include:

- How children are seen by our culture compared to how adults are seen;
- How parents discipline and guide children;
- What values parents and the culture model for children about how to live; and
- How parents substitute themselves with all types of distractions that don't fill children's needs.

These beliefs, trends and practices also include forcing children to grow up in ways that are not appropriate to their development and failing to allow children to develop and grow naturally.

## Child trauma and PTSD

Many children in our culture suffer symptoms of trauma and Post Traumatic Stress Disorder from distressing and frightening treatment such as physical punishment, severe abuse and neglect. Trauma affects all areas of a child's development and actually rewires the child's brain, causing emotional problems that may be misdiagnosed. Trauma is believed to be stored in parts of the brain that prevent therapy, maturity, learning and insight from healing it, causing symptoms to last for decades. A special kind of therapy, called EMDR, can help heal trauma.

## Extreme breaks in attachment: Foster care, institutional facilities and adoption

Children who have been adopted or who live in orphanages, foster homes, institutions and programs have suffered extreme attachment disruption and often have severe emotional and behavioral problems as a result. These are the children who our culture has failed the most, as they are some of the most damaged and hurting people in our societies.

## Our children do not have brain disorders— Our culture is disordered!

Most children in our culture who act out their distress are misdiagnosed with mental illnesses and brain disorders such as ADHD, learning disabilities, bipolar disorder and oppositional defiant disorder. They are often forced to take powerful, mindaltering drugs once they are diagnosed. However, most of the symptoms that these children are expressing are actually symptoms of a disrupted attachment, a developmentally inappropriate educational environment and Post Traumatic Stress Disorder. Although our culture views these children as "brain disordered", it is actually our *culture* that is disordered. Diagnosing and medicating children does not heal the *causes* of their distress. The symptoms that children show are actually *natural responses to an unnatural and intolerable life circumstances*!

## Repairing attachment and healing trauma

It is possible for parents to repair attachment and heal trauma with children of all ages! Basic principles of healing, such as physical affection, empathizing and showing compassion to our children, plus getting help for ourselves, are necessary parts of repairing attachment and trauma. Other necessities include:

- Attachment parenting;
- Instilling family principles, self discipline and responsibility through respectful guidance and strong modeling;

- Learning nonviolent forms of emotional expression and communication with children;
- Finding alternatives to traditional schooling such as unschooling, or schools that respect play and children's development;
- EMDR treatment to heal trauma;
- Neurofeedback to retrain the brain;
- Natural attachment therapy to help repair insecure attachment;
- Holistic and body-centered treatments to heal imbalances; and
- Learning about the dangers of diagnosing and medicating children's behavior.

## Re-parenting children with severe attachment disruption and RAD

Even children who have been adopted or children who suffer from severe attachment disruption or Reactive Attachment Disorder can heal and grow to attach strongly to their parents! Parents must make a permanent commitment to their children, secure a support system for themselves and find an attachment specialist, to start this very challenging process.

Parents must be willing to provide their children with re-parenting experiences that meet their children's unmet early developmental needs, including intense physical affection. Parents must have a strong set of family principles in place, and an understanding of how to use consequences and restitution so that they are not punishing their children. In order to help their children develop emotional stability, tools for nonviolent emotional expression can be learned and practiced by every family member. Adoptive parents and parents of children with severe attachment disruption should expect severe testing behaviors and relapse cycles as children grow to deeper and deeper levels of attachment.

### Healing our culture now

In order for our culture to heal itself, parents, professionals and law makers must prioritize healing our children and our young adults rather than labeling, punishing, medicating, confining and incarcerating them. As citizens, we all have a responsibility to take part in demanding that mental health professionals, social workers, doctors, scientists, our state's human service agencies and our state legislators prioritize:

1. Meeting all children's needs *now*;
2. Healing the damage already done to children; and
3. Helping and mentoring young adults with trauma histories in order to prevent damage to the next generation.

## What we must do to make changes in our lives

Our culture is the collective entity of the beliefs and actions of generations of human beings, including ourselves, who have diverged from natural ways of living and parenting. Our culture is truly mentally ill and "brain" disordered! However, a giant bottle of Adderoll, Celexa or Risperdol isn't what our culture needs...

Our culture is saturated by violence and anger, leading to disrespect for other human beings, disrespect for other living creatures and disrespect for our own natural environment. Our culture is consumed with shame about sexuality and the human body, leading to rigid, uptight bans on sexuality on one hand and a relentless obsession and adolescent-like mockery of it on the other hand. Each generation passes this sickness of violence, shame and rage onto the next generation, creating materialism, self-obsession, money obsession, work obsession, academic obsession, substance obsession, media obsession and war obsession. More programs, prisons, schools, rules, medications, laws and punishments will *not* stop it. *We must start by raising human beings to think and feel differently.*

### *You have the power!*

If you put this book down and choose not to make a conscious commitment to healing your attachment to your children, this information will be quickly drowned out by all of the influences in your life that keep you and your children hurt, distressed and frustrated.

You have a tremendous power in you. It is the power to make choices that will alter the course of your life and your children's future. You have the instinctual power to choose to face a difficult but honest truth about your children: *They need you in a desperate way, in a way that is wildly different than what you've been taught to give them; in a way that you were never given.*

You have the intelligent power to choose to take some steps in a new direction; to meet many of your children's unmet needs and heal your attachment. You have the power to re-read this book or read other books that will help you learn what you need to do in order to heal your children. You have the power to talk to your spouse or partner about parenting in a way that is more in-tune with nature's intent for humans. You have the power to give up yelling, hitting, rough handling and punishing your children. You have the power to give up our culture's cold beliefs that babies belong in cribs, fed by bottles. You have the power to challenge harmful trends, including the belief that the sarcastic cartoons on TV are "fine" for your children to watch.

You have the "mother-bear" power to challenge our culture's apathetic notions that children belong in school and that your children "learn more" at school than at home. You have the parental power to tell your children's teachers that you will not be allowing homework in your home. You have the power to connect with the unschooling or homeschool groups in your area to find out how easy and freeing it can be to allow your children to learn at home and out in the community. You have the power to search for a school for your children that *you* would have *loved* as a child; a school that will allow your children to keep their natural love for learning; a school that your children would find true joy in.

You have the instinctual, loving power to cuddle and nurture your children daily and re-parent their earlier unmet needs. You have the courageous power to deeply listen to your children and find out what they *need*, instead of what you *believe*. You have the healing power to not blame yourself, to not blame others, to not blame brain disorders and to not blame your *children* for the way things are now. You have the power to get the help you need in order to help your children.

Most importantly, you have the life-changing power to take responsibility for moving in a direction that will naturally reward you and your family more happiness and a deeper connection to each another.

> *"You may never know what results come of your action, but if you do nothing there will be no result"*
> *–Mahatma Gandhi*

# How to become involved with helping children and changing laws

*"The best way to find yourself is to lose yourself in the service of others." –Mahatma Gandhi*

If we desire to help others and make a difference in our world, we must start at home, with the way we treat our children and other family members. Once we begin to heal ourselves and our closest relationships, we can offer ourselves to helping to ease the suffering of others. Here are some ideas:

### Speak out politically about attachment, trauma and children's needs and rights!

- Write letters to the editor of your local newspaper;
- Write letters to your state legislators and other politicians;
- Speak out at school meetings and town meetings;
- Research politicians before you vote, and vote for politicians that are most likely to support children's rights;
- Start a rally in your community if there is a community child advocacy issue that needs to be addressed;
- If you are politically savvy or are willing to learn, consider drafting a bill; or
- Search the Internet for information about how to contact your state representatives and how to take political action in your state.

### Mentor or volunteer!

- Become a Big brother or Big Sister. Contact: Big Brothers Big Sisters of America at www.bbbsa.org or Big Brothers Big Sisters of Canada at www.bbsc.ca;

- Contact your state child protective services and inquire about mentoring a child in state custody;

- Contact any independent living programs, residential, detention or group homes in your area, and inquire about mentoring a child in one of these institutions;

- Research on the Internet and locate child advocacy organizations that could use your help; or

- Call your state department of social services and ask about local volunteer organizations or programs that could use your help.

## Become an adoptive or foster parent to children in the foster care system!

In the USA, there are thousands of children in the foster care system who are in desperate need of a temporary or permanent home. The majority of these children have been removed from their biological families due to severe abuse, neglect or abandonment.

Most of the children waiting in state custody are between the ages of 6-18. Most prospective adoptive families are eager to adopt infants and toddlers, causing it to be very difficult to find homes for older children, especially boys and older adolescents. The problem of finding permanent homes for waiting children is also compounded by the difficult emotional and behavioral problems that many of these children exhibit due to their histories of extreme attachment disruption, trauma and multiple foster care placements. However, with fiercely committed, attachment-minded adoptive parents, traumatized children can begin the healing process necessary to become reciprocal members of a loving family.

Foster parents provide a child with a temporary home until it is safe for the child to return to the biological home, or until an adoptive home can be found for the child. Foster parents are paid a stipend to cover the child's living expenses.

Adoptive parents provide an abused, neglected or abandoned child who is unable to return to the biological family with the ultimate gift: A permanent family to love and care for him or her. There are generally no adoption fees when adopting children in state custody. Parents adopting children with disabilities may be eligible for financial assistance. For more information, visit: www.adopt.org

*Note: There are training and legal requirements that prospective foster and adoptive families must meet in order to be eligible to foster or adopt. The entire process, including matching up with a child, can take from 6-12 months.*

### Work in a related field!

There are multiple careers that are in dire need of strong child advocates. In order to research careers in the child advocacy fields, and to find out degree and educational requirements, contact your state university, local college or interview people in the fields in which you have an interest. You can also contact your state social service agency or research careers on the internet. Many of these careers will require college, graduate school and an educational internship.

### Use your talents for a good cause

- If you have a special talent, skill or provide a service to the community, donate your skills and services to children in state custody (tutoring; visits with animals; apprenticeships; art and photography lessons; skateboard lessons; sports or fitness lessons; computer lessons; free haircuts; free snacks and pizzas; free tickets to sporting events, movies, concerts, amusement parks; fundraising help, etc.).

- Use your writing skills to write letters to your state legislators or draft a bill to strengthen child protection laws.

- Use your public speaking talents to speak out at political events, PTA's, town meetings, etc. about child advocacy issues.

- Use your organizational skills to form a child advocacy organization or a task force to target a child advocacy issue in your community.

- Offer professional pro bono services to the community (legal, technological, medical, mental health, etc.) to further child advocacy efforts.

## If you witness or suspect child abuse, intervene!

- <u>If you suspect that a child may be experiencing some form of abuse or neglect</u>, document all suspicious incidents and contact your local state child protective services to file a report. You can obtain the number by contacting the information operator. If you feel that the child is in immediate danger, contact the police or dial 911. In the meantime, do what you can to support, protect and shelter the child until help can be obtained.

- <u>If you witness child maltreatment in public</u> and it is safe for you to do so, consider intervening in a calm and non-threatening manner by saying something such as, "It can be difficult to shop with kids when they get tired and bored... Could I tell you what's worked for me?", or "I can see that you are really frustrated, is there anything I can do to help?". Try to make eye contact with the child and smile at him or say something comforting. If you feel that it is unsafe to intervene, or if you feel the child is in danger of being hit again, seek out store security or call the police. Please understand that if you choose to intervene, the parent is likely to respond to your attention by swearing at you, telling you to mind your own business or by becoming belligerent. However, your intervention may make a difference in the life of a child who is unable to obtain help in any other manner.

- <u>If child maltreatment is happening in your family</u> you have a moral, and in some states, a legal obligation to protect the children affected and to support the involved adult family members to get the help they deserve. Try to talk to your family member to express your concerns. Offer emotional support, child care, parenting resources in your community, treatment resources and attachment parenting books. Try to involve any emotionally healthy family members to assist you, if possible. If the maltreatment continues despite your efforts, let your family member know that if the maltreatment does not cease, you will need to report the maltreatment to the local state child protective services. This can be an excruciating decision that may result in family members ostracizing and alienating you in their efforts to keep the maltreatment secretive. *Recognize that the safety of the children involved is the priority— Children are unable to defend themselves or leave aggressive parents.* You will be helping to put a stop to a multi-generational pattern of adults defending adults who hurt children and changing it to a pattern of adults defending children and ending child maltreatment.

*"Spread love everywhere you go: first of all in your own house. Give love to your children, to your wife or husband, to a next door neighbor... Let no one ever come to you without leaving better and happier..." –Mother Theresa*

# Resources and information on specific topics

I have listed books and websites below that I recommend or highly recommend for helping parents on their journey of understanding their children and healing their relationships with their children. It is my hope that you read many of these books and visit some of these websites. *Note: On my website you will find this list of resources annotated.*

If any book or website that you read ever leads you to information or other resources that appear out of line with natural attachment parenting and natural learning, be skeptical and disregard the information. Always ask yourself if the information is respectful of children, in line with nature's intent and if it will bring you closer to your children. The wonderful thing about books is that you can take what is helpful and leave the rest!

I list resources and information on the following topics:

- Attachment parenting
- Alternatives to traditional school
- Why traditional school and homework are harmful to children
- Nonviolent and non-defensive communication
- Positive, nonviolent discipline
- Parenting adoptive children, foster children and children with severe attachment disruption
- Attachment treatment
- EMDR
- Neurofeedback
- Strength-based residential programs in the USA
- Psychiatric medication: dangers and alternatives
- ADHD and mental illness diagnosis fraud

- Naturopathic and homeopathic alternatives
- Body-centered alternatives
- Tribal cultures and mammal parenting
- Natural, organic living
- Information about child abuse and trauma and its effects on children
- Abolishing physical punishment of children
- The detriments of TV, media and fast food
- Information about today's toxic peer culture
- How society fails youth and how to heal it
- Help for parents who had traumatic childhoods
- Autobiographies and biographies of survivors of severe child abuse

Additional resources can be found in the Appendices and Bibliography.

*Note: As of this printing, all of the Internet links provided here were active.*

If any of the provided links do not work:

- Try erasing the end of the URL (web address). For example, if www.childadvocate.org/1a.htm does not work, try removing /1a.htm.
- Run a search online for the resource or website using the keywords in the title
- If the website is truly no longer available, find a similar website by running a search for the topic you wish to research.

## Attachment Parenting

*America's Lost Dream: 'Life Liberty and the Pursuit of Happiness':
Current research and Historical Background on the Origins of Love
and Violence* by James W. Prescott. This paper can be accessed in
PDF format at: www.ttfuture.org/pdf/members/Prescott_ALD.PDF

*Attachment Parenting: Instinctive Care for Your Baby and Young Child*
by Katie Allison Granju

*Attachment Parenting International*, www.attachmentparenting.org

*Connection Parenting: Parenting through Connection instead of
Coercion, Through Love instead of Fear* by Pam Leo

*Kindred magazine*, www.kindredmagazine.com.au

*La Leche League*, www.lalecheleague.org

*The Mother magazine*, www.themothermagazine.co.uk

*Mothering magazine*, www.mothering.com

*Natural Child magazine*, www.naturalchildmagazine.com

*The Natural Child: Parenting from the Heart* by Jan Hunt

*The Natural Child Project*, www.naturalchild.org

*Natural Family Living* by Peggy O'Mara

*Nonviolent Communication, a Language of Life: Create Your Life, Your
Relationships, and Your World in Harmony with Your Values* by
Marshall B. Rosenberg

*Organic Parenting essay* by Geraldine and Gaetano Lyn-Piluso
www.primalspirit.com/ps3_1lyn-piluso.htm

*The Origins of Peace and Violence*, www.violence.de

*Primal Parent magazine*, www.primalparentingmagazine.com

*Raising Our Children, Raising Ourselves: Transforming Parent-child
relationships from Reaction and Struggle to Freedom, Power and Joy*
by Naomi Aldort

*Taking Children Seriously*, www.takingchildrenseriously.com

*Why Love Matters: How Affection Shapes a Baby's Brain* by Sue
Gerhardt

## Alternatives to Traditional School

*American Montessori Society*, www.amshq.org

*Association of Waldorf Schools of North America*, www.awsna.org

*The Autonomous Child*, www.autonomouschild.co.uk

*Challenging Assumptions in Education* by Wendy Priesnitz

*Connections Ezine*, www.connections.organiclearning.org

*Democratic School*, www.educationrevolution.org/lisofdemscho.html

*DeSchooling Our Lives* by Matt Hern

*Dumbing Us Down: The Hidden Curriculum of Compulsory Schooling* by John Taylor Gatto

*The Education Revolution*, www.educationrevolution.org

*The Exhausted School* by John Taylor Gatto

*Family Unschoolers Network*, www.unschooling.org

*Free at Last: The Sudbury Valley School* by Daniel Greenberg

*Guerrilla Learning: How to Give Your Kids a Real Education With or Without School* by Grace Llewellyn and Amy Silver

*The Happy Child: Changing the Heart of Education* by Steven Harrison

*Home Education magazine*, www.homeedmag.com

*Homeschooling on a Shoestring* by Melissa L. Morgan and Judith Waite Allee

*Homeschooling our Children, Unschooling Ourselves* by Alison McKee

*The International Montessori Index*, www.montessori.edu

*Life Learning magazine*, www.lifelearningmagazine.com

*Live Free, Learn Free magazine*, www.livefreelearnfree.com

*Living Joyfully with Children* by Win and Bill Sweet

*The Montessori Foundation*, www.montessori.org

*On-line Schools and Classes* www.geocities.com/Athens/8259/skonet.html

*Sudbury Valley School*, www.sudval.org

*Summerhill School* by A. S. Neill

*Teach Your Own* by John Holt and Patrick Farenga

*The Teenage Liberation Handbook* by Grace Llewellyn

*Unschooling.com*, www.unschooling.com

*The Unschooling Handbook* by Mary Griffith

*Waldorf Education in Canada*, www.waldorf.ca

## Why Traditional School and Homework are Harmful to Children

*The Case Against Homework: How Homework is Hurting Our Children and What We Can Do About It* by Sara Bennett and Nancy Kalish

*Closing the Book on Homework* by John Buell

*Creating Emotionally Safe Schools* by Jane Bluestein

*Dumbing Us Down: The Hidden Curriculum of Compulsory Schooling* by John Taylor Gatto

*The End of Homework: How Homework Disrupts Families, Overburdens Children, and Limits Learning* by Etta Kralovec and John Buell

*The Exhausted School* by John Taylor Gatto

*The Happy Child: Changing the Heart of Education* by Steven Harrison

*The Homework Myth: Why Our Kids Get Too Much of a Bad Thing* by Alfie Kohn

*In Their Own Way: Discovering and Encouraging Your Child's Multiple Intelligences* by Thomas Armstrong

*What Happened to Recess and Why Are Our Children Struggling in Kindergarten?* by Susan Ohanian

## Nonviolent/Non-Defensive Communication

*Nonviolent Communication, A Language of Life: Create Your Life, Your Relationships, and Your World in Harmony with Your Values* by Marshall B. Rosenberg

*Parenting from the Heart: Sharing the Gifts of Compassion, Connection, and Choice* by Inbal Kashtan

*Raising Children Compassionately: Parenting the Nonviolent Communication Way* by Marshall B. Rosenberg

*Taking the War Out of Our Words: The Art of Powerful Non-Defensive Communication* by Sharon Ellison

## <u>Positive, Nonviolent Discipline</u>

*Connection Parenting: Parenting through Connection instead of Coercion, Through Love instead of Fear* by Pam Leo

*The Disadvantages of Time-Out article* by Aletha Solter
http://www.awareparenting.com/timeout.htm

*Discipline that Works: Promoting Self-Discipline in Children* by Thomas Gordon

*Empathic Parenting, www.empathicparenting.org*

*No Disposable Kids* by Larry K. Brendtro, Arlin Ness and Martin Mitchell

*The Nonviolent Christian Parent: Raising Children with Love, Limits and Wisdom* by Dr. Teresa Whitehurst, Debbie Haskins and Al Crowell www.nospank.net

*No Such Thing as a Bad Kid: Understanding and Responding to the Challenging Behavior of Troubled Children and Youth*
by Charles D. Appelstein

*The Nurturing Parent, www.nurturingparenting.com*

*Parenting in Jesus' Footsteps, www.parentinginjesusfootsteps.org*

*Parenting without Punishing, www.nopunish.net*

*The Power of Peace, www.nospank.net*

*Raising Healthy Children:   A Mini-Guide to Good Parenting and Positive Non-Violent Discipline, www.psychealthltd.com*

*Raising Our Children, Raising Ourselves: Transforming Parent-child relationships from Reaction and Struggle to Freedom, Power and Joy* by Naomi Aldort

*Unconditional Parenting: Moving from Rewards and Punishments to Love and Reason* by Alfie Kohn

## <u>Parenting Adoptive Children, Foster Children and Children with Severe Attachment Disruption</u>

*Adopting on Your Own: The Complete Guide to Adopting as a Single Parent* by Lee Varon

*Angry Young Men* by Aaron Kipnis

*Attaching in Adoption* by Deborah Gray

*Attachment-Focused Family Therapy* by Daniel A. Hughes

*Attachment, Trauma and Healing: Understanding and Treating Attachment Disorder in Children and Families* by Terry M. Levy and Michael Orlans

*Challenging the Limits of Care* edited by Richard W. Small and Floyd J. Alwon

*The Effect of Childhood Trauma on Brain Development*

*Facilitating Developmental Attachment* By Daniel Hughes

*Healing Resources.info*
www.healingresources.info/emotional_trauma_online_video.htm

*La Leche League,* www.lalecheleague.org

*No Disposable Kids* by Larry K. Brendtro, Arlin Ness and Martin Mitchell

*No Such Thing as a Bad Kid: Understanding and Responding to the Challenging Behavior of Troubled Children and Youth* by Charles D. Appelstein

*Our Own: Adopting and Parenting the Older Child* by Trish Maskew

*The Nurturing Parent* www.nurturingparenting.com

*The Primal Wound* By Nancy Newton Verrier

*The Reclaiming Youth Network*
www.reclaiming.com

*Understanding the Effects of Maltreatment on Early Brain Development*
www.childwelfare.gov/pubs/focus/earlybrain/earlybrain.pdf

*Why Love Matters: How Affection Shapes a Baby's Brain* by Sue Gerhardt

## Attachment Treatment

*Center for Family Development,* www.center4familydevelop.com

*Bonding and Attachment in Maltreated Children: Consequences of Emotional Neglect in Childhood* by Bruce D. Perry

www.childtrauma.org/CTAMATERIALS/Attach_ca.asp

*Dyadic Developmental Psychotherapy*
http://danielahughes.homestead.com

*EEG Info: The Complete Neurofeedback Resource*
http://directory.eeginfo.com

*EEG Spectrum International, www.eegspectrum.com/IntroToNeuro/*

*The EMDR Institute,* www.emdr.org

*The EMDR International Association (EMDRIA)*, www.emdria.org

*Family Attachment Narrative Therapy*
www.familyattachment.com/pages/narrative.html

*The Nurturing Parent*, www.nurturingparenting.com

*Theraplay*, www.theraplay.org

*The White Paper on Coercion in Treatment*
*www.attach.org/WhitePaper.pdf*

## EMDR

*The EMDR Institute*, www.emdr.org

*The EMDR International Association (EMDRIA)*, www.emdria.org

## Neurofeedback

*EEG Info: The Complete Neurofeedback Resource*
http://directory.eeginfo.com

*EEG Spectrum International*
*www.eegspectrum.com/IntroToNeuro/*

*International Society for Neurofeedback and Research*
www.isnr.com

*Neurofeedback Today*
http://neurofeedbacktoday.com/media.htm

## Strength-Based Residential Programs in the USA

*Note: Most residential, "rehabilitative" and "boot camp" programs for "troubled youth" are severely punitive, confrontational, use obedience-based "level systems" and in many cases, can be abusive. Before entering your child into any program, find out how closely they follow an attachment or strength-based, non-punitive model. Parents should be the most important part of the child's treatment. I have visited programs that claim to be "strength" or "attachment"-based, but most of the programs were just as punitive and as lacking in affection as their counterparts.*

*American Association of Children's Residential Centers*
*www.aacrc-dc.org*

*Cunningham Children's Home*, www.cunninghamhome.org

*Eckerd Youth Alternatives Programs*, www.eckerdyouthalternatives.org

*Forest Heights Lodge*, www.forestheightslodge.org

*Girls and Boys Town*, www.girlsandboystown.org

*KidsPeace*, www.kidspeace.org

*Starr Commonwealth*, www.starr.org

*UMFS*, www.umfs.org

## Psychiatric Medication: Dangers and Alternatives

*Alpha-Stim*, www.alpha-stim.com

*The Biofeedback Network*, www.biofeedback.net

*The Citizens Commission on Human Rights: Investigating and Exposing Psychiatric Human Rights Abuse* www.cchr.org/index.cfm/9317

*Commonsense Rebellion: Taking Your Life Back from Drugs, Shrinks, Corporations and a World Gone Crazy* by Bruce E. Levine

*Death from Ritalin: The Truth Behind ADHD*
http://ritalindeath.com/ADHD-Drug-Deaths.htm

*The Drugging of Our Children documentary* by Gary Null
http://video.google.com/videoplay?docid=-3609599239524875493

*EEG Info: The Complete Neurofeedback Resource*
http://directory.eeginfo.com

*EEG Spectrum International*
www.eegspectrum.com/IntroToNeuro/

*FDA Public Health Advisory: Suicidality in Children and Adolescents Being Treated with Antidepressant Medications*
www.fda.gov/CDER/DRUG/antidepressants/SSRIPHA200410.htm

*International Coalition for Drug Awareness*
www.drugawareness.org

*The Myth of the ADD Child: 50 Ways to Improve Your Child's Behavior and Attention Span Without Drugs, Labels, or Coercion* by Thomas Armstrong

*Reclaiming Our Children: A Healing Plan for a Nation in Crisis*
by Peter R. Breggin, M.D.

*Ritalin Free Kids: Safe and Effective Homeopathic Medicine for ADHD and Other Behavioral and Learning Problems* by Judyth Reichenberg-Ullman ad Robert Ullman

*Talking Back to Ritalin: What Doctors Aren't Telling You about Stimulants and ADHD* by Peter R. Breggin, M.D.

*Toxic Psychiatry* by Peter R. Breggin, M.D.

*The Wildest Colts Make the Best Horses: The Truth about Ritalin, "ADHD" and other "Disruptive Behavior Disorders"*
*Wildest Colts Resources*, www.wildestcolts.com/index.htm

*Without Ritalin: A Natural Approach to ADD* by Samuel A. Berne

## ADHD and Mental Illness Diagnosis Fraud

*ADHD Fraud.org*, www.adhdfraud.org

*ADHD Fraud videos*, www.adhdvideo.org

*Alliance for Human Research Protection* www.ahrp.org/info-mail/04/12/03.php

*Death from Ritalin: The Truth Behind ADHD*
http://ritalindeath.com/ADHD-Drug-Deaths.htm

*The Myth of the ADD Child: 50 Ways to Improve Your Child's Behavior and Attention Span Without Drugs, Labels, or Coercion* by Thomas Armstrong

*The Necessity of Madness and Unproductivity: Psychiatric Oppression or Human Transformation*
www.wildestcolts.com/john/madness.html

*Talking Back to Ritalin: What Doctors Aren't' Telling You about Stimulants and ADHD* by Peter Breggin, MD

*There is No Such Thing as a Psychiatric Disorder... (paper)*
www.pubmedcentral.nih.gov/articlerender.fcgi?artid=1518691

*Toxic Psychiatry* by Peter Breggin, MD

*Wildest Colts Resource*, www.wildestcolts.com/index.htm

## Naturopathic and Homeopathic Alternatives

*Without Ritalin: A Natural Approach to ADD* by Samuel A. Berne

*Ritalin-Free Kids: Safe and Effective Homeopathic Medicine for ADHD and Other Behavioral and Learning Problems* by Judyth Reichenberg-Ullman and Robert Ullman

*The Myth of the ADD Child: 50 Ways to Improve Your Child's Behavior and Attention Span Without Drugs, Labels, or Coercion* by Thomas Armstrong

*Homeopathic Treatment of Children with ADHD Study*
www.springerlink.com/content/t512515754w83686

*The American Association of Naturopathic Physicians*
www.naturopathic.org

*Natural Herbs Guide.* www.naturalherbsguide.com

*Candida-Free* www.candidafree.net

## Body-Centered Alternatives

*Discovering the Body's Wisdom* by Mirka Knaster

*Bodywork and Movement Healing Therapies Internet Resources*
www.holisticmed.com/www/bodywork.html

*Acupuncture,* www.acupuncture.com

*CranioSacral Therapy,* www.iahe.com/html/therapies/cst.jsp

*The Home of Reflexology,* www.reflexology.org

*The International Center for Reiki Training,* www.reiki.org

*International Taoist Tai Chi Society,* www.taoist.org

*Massage Therapy,* www.massagetherapy.com

*The Qigong Institute,* www.qigonginstitute.org

*The Rolf Institute,* www.rolf.org

*World Center for EFT, www.emofree.com*

*Yoga Movement,* www.yogamovement.com/links/index.html

## Tribal Cultures and Mammal Parenting

*America's Lost Dream: 'Life Liberty and the Pursuit of Happiness':
Current research and Historical Background on the Origins of Love
and Violence* by James W. Prescott
www.ttfuture.org/pdf/members/Prescott_ALD.PDF

*Bonobo: Forgotten Ape* by Frans B. M. de Waal

*The Continuum Concept* by Jean Liedloff

*Cultural Survival Quarterly,* www.cs.org

*Organic Parenting,* www.primalspirit.com/ps3_1lyn-piluso.htm

*Saharasia: The 4000 BCE Origins of Child Abuse, Sex-Repression,
Warfare and Social Violence in the Deserts of the Old World*
by James DeMeo

## Natural, Organic Living

*Gentle Spirit magazine,* www.gentlespirit.com

*Informed Voice magazine,* www.avn.org.au

*Kindred magazine,* www.kindredmagazine.com.au

*Natural Life magazine,* www.life.ca

*Organic Family Magazine,* www.organicfamilymagazine.com

*Primal Parent magazine,* www.primalparentingmagazine.com

## Information about Child Abuse and Trauma and Effects on Children

*Abused Boys: The Neglected Victims of Sexual Abuse* by Mic Hunter

*The Body Never Lies: The Lingering Affects of Cruel Parenting* by Alice Miller

*The Effect of Childhood Trauma on Brain Development* www.leadershipcouncil.org/1/res/brain.html

*For Your Own Good: The Hidden Cruelty in Child-rearing and the Roots of Violence* by Alice Miller

*From Victim to Offender* by Freda Briggs

*Female Sexual Abuse of Children* by Michele Elliot

*The Origins of Peace and Violence,* www.violence.de

*Rewiring the Brain: Early Deprivation and Child Development* by Sasha Aslanian

*Saharasia: The 4000 BCE Origins of Child Abuse, Sex-Repression, Warfare and Social Violence in the Deserts of the Old World* by James DeMeo

*Spare the Child: The Religious Roots of Punishment and the Psychological Impact of Physical Abuse* by Philip Greven

*Understanding the Effects of Maltreatment on Early Brain Development* www.childwelfare.gov/pubs/focus/earlybrain/earlybrain.pdf

*Why Love Matters: How Affection Shapes a Baby's Brain* by Sue Gerhardt

## Abolishing Physical Punishment of Children

*Beating the Devil Out of Them* by Murray Straus

*The Case Against Spanking* by Irwin A. Hyman

*Children Are Unbeatable! Alliance*, www.childrenareunbeatable.org.uk

*Eliminating Corporal Punishment: The Way Forward to Constructive Child Discipline* edited by Stuart N. Hart, with Joan Durrant, Peter Newell and F. Clark Power

*EPOCH-USA End Physical Punishment of Children* www.stophitting.com

*Global Initiative to End All Corporal Punishment of Children* www.endcorporalpunishment.org

*The Hitting Stops Here!*, www.thehittingstopshere.com

*NeverHitAChild.org*, www.neverhitachild.org

*People Opposed to Paddling Students*, www.nospankingzone.org

*Plain Talk about Spanking* by Jordan Riak

*Project NoSpank*, www.nospank.net

*Spare The Child: The Religious Roots of Punishment and the Psychological Impact of Abuse* by Philip Greven

*Stop the Rod*, www.stoptherod.net

*Why Spanking Doesn't Work: Stopping this Bad Habit and Getting the Upper Hand on Effective Discipline* by Michael J. Marshall

## The Detriments of TV, Media and Fast Food

*Commonsense Rebellion: Taking Your Life Back from Drugs, Shrinks, Corporations and a World Gone Crazy* by Bruce E. Levin

*Fast Food Nation: The Dark Side of the All-American Meal* by Eric Schlosser

*Generation MySpace: Helping Your Teen Survive Online Adolescence* by Candice M. Kelsey

*The Plug-In Drug: Television, Computers and Family Life* by Marie Winn

## Information About Today's Toxic Peer Culture

*And Words Can Hurt Forever: How to Protect Adolescents from Bullying, Harassment, and Emotional Violence* by James Garbarino and Ellen deLara

*The Breakfast Club (1985- Rated R)*

*Generation MySpace: Helping Your Teen Survive Online Adolescence* by Candice M. Kelsey

*Odd Girl Out: The Hidden Culture of Aggression in Girls* by Rachel Simmons

## How Society Fails Youth and How to Heal it

*Angry Young Men* by Aaron Kipnis

*Children First: What Society Must Do—and is Not Doing—for Children Today* by Penelope Leach

*The Coalition Against Institutionalized Child Abuse* http://www.caica.org/index.htm

*The Men They Will Become: The Nature and Nurture of Male Character* by Eli Newberger

*No Disposable Kids* by Larry K. Brendtro, Arlin Ness and Martin Mitchell

*Reclaiming Our Children: A Healing Plan for a Nation in Crisis* by Peter R. Breggin, M.D.

*The Reclaiming Youth Network,* www.reclaiming.com

*The Scapegoat Generation: America's War on Adolescents* by Mike A. Males

*Violence: Reflections on a National Epidemic* by James Gilligan

*Why Love Matters: How Affection Shapes a Baby's Brain* by Sue Gerhardt

## Help for Parents who had Traumatic Childhoods

*The Body Never Lies: The Lingering Effects of Cruel Parenting* by Alice Miller

*Connection Parenting: Parenting through Connection instead of Coercion, Through Love instead of Fear* by Pam Leo

*Dialectical Behavioral Therapy (DBT) Self Help,* www.dbtselfhelp.com

*The EMDR Institute,* www.emdr.org

*The EMDR International Association (EMDRIA),* www.emdria.org

*Emotional Intelligence: Why it Can Matter More than IQ* by Daniel Goleman

*Neurofeedback*
www.eegspectrum.com/IntroToNeuro/

*HelpGuide.org Emotional Intelligence in Communication*
ww.helpguide.org/mental/improve_relationships.htm

*The Practice of Relaxation*
www.psychealthltd.com

*Radical Parenting: Seven Steps to a Functional Family in a Dysfunctional World* by Brad Blanton

*Raising Our Children, Raising Ourselves: Transforming Parent-child relationships from Reaction and Struggle to Freedom, Power and Joy* by Naomi Aldort

*What the Bleep Do We Know!?*
www.whatthebleep.com

*Why Love Matters: How Affection Shapes a Baby's Brain* by Sue Gerhardt

## Autobiographies and Biographies of Survivors of Severe Child Abuse

*A Child Called "It"* by Dave Pelzer

*The Lost Boy* by Dave Pelzer

*A Man Named Dave* by Dave Pelzer

*Death From Child Abuse... And No One Heard* by Eve Krupinski and Dana Weikel

*The God Squad* by Paddy Doyle

*The Magic Castle* by Carole Smith

*Orphan: A True Story of Abandonment, Abuse, and Redemption* by Roger Dean Kiser, Sr.

*Sleepers* by Lorenzo Carcaterra

*Sybil* by Flora Rheta Schreiber

*They Cage the Animals at Night* by Jennings Michael Burch

*Wayne: An Abused Child's Story of Courage, Survival, and Hope* by Wayne Theodore

# Appendix A
# A Child's Perspective on Corporal Punishment

Following is a speech that my son presented at the age of 12 at The Child and Nonviolence Summit at the Hartgrove Hospital in Chicago, Illinois, on April 7, 2006. If anyone at the conference believed that any form of physical punishment was acceptable prior to his speech, it was his hope and mine that the audience members would have no conscientious way of justifying physical punishment after they heard his own heart-felt words. It is vital that we listen to the words of children, what they are telling us that they need and to how our punitive, aggressive practices feel to them. After all, as adults, we must ask ourselves, would we wish to be treated the way we treat our children?

*Note: I have left my son's original grammar intact as he edited this speech before the conference to his satisfaction.*

### A Child's Perspective on Corporal Punishment
by Brycen Robert Rylan Couture
A speech presented at The Child and Nonviolence Summit, Chicago, IL
April 7, 2006

Hello my name is Brycen Robert Rylan Couture. I am 12 years old and I am homeschooled. I am going to tell you a child's perspective of corporal punishment. When I talk about corporal punishment, I'm talking about child abuse because that's exactly what it is. If a husband hits a wife or a wife hits a husband, it's illegal, but if a mother or father hits a child, it's legal. Why is there a difference when two spouses hit each other than when a parent is violent towards a child? What is the difference?

Some adults like to use the word "spanking" so the child gets the impression that what the adult is doing is right. But if the adult uses the word "hit", the child knows it's wrong. I believe that we need to start calling "spanking" what it really is: Spanking is hitting!

Now I am going to tell you a child's perspective. My Mom is Laurie Couture. She is my special adoptive Mom. I was in several foster families. When I was in my biological family I got hit all the time. I also saw my brothers get hit and I hated it. Sometimes at night my step father would come in to "spank" us and we'd all dart under the bed. The only emotion I felt was fear... sheer and utter fear! And sometimes when one of my brothers would do something "wrong" my birthmother and step father would tell me to hit him. I even got hit in one of my foster homes, a place that was supposed to be protecting me from abuse!

When a child is getting hit, he feels like he is hated and no one loves him. He really feels like no one loves him. Over time, children start putting up bricks around their heart. They start shutting everyone out and they learn to dissociate. When they get older they may become a cold and callous person who can't love. Hitting really does not help their behavior. When people really do tell them wrong from right, they ignore it all. Prisoners may have emotional problems from being hit. Not everyone turns out like that because they may have one person that really loves them.

When children get hit, the first feeling is fear, "I'm going to get pain". It is fear because it means violence. A kid's definition of it is pain. They get that fear that clutches their heart like an iron grip. And that iron grip stays and it hardens over their heart and it just shuts them down. They feel angry, rage. They feel like they just want to get revenge and inflict pain on the one that inflicted pain on them. They feel sadness. The one who gave them the pain is the one who is supposed to protect them from pain. They feel distrust, they can't trust anyone. Their natural feeling when they are with someone who cares is to trust, but when that very person that is supposed to protect them from pain, hurt and sadness *hits* them, the trust just disappears. They destroy all that trust. Unless someone shows they care who doesn't hurt them, who uses strong but caring words, unless children have that type of person, they are going to stay that way.

Corporal punishment isn't only about hitting. When a teacher or adult won't let a child go to the bathroom when their body is telling them it is time to go, a child feels anger because they feel, "I NEED TO GO!" and the teacher won't let you! You feel like you want to punch them because the adult is ignoring your body's needs. The pain causes you to not be able to concentrate on what they are asking you to do. You feel pain and anger. Then you get scared when you have to go to the bathroom because you'll get in trouble, so then you don't ask and you start trying to rush through your work. That whole cycle of fear, sadness and rage starts all over again. When you start holding it, it desensitizes you to that feeling and you ignore your body's feelings.

Now I'm going to talk about what children need. They need someone who can show them love and care without hurting them. Show them firmness in a gentle but strong way. That's how they'll feel loved and how they'll learn to be a good parent. You have to show the care by giving discipline with strong, firm gentle words. You have to show you can master all your anger by taking deep breaths, changing your negative thoughts and saying sorry to your child. They'll learn to trust. If children feel they are loved by you then they won't do wrong in the first place because they will want to be cooperative and not be oppositional. If there's a little problem, you calmly tell them the right way.

Parents need to set the example and be a role model, as some people call it. Show that mistakes are ok but acting out your feelings in a hurtful way is wrong. If they see you take deep breaths, changing your negative thoughts and doing grounding exercises, they'll copy you.

First of all, STOP the angry yelling at children! I just feel like I want to run to the child's defense and yell at the one who's yelling at the child and stop it! If you've been hitting or hurting them, let them know you are sorry. If they are aggressive to you back, don't try to use karate moves. Calmly walk away. Keep up the cycle of being caring and loving and process with them. Eventually they'll start saying how upset and angry they are at you and open up and tell you their feelings. You have to show you are sorry and that you really are wanting a second chance to show love and care and you're really sorry for the pain you inflicted on them.

After apologizing is done then you need to create a feeling of safety so they know they can trust you near them, so they won't just shut down on you and close you out of their heart. Be gentle, loving and ready to show it. You need to be playful. Play is part of growing up! Also, stop punishment and use more consequences. When I'm oppositional my Mom gives me a consequence suitable to what I have done. And that teaches me. Then we process it, why I did it, what I could do next time and how to cope with the feeling that started it all. Because it's almost always a feeling that started it! Then we can have a good day! This way teaches that parents need to be the parent, that everyone loves everyone and parents and children are respected and loved.

Kids really do need their hugs and praise every day. They need that special touch from the person they are loved by. Any age kids are needing of hugs and cuddling. Me and my Mom cuddle every day. When children know they are loved they want to please their parents and be cooperative. That makes a difference!

The reason I think corporal punishment should be banned is because it is wrong and it's not equal. It pushes kids away. Adults can't hit adults, so why is it ok for adults to hit kids? It's not equal rights! When an adult hits a child, why can't a child hit the adult back, because the child is copying what the adult just taught them is right! It makes the child feel if adults are allowed to hit, "so can I". It creates a cycle. Corporal punishment is disrespectful. When an adult hits a child, is the adult treating the child how the adult wants to be treated?

So, if you stop hurting children, then they won't close their heart. They will be more accepting and trusting and they will give that love to another person. They will be more loving so the next generation and then the next and the next will do the same thing. Then there will be peace. If you start with the children a whole chain link starts of love, care, give and take. They won't have all that anger stocked up in them and no one will be angry enough to start wars.

So you see, to save the world, you need to save the children!

# Appendix B
# Facts about corporal punishment and national and international law

## Corporal punishment by USA parents

*Fact:* It is *legal* in all 50 states for a parent to spank, smack, hit, belt, paddle and whip or otherwise inflict punitive pain on a child, as long as the corporal punishment does not meet the individual state's definition of "child abuse".

*Fact:* It is illegal in all 50 states for an adult to strike or to otherwise inflict any type of punitive pain upon another adult citizen, including spouses, domestic partners, employees, teachers, senior citizens, patients in psychiatric facilities, soldiers and prisoners. The same does not apply to persons under the age of 18.

*Fact:* The United States and Somalia are the only two countries in the United Nations who refuse to ratify The United Nations Convention on the Rights of the Child.

*Fact:* Minnesota is the only state in which parents tried for child abuse cannot defend their abusive actions by claiming they were exercising their right to corporally punish their child.

*Fact:* The states of Nevada and Oklahoma recently renewed their laws allowing parents the right to strike their children.

*Fact:* Boys are the victims of the majority of parental corporal punishment; their punishments are more severe, more frequent and more aggressive than punishments administered to girls.

*Fact:* Both mothers and fathers are more likely to hit their sons than their daughters, with mothers doing the majority of the hitting of both sons and daughters. Fathers are least likely to hit daughters.

*Fact:* African American children suffer more corporal punishment at home than European American children.

*Fact:* The first publicly documented victim of child abuse required protection under the Society for the Prevention of Cruelty to Animals in 1871, as there was no such protection agency for children until 1874!

## **Corporal punishment in USA schools**

*Fact:* It is legal in 21 states for public schools to paddle or use other forms of corporal punishment on a child.

*Fact:* The following 29 states have formally *banned* corporal punishment in public schools. They are recognized as:

- Alaska
- California
- Connecticut
- Delaware
- Hawaii
- Illinois
- Iowa
- Maine
- Maryland
- Massachusetts
- Michigan
- Minnesota
- Montana
- Nebraska
- Nevada
- New Hampshire
- New Jersey
- New York
- North Dakota
- Oregon
- Pennsylvania
- Rhode Island
- South Dakota
- Utah
- Vermont
- Virginia
- Washington
- West Virginia
- Wisconsin

In all other states it is legal for children to be physically punished by school teachers or school administrators, and in some states, residential facility workers, foster parents, day care providers and youth detention workers, as permitted by state law or individual school districts. Please note: Some of the above states may not have banned corporal punishment in private religious or youth "treatment" schools.

*Fact:* Seven states stand out as being the most violent towards school children, all of which overwhelmingly administer the most school corporal punishment in the United States:

- Texas
- Florida
- Mississippi
- Indiana
- Arkansas
- Louisiana
- South Carolina

*Fact:* Boys of all races are the victims of the majority of school corporal punishment; their punishments are more severe, more frequent and more aggressive than punishments administered to girls. African-American boys receive the most corporal punishment in schools.

For specific USA statutes and the most up-to-date info on school CP law, visit The Global Initiative to End All Corporal Punishment of Children at: www.endcorporalpunishment.org  or The Center for Effective Discipline at www.stophitting.com.

## Corporal Punishment by parents: International laws

*Fact:* Sweden was the first country to fully protect children against assaults by adults. In 1979, Sweden formally banned parents from using any form of corporal punishment on their children.

*Fact:* It is *illegal* in the following 24 countries for a parent, teacher or caretaker to use any form of corporal punishment on a child:

- Sweden (1979)
- Finland (1983)

- Denmark (1985)
- Norway (1986)
- Austria (1989)
- Cyprus (1994)
- Croatia (1996)
- Italy (1996)
- Latvia (1998)
- Germany (2000)
- Israel (2000)
- Bulgaria (2000)
- Iceland (2003)
- Romania (2004)
- Ukraine (2004)
- Hungary (2004)
- Greece (2006)
- The Netherlands (2007)
- New Zealand (2007)
- Portugal (2007)
- Uruguay (2007)
- Venezuela (2007)
- Spain (2007)
- Chile (2007)

For specific statutes and the most up-to-date info on CP International law, visit: The Global Initiative to End All Corporal Punishment of Children at: www.endcorporalpunishment.org or The Center for Effective Discipline at www.stophitting.com/laws/legalReform.php.

# Appendix C
# The School Student's Bill of Rights

Here is an example of a student bill of rights that would be in line with the principles of the United States Constitution, as well as with developmentally appropriate practice and respect of children's humanity and dignity.

## The School Student's Bill of Rights
© 2004-2008 Laurie A. Couture

*Article 1:* All young people have a right to a democratic education, as the United States of America is a democracy. This includes the right to individual thought, idea and free speech, even as it differs from the educator's, and the right to all the responsibilities associated with free speech. This also includes the right to question their educator's ideas and statements without punishment; the right to develop an individualized curriculum; the right to question and dispute the validity of the teacher's/school's curriculum as it applies to the individual, and the right to develop an alternative independent study if the current curriculum fails to stimulate interest.

*Article 2:* All young people have an inherent right to safety of their person and to have their physiological needs met and respected. This includes the right to be free of physical punishment; the right to eat if hungry; the right to have water at all times; the right to eliminate bodily waste whenever the need arises, without restriction and the right to rest and exercise. These physiological necessities cannot be withheld as a form of punishment or containment, nor presented as "privileges" that must be earned.

*Article 3:* All young people have the right to freedom of movement and physical activity. This includes the right to move freely around the classroom and building without confinement unless there is a specific emergency at hand; the right to shift to a more comfortable seating arrangement, such as on the floor and the right to periods of unstructured outdoor and physical activity at least three times during the school day. The need for outdoor and physical activity cannot be withheld as a form of punishment, nor presented as "privileges" that must be earned.

*Article 4:* All young people have the right to have their individual learning styles and learning needs met according to their strengths. This includes the right to receive information and demonstrate understanding of the information through the sensory channels most appropriate to the needs of the individual, including movement ("hands-on"). This includes the right to receive information and demonstrate understanding of the information through the intelligence channels most appropriate to the needs of the individual, including artistic, visual, kinesthetic, verbal, musical, logical, introspectively and intraspectively (group work) and the right to proceed at each learning task at a pace suitable to the needs and abilities of the individual.

*Article 5:* All young people have the right to be respected as individuals. This includes the right to wear the clothing and hair style that the individual chooses, as long as the dress style is legal, respectful of others and appropriate to wear in public. This also includes the right to be valued as one is and not according to how well one conforms to the rules, needs and desires of a teacher.

*Article 6:* All young people have the right to emotional and social respect. This includes the right for the individual's behavior to be understood and viewed in the context of the individual's life circumstances and needs; the right for firm and vigorous protection by the school system from peer harassment and from teacher ridicule, discrimination and disrespect; the right to real human relationships with teachers based on nurturance, respect and caring and the right to have one's developmental social needs met during the school day (the need to socialize).

*Article 7:* All young people have the right to real world experience in every aspect of their curriculum. This includes the right to spend the school day pursuing self-directed learning, education and resources outside of the school; the right to spend the school day in apprenticeships in fields of individual's interest, and the right to have school life follow a community model rather than a prison model.

*Article 8:* All young people have the right to free time and solitude. This includes the right to large amounts of free time and space for solitude and socialization through out the school day; the right to own one's time outside of school and to be free from intrusions such as homework, projects and study, unless the individual chooses this as part of the individual's curriculum.

*Article 9:* All young people have the right to sanctity of the home. This includes the right to be free from school intrusions in the home such as homework, projects and studying unless the individual child chooses this as part of the individual's curriculum. In the case of children whose parents are punitive or harsh, this includes the right for children's behavioral issues to be addressed at school and to remain the private business of the child unless the individual chooses to share these with their parents (or unless a serious medical, emotional or legal issue, or child abuse, is suspected). This also includes the right of the child to full advocacy by their parents untainted by negative reports and evaluations by the teacher.

*Article 10:* All young people have the right to opt out of any educational experience that does not meet the individual's needs and personal goals in order to pursue a an educational experience that meets their needs and goals.

*Article 11:* All young people have the right to have their work evaluated in a constructive and individualized manner free from tests and grading. This includes the right to a comprehensive evaluation, taking into account all areas of a child's being, needs, experience, learning styles, sensory channels, talents, efforts, strengths, challenges and individual goals; this includes the right of the child to participate in self evaluation as part of the overall evaluation; this includes the right of the child to include in the self-evaluation an evaluation of how well the teacher supported the individual's learning goals, strengths and needs, and the right of the child to dispute and appeal the teacher's evaluation.

*Article 12:* All young people have the right to privately evaluate the competency, effectiveness and behavior of the teacher and the right to influence the firing of any teacher who consistently fails to treat children with respect and dignity. Children should also have a say in hiring new teachers and keeping caring, maverick teachers.

# Appendix D
# Forced Retention of Bodily Waste

This Appendix will discuss:

- The medical risks to children when school teachers and other caretakers deny children their basic need and right to eliminate bodily waste;

- Medical advice for preventing urinary and digestive problems;

- What parents can do if their child's teacher delays or denies their child the right to use the toilet at school;

- Teacher arguments along with commonsense rebuttals; and

- The case of a high school senior and his mother who advocated for the youth's right to use the toilet in class without punishment.

Please note, this is a partial list of information. For more comprehensive information on forced retention of bodily waste, please visit www.childadvocate.org.

## Forced retention of urine

### Medical advice for prevention of urinary health problems

"It is important that... children (who infrequently void) go to the bathroom frequently. Trying to 'hold on' can damage the bladder and kidneys and teach the child improper voiding." (Christopher S. Cooper, M.D., 2000, Pediatric Urologist)

"Ensure your child voids frequently... Nature's own cleansing mechanism works well if it works often. Every two hours is suggested... The child should be encouraged to drink at least eight glasses of fluid per day..." (Children's Hospital Medical Center of Akron, 2002)

"Urinate when you feel the need; don't resist the urge to urinate." (National Kidney and Urologic Diseases Information Clearinghouse, 2000)

"Voiding less than four times a day or having more than four hours between voids... is abnormal [for children and adolescents]." (Wan and Greenfield, 1997, Pediatric Bulletin)

"Its very possible the child is not going to the bathroom often enough during the day. Parents should try to find out about their child's bathroom habits during the school day." (William Strand, M.D., Parenthood.com)

## Health risks associated with infrequent, delayed or rushed urination:

- Overflow urinary incontinence
- Urinary tract infection
- Overextension of the bladder muscle
- Weakening of the brain-bladder signals
- Incomplete voiding (frequency)
- Bladder contracting against closed sphincter (uncoordinated voiding)
- Urinary reflux
- Renal (kidney) failure

## How does delaying urination put a young person at risk?

"Some children do not void frequently enough and their bladders hold a larger than normal amount of urine. Normally, as our bladder fills it sends signals to the brain and we become aware that we will soon need to go to the bathroom. By ignoring these signals over a long period of time some bladders become stretched out and floppy. Children with bladders like this may not notice that they need to go to the bathroom until the bladder is so stretched that it just can't hold any more urine." (Christopher S. Cooper, M.D., 2000, Pediatric Urologist)

"Retaining urine sets the stage for urinary tract infections." (National Kidney and Urologic Diseases Information Clearinghouse, 2000)

"Since the bladder may become overstretched in people who do not empty it very often, your child may say that he/she does not have to go as often as necessary." (The Detroit Medical Center Department of Urology, n.d.)

"...Some... children try and delay urination by learning to contract down their sphincter muscles when the bladder feels full or contracts. Unfortunately, this can generate high pressures in the bladder which can damage the bladder or kidneys..." (Christopher S. Cooper, M.D., 2000, Pediatric Urologist)

"Poor toilet habits such as infrequent voiding... are found in 90% of children who have had a UTI but whose imaging studies are negative for anatomic abnormalities.... When taken to extremes, this dysfunctional behavior (infrequent voiding) can lead to both upper and lower tract damage... Large surges in bladder pressure can result and lead to dilation of the ureters and kidneys and reflux of urine." (Wan and Greenfield, 1997, Pediatric Bulletin)

## Forced retention of bowel waste

### Medical advice for prevention of bowel health problems

"Drink one and 1/2 to 2 quarts of water... every day. Drink extra fluids in the morning... urges usually occur sometime after meals. Establish a daily routine... Go when you feel the urge. Your bowels send signals when a stool needs to pass. If you ignore the signal, the urge will go away and the stool will eventually become dry and difficult to pass." (Healthwise Handbook, 1999)

"Drink at least six to eight glasses of water or other liquids every day... Do not resist the urge to move your bowels... To reduce your risks of fecal impaction... heed the first urge to defecate." (Mayo Clinic Family Health Book, second edition, David E. Larson, MD, Editor-in-Chief, 1996)

"Make a conscious effort to go to the toilet promptly whenever you feel the need." (The American Medical Association: Guide to Your Family's Symptoms, Clayman and Curry, Medical Editors, 1992)

"Ideally, constipation should be prevented by attention to the diets of young children, by providing advice to parents on pot training, and by revolutionizing the design of school lavatories and the rules about their use... *a more child-oriented provision of lavatory facilities in schools and public buildings...*" (Pediatric Gastrointestinal Disease, Vol. One Second Edition, Chapter 20, Murphy and Clayden, 1996) [Italics added]

"It goes without saying that the best treatment for encopresis is to avoid stool withholding..." (Joseph Levy, MD, 2004 My Tummy Hurts)

## Health risks associated with fecal retention

- Constipation
- Stool impaction
- Encopresis (bowel incontinence)
- Weakening of the brain-bowel signals
- Bowel obstruction

## How does delaying elimination put a young person at risk?

"Constipation is a very common problem: probably one of every four patients seen by a gastroenterologist is there for stooling difficulties... When a child is constipated, stool builds up and overfills the large intestine. The consequent overstretching causes a diffuse pain below the bellybutton... Prevention is one of the best treatments for constipation... An effective routine to avoid constipation involves attention to the following areas: Sufficient fluid intake, sufficient fiber intake, regular exercise (and) anticipatory guidance to prevent stool withholding." (Joseph Levy, MD, 2004 My Tummy Hurts)

"Encopresis is usually caused by chronic constipation. When stool is withheld, the rectum is progressively overstretched until the child loses the ability to sense the presence of stool. When the message is consistently disregarded, the brain eventually grows to accept the distension as the normal state, and ignores the signals." (Joseph Levy, MD, 2004 My Tummy Hurts)

## What to do if your child's teacher restricts or denies toilet use

I receive many letters every week through ChildAdvocate.org from parents requesting assistance with how to protect their children from a teacher or school that restricts or denies their children the right to use the toilet at school.

Here is the protocol for protecting your children if:

- Your child's teacher or school has a restrictive or regimented toilet use policy,
- Your child's teacher has denied your child use of the toilet,

- Your child has been punished in any way for using or needing to use the toilet,
- Your child has received a reward for NOT using the toilet, and
- Your child's school locks student bathrooms.

If you are not willing to remove your child from the school, here is the protocol that I recommend for advocating for your child:

- Take the issue seriously. Listen to your child. Get all the facts. Tell your child that he has a right to use the toilet whenever needed and that you will protect that right and seek justice for him. Tell your child to get up and walk out of class if a teacher denies him use of the toilet again.

- Contact your child's teacher. Explain to the teacher that toilet use is a right, not a privilege. State that your child is to be allowed to use the toilet whenever she has the need. Furnish information from the Medical Risks pages on ChildAdvocate.org about the medical and health risks of retaining bodily waste.

- If your child's teacher complains that your child has been misusing the bathroom pass, develop a plan for your child to use the toilet in the nurses' office for a few weeks. Never settle for your child's toilet use to be restricted!

- Follow up with a written letter. Do not use the words "bathroom privileges" when you discuss the problem- That is the language of schools. Toilet use is a RIGHT, not a privilege!

- E-mail your child's story to ChildAdvocate.org. PLEASE include your STATE, your country if out of USA, and your children's grade or age.

- If the teacher refuses to honor your request, contact the school principal and repeat the above protocol.

- Involve your child's school guidance counselor and nurse.

- Explain to the principal that you will not allow your child to serve any punishment in connection with using or needing to use the toilet.

- If the school principal refuses to honor your request, explain that you will contact the superintendent, school board, child protective services, the local media and if necessary, an attorney.

- Follow up with a written letter.

- Contact your child's pediatrician and request that she write a note to your child's school that your child is to be allowed to use the toilet anytime he has the need.

- If the school principal still refuses to honor your request, contact the superintendent's office and the school board and explain your child's situation and the school's refusal to honor your request.

- Report the teacher/school to your local state child protective services for neglect of basic biological needs and/or abuse if your child was denied toilet use as a form of punishment. You can get the phone number from the information operator. Often child protective services is not helpful in toilet use denial cases, however, it is important to document the incident. After several complaints, the state is often required to investigate. If the school is locking bathrooms, ask to file a report of institutional abuse and neglect.

- Rally support from other parents. Post a webpage, start a petition and...

- Take the matter to your local media. Contact your local newspaper, write a letter to the editor and call your local TV station. If they seem reluctant at first to take your story seriously, continue to call, encourage other parents to call and use the information on this site to build a case.

- Contact major news media (CNN, etc) for very serious situations. Insist that they not use degrading or childish words, puns or jokes (i.e.: "potty passes") when delivering the story.

- Contact an attorney until you find one that will advise you on your child's situation. Or, contact a legal referral service and ask for the name of a children's rights attorney in your state.

- In order to protect your child, consider removing your child from the classroom or from the school and place your child in a child-centered school. Better yet, cut the chains of the school from your family and homeschool your child!

- Consider contacting your state's Civil Liberties Union and report your child's situation. You can search for your state at www.aclu.org. Please note that the Civil Liberties Union only deals with constitutional violations, so you may need to appeal and try to make a case. If enough parents and children contact them, they may realize the scope of the problem.

## Teacher arguments about toilet use restrictions & research-based answers

I received the following letter from a public middle school teacher in Washington D.C. It is typical of the types of responses I hear from school teachers who believe that toilet use should be regimented or denied. Below is her letter in its entirety. My answer follows her letter:

February 10, 2004 (Washington D.C., USA)

"Face it, even a four year old can sleep through the night (8 hours) without going to the bathroom. In my school, and every school I have ever heard of, students have free and unlimited use of bathrooms during lunch and recess. The teachers certainly don't get to go to the bathroom any other time. My argument is not so much that students shouldn't be able to use the bathroom, but that the problem just isn't this serious. Going to the bathroom whenever you want all school day? Ridiculous. It would be abused. As a secondary argument, who supervises the children en route to and in the bathroom? Were you aware that the teacher is legally responsible for the student even when the student is out of his site? For instance, a child gets hurt or attacked in the bathroom = teacher's fault. They WILL be sued and they will lose! That is why many teachers are hesitant to let students go by themselves."

Response by Laurie A. Couture, February 10, 2004

Dear _____,

You raised several issues in your e-mail and I will attempt to address them all:

1. You stated that based on the fact that some four year olds "can sleep through the night without going to the bathroom", that school children, during waking hours, should be expected to retain waste for presumably as long. Some basic research on how the human body functions during nocturnal sleep vs. during the waking day would indicate that during the state of sleep, the body is not taking in any fluids or food, nor is it subjected to the numerous other physiological

influences that it encounters during waking hours that effect urine and stool production.

Additionally, during sleep, the body produces an increase in levels of the hormone vasopressin ADH, which suppresses and slows nighttime urine production. This allows some people to sleep through the night without the need to urinate. However, many children and adults alike wake once or twice during the night to use the toilet.

2. You state that "in my school, and every school I have ever heard of, students have free and unlimited use of bathrooms during lunch and recess." I am glad to hear that in your school, and those you have heard of, the human rights of children are respected during recess and lunch times. However, in many schools, including some I work in, this is absolutely NOT the case. Additionally, because every human body is different, to expect that every individual child in a class or school can synchronize his or her unique urinary and digestive systems to the time schedule of the school is contrary to facts about the human body.

3. You state that "the teachers certainly don't get to go to the bathroom any other time", indicating to me that you are implying that the needs and bodies of young people should conform to adult-level needs and expectations. Your statement also indicates that you feel that if teachers are restricted in toilet breaks, children should also suffer this indignity. In fact, teachers do have a legal right, mandated by OSHA laws, that they are to be allowed to use the toilet when ever needed. Teachers have the legal backing if they wish to pursue this matter. Children's needs, however, are at the mercy of the whims of teachers. Teachers also freely choose their professions, understanding full well the restrictions that will be placed upon them by their profession. Children do not have a choice about going to school- They are held hostages.

4. You state that "the problem (of toilet use denial) just isn't this serious." Unfortunately, the problem is very serious, it is pervasive and it results in real suffering, emotionally and physically as well as real medical problems (urinary tract infection, constipation, fecal impaction, urinary reflux, weakening of the brain-bladder/bowel signal, etc). In fact, in extreme cases, young people have been forced to urinate in their pants or in garbage cans because they were adamantly refused to be allowed to relieve themselves despite pleading several times. Some kids who have left the classroom in distress have been suspended.

I strongly encourage you to visit ChildAdvocate.org and view the letters sent in by parents whose children are suffering this type of abuse in the classroom so that you may see that in fact, this issue is a real problem that causes real distress for children. I also invite you to view the page of letters by people who have suffered this abuse. In fact, a large percentage of all pediatric urinary dysfunction is caused by unhealthy voiding patterns taught in schools. I invite you to research this for yourself on my page of medical risks of retaining urine, including urinary tract infection, over stretching of the bladder muscle, and other voiding dysfunction.

5. Your next comment troubles me, and shows a lack of empathy to the physiological needs and the distress of children: "Going to the bathroom whenever you want all school day? Ridiculous. It would be abused." What is ridiculous and inhumane is that school schedules are set up contrary to the physiological needs of children, with hundreds or thousands of individual human beings expected to conform their largely involuntary internal systems (and internal homeostasis) to a mechanical routine, rather than the school being structured around and dictated by the physiological needs of children.

Many teachers who are successful at functioning with an open bathroom-use policy state that children do not "abuse" the right when their rights are respected. If individuals do "abuse" the right, it could mean that the child needs a break, the classroom material isn't stimulating or there is some other issue that should be addressed individually. If children appear to be "abusing" the right, they can be asked to use the toilet in the nurse's office (with a pass signed by the nurse) for one week. The solutions are simple if one desires to put the needs of children before the teacher's need for dominance and control. Unfortunately what is truly being "abused" in schools is the human rights of children in the name of control and routine.

6. Lastly, you stated that teachers are legally responsible for children in their classroom, even if they leave the room. You stated a fear of legal action if a child was assaulted or hurt in the bathroom. If this is a real problem that prevents children from using the toilet when the need arises, then schools need to be redesigned to either have a toilet in each class, or to employ hall monitors to keep the halls and bathrooms safe.

I agree that teachers, as ex facto parents during the school day, have a legal responsibility to keep the children in their care safe. By denying children the right to respond to their body's individual needs to urinate and defecate, teachers are putting their students at harm. Teachers who deny a child the right to use the toilet are not providing a safe environment- They are controlling a child's body and inflicting pain upon that child (which is illegal in most states). Teachers open themselves to legal action when neglecting a child in this manner.

...It is my hope that, rather than trying to force your children's bodies to conform to your routines, whims, biases, frustrations and arguments, that you instead advocate for the rights and very real health needs of your students and find creative ways to let children assume control over their own needs. Deal with individual problems that arise, without punishing every child preemptively for what a few limit-testers may do.

The other issue I wanted to raise relates to the work of Abraham Maslow, whose research states that when the basic human needs of the body are denied, higher level functions, such as learning, cannot take place. How can a child concentrate and learn when he or she is forced (or intimidated) to sit with uncomfortable bladder and bowels? The only learning taking place at such a time is learning how to ignore internal signals to the detriment of the body. I work in five different schools, and have visited over 50 others, in addition to dialoging with thousands of children and hundreds of teachers and parents. I have researched this issue extensively in hopes of bringing more sensitivity to the issue by teachers and school administrators. I hope this response answered all of your questions.

-Laurie A. Couture


## A mother and son advocate and change inhumane school toilet-use policies.

The mother and son in the following letter both granted permission for their names and locations to be used:


May 19, 2007 (North Carolina, USA)

"Dear Laurie,

We are making a dent here in Union County with the issue of bathroom use. I am very proud of the part that my son Mike played in effecting change. Please share this story if you can.

Three weeks ago, my 18 year old son, Mike was one hour into his first period class and had to urinate. He raised his hand and asked to be excused. The teacher informed him that he did not have any "potty passes" left, and could not go. Mike wisely negotiated with this teacher, and told her that he did not wish to be disrespectful, but that it was his human right to urinate if he had the need, and that it was not a privilege for her to dole out at will. She finally allowed him to go, but told him that he would serve a detention, since he was out of passes for the year. Mike told her that he would be gone a few extra minutes, as he wished to stop by the office and plead his case with a school administrator. The teacher refused to allow this. My son obeyed, and upon return to the classroom, found his name on the board for all to see. This constant reminder stayed on the board for almost three weeks.

Mike went to the principal's office after school that same day, and told an administrator what had happened. He was told to serve the detention or he would be suspended. Mike has politely refused to serve the detention, and his name has remained on the board for all students in all class periods to know that he has a pending punishment for urinating. The teacher never talked to him or gave him a time to serve this detention, so Mike just let the topic rest. He refused to let me negotiate on his behalf, hoping it would just go away. I knew better.

Sure enough, yesterday, I got a call from the vice principal at __ High School, Mr. __. He told me that Mike was referred to the office by his teacher for refusing to serve the detention and for being 'disrespectful' to her in class by telling her that he would not serve it. I told this administrator that I backed my son 100% and gave him information on bathroom use as it pertains to human rights. I also told him that it was my understanding that as a result of numerous parent and student complaints in our district, and after children have urinated, defecated, and menstruated in their seats when denied bathroom use, an administrative directive had been communicated to all principals in the county. I was under the impression that children were not to be denied bathroom use, or punished for asking to go. This vice principal had no knowledge of such.

The best news is this: The assistant superintendent of Union County Schools, __, sided with Mike, and I got the call an hour later that not only was Mike not to be punished, but this teacher would be changing her classroom policy! Dr. Ellis also emailed me to let me know that the principal was to warn this teacher not to speak of this or retaliate against Mike for standing up for his human right to urinate. I also contacted several school board members, and there is talk that a policy is needed to protect our children, as the administrative directive was ignored and /or not communicated. I feel so empowered, and so does my son. A school board member told me that she is very proud of Mike for taking a stance and that this will, in the end, protect other children.

We would not have had the power or knowledge to know how to negotiate this situation without two important factors. First, a big thank you to you for your wisdom and for [your web] site. I would also like to thank those children who paved the way for change, who were not as fortunate as our son, Mike. Here's to all the children in Union County who have been humiliated beyond belief, denied bathroom use, punished for going to the bathroom, or had points added to the end of grade average for not using the bathroom. Those days are gone. We are making progress in Union County, NC.

Thanks,

Peggy Dean, RN"

More information about Forced Retention of Bodily Waste, including helpful resources, are available at: www.childadvocate.org.

# Bibliography and Further Resources

Aka Pygmies "Best dads in the world". (2005, June 16). *Afrol News.* Retrieved on April 19, 2007 from http://www.afrol.com/articles/16592

Aldort, N. *Raising Our Children, Raising Ourselves: Transforming parent-child relationships from reaction and struggle to freedom, power and joy.* Book Publishers Network, 2006.

American Civil Liberties Union of Colorado. (1998, September 2). Amnesty International Criticizes El Paso County Sheriff's Use of Restraint Board. *American Civil Liberties Union of Colorado Press Release.* Retrieved on November 29, 2002 from http://www.aclu-co.org/news/pressrelease/release_amnesty.htm

Angier, N. (n.d.) *Bonobo Society: Amicable, Amorous and Run by Females.* Retrieved on April 19, 2007 from http://www.unl.edu/rhames/bonobo/bonobo.htm

Appelstein, C. D. *No Such Thing As a Bad Kid: Understanding and Responding to the Challenging Behavior of Troubled Children and Youth.* The Gifford School, 1998.

Armstrong, T. *In Their Own Way: Discovering and Encouraging Your Child's Multiple Intelligences.* Jeremy P. Tarcher/Putman, 2000.

_____. *The Myth of the A.D.D. Child: 50 Ways to Improve Your Child's Behavior and Attention Span Without Drugs, Labels, or Coercion.* Plume, 1995.

Aslanian, S. (2006). Rewiring the Brain: Early Deprivation and Child Development. *American Public Media/American RadioWorks.* Retrieved on December 27, 2007 from http://americanradioworks.publicradio.org/features/romania/index.html

Barlow, D.H., Durand, V.M. *Abnormal Psychology: An Integrative Approach.* Brooks/Cole Publishing Company, 1995.

Batmanghelidj, F. *Your Body's Many Cries for Water: You Are Not Sick, You Are Thirsty! Don't Treat Thirst with Medications.* Global Health Solutions, 1997.

Bavolek, S.J. *Red White and Bruises: Spanking in the U.S.A.* Family Development Resources, Inc, 1994.

Bennett, S., Kalish, N. *The Case Against Homework: How Homework is Hurting Our Children and What We Can Do About It.* Crown Publishers, 2006.

Berman, S. (2002, January 25). How Can I Help My Child Stop Bedwetting/Wetting His or Her Pants? *Plateau Pediatrics.com.* Retrieved on March 13, 2003 from http://www.plateaupediatrics.com/enuresisinfo.html

Berne, S. A. *Without Ritalin: A Natural Approach to ADD.* Keats Publishing, 2002.

Black, J.K., Puckett, M.B. *The Young Child: Development from Prebirth Through Age Eight.* Merrill, 1996.

Blanton, B. *Radical Parenting: Seven Steps to a Functional Family in a Dysfunctional World.* Sparrowhawk Publications, 2002.

Bluestein, J. *Creating Emotionally Safe Schools: A Guide for Educators and Parents.* Health Communications, Inc., 2001.

Bodily Elimination Needs: No Laughing Matter. (n.d.). *Parenthood.com.* Retrieved on April 12 2003 from http://www.parenthood.com/articles.html?article_id=2456

Bredekamp, S., Copple, C. (Eds.) *Developmentally Appropriate Practice in Early Childhood Programs Revised Edition.* NAEYC, 1997.

Bredekamp, S., Rosegrant, T. (Eds.) *Reaching Potentials: Appropriate Curriculum and Assessment for Young Children Volume One.* NAEYC, 1992.

Breggin, P. R. *Reclaiming Our Children: A Healing Plan for a Nation in Crisis.* Perseus Publishing, 2000.

_____. *Talking Back to Ritalin: What Doctors Aren't Telling You About Stimulants and ADHD.* Perseus Publishing, 2001.

_____. *Toxic Psychiatry.* St. Martin's Press, 1991.

Brendtro, L. K., Ness, A., Mitchell, M. *No Disposable Kids.* Sopris West, 2001.

Briere, J., Berliner, L., Buckley, J.A., Jenny, C., Reid, T. *The APSAC Handbook On Child Maltreatment.* Sage Publications, 1996.

Briggs, F. (Ed.) *From Victim to Offender: How Child Sexual Abuse Victims Become Offenders.* Allen & Unwin, 1995.

Buell, J. *Closing the Book on Homework: Enhancing Public Education and Freeing Family Time.* Temple University Press, 2004.

Burch, J. M. *They Cage the Animals at Night: The True Story of a Child Who Learned to Survive.* Signet, 1984.

Carcaterra, L. *Sleepers.* Ballantine Books, 1995.

Carson, M. L., Goodfield, R. K. The Children's Garden Attachment Model. In Small, R. W., Alwon, F.J. (Eds.). *Challenging the Limits of Care* (pp. 115- 126). The Albert E. Trieschman Center, 1988.

Chaffin, M., Hanson, R., Saunders, B.E., Nichols, T., Barnett, D., Zeanah, C., Berliner, L., Egeland, B., Newman, E., Lyon, T., LeTourneau,

E., Miller-Perrin, C. (2006). Report of the APSAC Task Force on Attachment Therapy, Reactive Attachment Disorder, and Attachment Problems. *Child Maltreatment, 11*, 76-89.

Chalker, R., Whitmore, K.E. *Overcoming Bladder Disorders.* HarperPerennial, 1990.

Chomsky, N., Macedo, D. (Ed.). *Chomsky on MisEducation.* Rowman and Littlefield Publishers, 2000.

Chugani, H.T., Behen, M.E., Muzik, O., Juhasz, C., Nagy, F., Chugani, D. C. (2001). Local Brain Functional Activity Following Early Deprivation: A Study of Postinstitutionalized Romanian Orphans. *Neurolmage, 14*, 1290-1301.

Clayman, C. B., Curry, R. H. (Eds.). *The American Medical Association: Guide to Your Family's Symptoms.* Random House, 1992.

Constipation, Age 12 and Older- Prevention. (2006, December 14). *WebMD.* Retrieved on December 16, 2007 from http://www.webmd.com/digestive-disorders/tc/constipation-age-12-and-older-prevention

Cook, P. (1978). Childrearing, Culture and Mental Health: Exploring an Ethological-Evolutionary Perspective in Child Psychiatry and Preventative Mental Health with Particular Reference to Two Contrasting Approaches to Early Childrearing. *The Medical Journal of Australia, special supplement, 2*, 3-14. Retrieved on April 19, 2007 from http://www.naturalchild.org/peter_cook/childrearing.html

Cook, P. (1997). The Species-Normal Experience for Human Infants - A Biological and Cross-cultural Perspective. *The Natural Child Project.* Retrieved on April 19, 2007 from http://www.naturalchild.org/peter_cook/ecc_ch1.html

Cooper, C. S. (2000, May). Daytime Wetting and Voiding Dysfunction in Children. *Children's Virtual Hospital: A Digital Library of Pediatric Information.* Retrieved on March 13, 2003 from http://www.vh.org/pediatric/patient/urology/faq/voidingdysfunction.html

Cooper, C. S., Abousally, C. T., Austin, C., Boyt, M. A., Hawtrey, C. E. (2003, September). Do Public Schools Teach Voiding Dysfunction? Results of an Elementary School Teacher Survey. *The Journal of Urology, 170*, 956-958.

Currie, E. *Crime and Punishment in America: Why the Solutions to America's Most Stubborn Social Crisis Have Not Worked- and What Will.* Owl, Henry Holt and Company, Inc., 1998.

Dale, S. (1993). Spanking Is An Addiction. *Mothering, 69*, 31-35.

Danso, H., Hunsberger, B., Pratt, M. (1997). The Role of Parental Religious Fundamentalism and Right-Wing Authoritarianism in Child-Rearing Goals and Practices. *Journal for the Scientific Study of Religion, 36*, 496-511.

Davison, G.C., Neale, J.M. *Abnormal Psychology*. John Wiley & Sons, Inc., 1998.

deMause, L. (1999). *The Journal of Psychohistory*. Vol. 26, No. 3.

DeMeo, J. *Saharasia: The 4000 BCE Origins of Child Abuse, Sex-Repression, Warfare and Social Violence in the Deserts of the Old World*. Natural Energy Works, 2006.

Dentan, R K. *The Semai: A Nonviolent People of Malaya*. Holt, Rinehart and Winston, 1979.

De Waal, F., Lanting, F. *Bonobo: The Forgotten Ape*. University of California Press, 1997.

*Diagnostic and Statistical Manual of Mental Disorders Fourth Edition DSM-IV*. American Psychiatric Association, 1994.

Dorsky, R., Dorsky, L. T. (1999, November/December). When "Little Accidents" Turn Serious: Understanding Fecal Incontinence. *Digestive Health and Nutrition*, 22-25.

Durrant, J.E. (1999). Evaluating the Success of Sweden's Corporal Punishment Ban. *Child Abuse and Neglect*, *23*, 435-448.

Elliot, M. *Female Sexual Abuse of Children*. The Guilford Press, 1993.

Ellison, S. *Taking the War Out of Our Words: The Art of Powerful Non-Defensive Communication*. Bay Tree Publishing, 2002.

*Ending Legalised Violence Against Children: Global Report 2006*. Global Initiative to End All Corporal Punishment of Children, 2006.

Englander, E. K. *Understanding Violence*. Lawrence Erlbaum Associates, 1997.

Fahlberg, V. I. *A Child's Journey through Placement*. Perspectives Press, 1991.

Fisher, S. (2007, January). FP02 and the Regulation of Fear. *Neuroconnections*, 13-17.

Flannery, M.E. (2000, February 3). Bathroom Policy Labeled 'Inhumane' to School Bus Drivers. *The Palm Beach Post*.

Fontana, V.J. *Somewhere a Child is Crying: Maltreatment- Causes and Prevention*. Mentor, 1983.

Fox, M. (2006, February 17). Orphanages Stunt Growth; Foster Care Better - Romania Study Concludes. *Reuters*. Retrieved on April 19, 2007 from http://www.performancevision.com/gery/StuntGrowth.htm

Garbarino, J. *Raising Children in a Socially Toxic Environment*. Jossey-Bass, 1995.

Garbarino, J., deLara, E. *And Words Can Hurt Forever: How to Protect Adolescents from Bullying, Harassment, and Emotional Violence.* The Free Press, 2002.

Gatto, J. T. *A Different Kind of Teacher: Solving the Crisis of American Schooling.* Berkeley Hills Books, 2002.

_____. (2003, September). Against School: How Public Education Cripples Our Kids, and Why. *Harper's Magazine, 307,* 33-38.

_____. *Dumbing Us Down: The Hidden Curriculum of Compulsory Schooling.* New Society Publishers, 1992- 2002.

_____ (Ed.). *The Exhausted School: Bending the Bars of Traditional; Education.* Berkeley Hills Books, 2002.

Gerhardt, S. *Why Love Matters: How Affection Shapes a Baby's Brain.* Routledge, 2004.

Gershoff, E.T. (2002). Corporal Punishment by Parents and Associated Child Behaviors and Experiences: A Meta-Analytic and Theoretical Review. *Psychological Bulletin, 128,* 539-579.

Gilligan, J. *Violence: Reflections on a National Epidemic.* Vintage Books, 1996.

Goleman, D. *Emotional Intelligence: Why it can matter more than IQ.* Bantam Books, 1995.

Gonnerman, J. (2007). School of Shock. *Mother Jones.* Retrieved on August 23, 2007 from http://www.motherjones.com/news/feature /2007/09/school_of_shock.html

Gordon, T. *Discipline That Work: Promoting Self-Discipline in Children.* Plume, 1989.

Granju, K. A., Kennedy, B. *Attachment Parenting: Instinctive Care for Your Baby and Young Child.* Pocket Books, 1999.

Gray, D. D. *Attaching in Adoption: Practical Tools for Today's Parents.* Perspectives Press, 2002.

Greenberg, D. *Free at Last: The Sudbury Valley School.* Sudbury Valley School Press, 1995.

Greven, P. *Spare the Child: The Religious Roots of Punishment and the Psychological Impact of Physical Abuse.* Vintage Books, 1990.

Griffith, M. *The Unschooling Handbook: How to Use the Whole World As Your Child's Classroom.* Prima Publishing, 1998.

Harrison, S. *The Happy Child: Changing the Heart of Education.* Sentient Publications, 2002.

Hart, S. N. (Ed.), Durrant, J., Newell, P., Power, F. C. *Eliminating Corporal Punishment: The Way Forward to Constructive Child Discipline.* UNESCO Publishing, 2005.

Helfer, R.E., Kempe, R.S. *The Battered Child.* The University of Chicago Press, 1987.

Hellerstein, S., Glasscock, E. L. (2002, April 25). Voiding Dysfunction. *eMedicine Journal.* Vol. 3, No. 4. Retrieved on April 12, 2003 from http://author.emedicine.com/ped/topic2414.htm

Hern, M. (Ed.) *Deschooling Our Lives.* New Society Publishers, 1996.

HFHS. "4 Year Old Female" Urology Expert Forum. (1999, September 17). *Medhelp.org.* Retrieved on April 12, 2003 from http://www.med-help.org/forums/Urology/messages/30114.html

Hobbs, C.J., Hanks, H.G.I., Wynne, J.M. *Child Abuse and Neglect: A Clinicians Handbook.* Churchill Livingstone, 1993.

Holt, J. Farenga, P. *Teach Your Own: The John Holt Book of Homeschooling.* Perseus Publishing, 2003.

Holt, J. *How Children Fail.* Merloyd Lawrence, Delta Seymour/Lawrence, 1964-1982.

_____. *How Children Learn.* Merloyd Lawrence, Delta Seymour/Lawrence, 1967-1983.

_____. *Instead of Education.* Sentient Publications, 2004.

Hughes, D. A. *Facilitating Developmental Attachment: The Road to Emotional Recovery and Behavioral Change in Foster and Adopted Children.* Rowman and Littlefield Publishers,1997.

Hunt, J. The *Natural Child: Parenting from the Heart.* New Society Publishers, 2001.

Hunter, M. *Abused Boys: The Neglected Victims of Sexual Abuse.* Fawcett Columbine, 1990.

_____. *The Sexually Abused Male Volume 1: Prevalence, Impact, and Treatment.* Lexington Books, 1990.

Hyman, I. A. *The Case Against Spanking: How to Discipline Your Child Without Hitting.* Jossey-Bass Publishers, 1997.

Hyman, I. A., Snook, P. A. *Dangerous Schools: What We Can Do About the Physical and Emotional Abuse of Our Children.* Jossey-Bass Publishers, 1999.

Incontinence and Voiding Problems in Children. (2003). *University Children's Hospital UCI Medical Center.* Retrieved on March 13, 2003 from http://www.ucihealth.com/healthcareservices/peduro11.htm

Jensen, D. *Walking on Water: Reading, Writing, and Revolution.* Chelsea Green, 2004.

Kalat, J. W. *Biological Psychology.* Brooks/Cole Publishing Company, 1995.

Karen, R. *Becoming Attached: First Relationships and How They Shape Our Capacity to Love.* Oxford University Press, 1998.

Kashtan, I. *Parenting From Your Heart: Sharing the Gifts of Compassion, Connection, and Choice.* PuddleDancer Press, 2003.

Keck, G. C., Kupecky, R. M. *Adopting the Hurt Child: Hope for Families with Special Needs Kids.* Pinon Press, 1995.

_____. *Parenting the Hurt Child: Helping Adoptive Families Heal and Grow.* Pinon Press, 2002.

Kelsey, C. M. *Generation MySpace: Helping Your Teen Survive Online Adolescence.* Marlowe and Company, 2007.

Kemper, D. W., Wiss, C. A. (Ed.), Schneider, S. L. (Ed.). *Healthwise Handbook: A Self-Care Manual for You.* Healthwise, Inc., 1999.

Kidney Stones- Prevention (2007, May 30). *WebMD.* Retrieved on December 13, 2007 from http://www.webmd.com/kidney-stones/kidney-stones-prevention

Kindlon, D., Thompson, M. *Raising Cain: Protecting the Emotional Life of Boys.* Ballantine Books, 1999.

Kipnis, A. *Angry Young Men: How Parents, Teachers, and Counselors Can Help "Bad Boys" Become Good Men.* Jossey-Bass Publishers, 1999.

Kiser, Sr. R. D. *Orphan: A True Story of Abandonment, Abuse, and Redemption.* Adams Media Corporation, 2001.

Knaster, M. *Discovering the Body's Wisdom: A Comprehensive Guide to More than Fifty Mind-Body Practices that Can Relieve Pain, Reduce Stress, and Foster Health, Spiritual Growth, and Inner Peace.* Bantam Books, 1996.

Knutson, L.L. (1998, April 18). Bathroom Breaks Mandated. *Las Vegas Review-Journal.* Retrieved March 25, 2000 from http://www.lvrj_home/1998?Apr-18-Sat-1998/business/7290654.html

Kohn, A. *The Homework Myth: Why Our Kids Get Too Much of a Bad Thing.* Da Capo Press, 2006.

_____. *The Schools Our Children Deserve: Moving Beyond Traditional Classrooms and "Tougher Standards".* Houghton Mifflin Company, 1999.

_____. *Unconditional Parenting: Moving from Rewards and Punishments to Love and Reason.* Atria Books, 2005.

Kralovec, E., Buell, J. *The End of Homework: How Homework Disrupts Families, Overburdens Children and Limits Learning.* Beacon Press, 2000.

Krupinski, E., Weikel, D. *Death From Child Abuse...and No One Heard.* Currier- Davis Publishing, 1986.

Larson, D. E. (Ed.). *Mayo Clinic Family Health Book.* William Morrow and Company, 1996.

Leach, P. *Children First: What Society Must Do- and is Not Doing- For Children Today.* Vintage Books, 1994.

Lee, N. *Parenting without Punishing.* Half Fast Press, 2002.

Leo, P. *Connection Parenting: Parenting through Connection instead of Coercion, Through Love instead of Fear.* Wyatt-MacKenzie Publishing, Inc., 2007.

Levine, B. E. *Commonsense Rebellion: Taking Back Your Life from Drugs, Shrinks, Corporations, and a World Gone Crazy.* The Continuum Publishing Group, 2001.

Levy, J. *My Tummy Hurts: A Complete Guide to Understanding and Treating Your Child's Stomachaches. Fireside,* 2004.

Levy, T. M., Orlans, M. *Attachment, Trauma, and Healing: Understanding and Treating Attachment Disorder in Children and Families.* CWLA Press, 1998.

Liedloff, J. *The Continuum Concept: In Search of Happiness Lost.* Da Capo Press, 1977.

Llewellyn, G. *The Teenage Liberation Handbook: How to Quit School and Get a Real Life and Education.* Element Books, 1997.

Lohn, M. (1999, July/August). The Scoop on Poop. *UTNE Reader,* 84-86.

Louv, R. *Last Child in the Woods: Saving Our Children from Nature-Deficit Disorder.* Algonquin Books of Chapel Hill, 2005.

Lyn-Piluso, G., Lyn-Piluso, G. (2004, February 25). Organic Parenting. *Primal Spirit.* Retrieved on April 19, 2007 from http://www.primalspirit.com/ps3_1lyn-piluso.htm

Males, M. A. *The Scapegoat Generation: America's War on Adolescents.* Common Courage Press, 1996.

Mander, J. *Four Arguments for the Elimination of Television.* Quill, 1978.

Maskew, T. *Our Own: Adopting and Parenting the Older Child.* Snowcap Press, 1999.

Maurer, A., Wallerstein, S. (1987). *The Influence of Corporal Punishment on Crime.* Retrieved April 24, 2000 from http://www.nospank.net

Maurer, A., Williams, G. (Guest Eds.). (1983). *Journal of Clinical Child Psychology Special Issue: Violence Against Children Reconsidered.* Vol. 12, No. 3.

McCracken, J.B. (Ed.) *Reducing Stress In Young Children's Lives.* NAEYC, 1998.

McElroy, S. (1983) Child-Raising in Non-violent Cultures. *In Context: A Quarterly of Humane Sustainable Culture.* Retrieved on April 19, 2007 from http://www.context.org/ICLIB/IC04/McElroy.htm

McKee, A. *Homeschooling Our Children Unschooling Ourselves.* Bittersweet House, 2002.

Mead, M. *Sex and Temperament in Three Primitive Societies.* Perennial, 1935-2001.

Miller, A. *The Body Never Lies: The Lingering Effects of Cruel Parenting.* W. W. Norton and Company, 2005.

_____. *For Your Own Good: Hidden cruelty in child-rearing and the roots of violence.* The Noonday Press, 1993.

Miller, R. *Free Schools, Free People: Education and Democracy After the 1960s.* State University of New York Press, 2002.

Montagu, A. (Ed.). *Learning Non-Aggression: The Experience of Non-Literate Societies.* Oxford, 1978.

Morgan, M. L., Allee, J. W. *Homeschooling on a Shoe String.* Harold Shaw Publishers, 1999.

Murphy, M. S., Clayden, G. Constipation. In Walker, W. A., Durie, P. R., Hamilton, J. R., Walker-Smith, J. A., Watkins, J. B. (Eds.). *Pediatric Gastrointestinal Disease: Pathology, Diagnosis, Management Volume One* (pp. 293- 317). Mosby, 1996.

National Safety Council. *First Aid and CPR for Infants and Children.* Jones and Bartlett, 1998.

Neill, A. S. *Summerhill School: A New View of Childhood.* St. Martin's Griffin, 1992.

Nelsen, J., Erwin, C., Duffy, R. *Positive Discipline for Preschoolers.* Prima Publishing, 1995.

Nelsen, J., Lott, L. *Positive Discipline for Teenagers: Empowering Your Teen and Yourself Through Kind and Firm Parenting.* Prima Publishing, 2000.

Nelsen, J., Lott, L., Glenn, H.S. *Positive Discipline A-Z*. Prima Publishing, 1999.

Newberger, E.H. *The Men They Will Become: The Nature and Nurture of Male Character*. Perseus Books, 1999.

Newman, B. M., Newman, P. R. *Development Through Life: A Psychosocial Approach*. Brooks/Cole, Wadsworth, 1999.

Newell, P. *Children Are People Too: The Case Against Physical Punishment*. Bedford Square Press, 1989.

Ohanian, S. *What Happened to Recess and Why are our Children Struggling in Kindergarten?*. McGraw-Hill, 2002.

O'Mara, P. *Mothering Magazine*. 1993-2008.

_____. *Natural Family Living: The Mothering Magazine Guide to Parenting*. Pocket Books, 2000.

Pelzer, D. *A Child Called "It": One Child's Courage to Survive*. Health Communications, Inc, 1995.

_____. *The Lost Boy: A Foster Child's Search for the Love of a Family*. Health Communications, Inc., 1997.

Perry, B. D. (1993, Spring). Neurodevelopment and the Neurophysiology of Trauma I: Conceptual Considerations for Clinical Work with Maltreated Children. *The Advisor: American Professional Society on the Abuse of Children*. Vol. 6, No. 1.

_____. (1993, Summer). Neurodevelopment and the Neurophysiology of Trauma II: Clinical Work Along the Alarm-Fear-Terror Continuum. *The Advisor: American Professional Society on the Abuse of Children*. Vol. 6, No. 2.

_____. (2001, July). Bonding and Attachment in Maltreated Children: Consequences of Emotional Neglect in Childhood. *The ChildTrauma Academy Caregiver Education Series V 3.0.*, Vol. 1, No. 4.

_____. Neurobiological Sequelae of Childhood Trauma: PTSD in Children. In M. M. Murburg (Ed.). *Catecholamine Function in Posttraumatic Stress Disorder: Emerging Concepts* (pp. 233- 250). American Psychiatric Press, 1994.

Pollack, W. *Real Boys: Rescuing Our Sons from the Myths of Boyhood*. Random House, 1998.

Popenoe, J. *Inside Summerhill*. Hart Publishing Company, 1970.

Postman, N., Weingartner, C. *Teaching as a Subversive Activity*. Delacorte Press, 1969.

Prescott, J. W. (2002, August 1). *America's Lost Dream "Life Liberty and the Pursuit of Happiness": Current Research and Historical Background on the Origins of Love and Violence.* Retrieved on April 18, 2007 from http://www.violence.de/prescott/appp/ald.pdf

Priesnitz, W. *Challenging Assumptions in Education.* The Alternate Press, 2000.

Priesnitz, W. (Ed.). *Life Learning Magazine.* Life Media, 2002-2008.

Quinn, D. *Beyond Civilization: Humanity's Next Great Adventure.* Three Rivers Press, 1999.

_____. *If They Give You Lined Paper Write Sideways.* Steerforth Press, 2007.

Reichenberg-Ullman, J., Ullman, R. *Ritalin Free Kids: Safe and Homeopathic Medicine for ADHD and Other Behavioral and Learning Problems.* Prima Publishing, 2000.

Renvoize, J. *Innocence Destroyed: A Study of Child Sexual Abuse.* Routledge, 1993.

Rogers, C. R. *On Becoming a Person.* Houghton Mifflin Company, 1961.

Rosenberg, M.B. *Nonviolent Communication a Language of Life: Create Your Life, Your Relationships, and Your World in Harmony with Your Values.* PuddleDancer Press, 2005.

Santrock, J. W. *Life-Span Development.* Brown and Benchmark Publishers, 1997.

Schlosser, E. *Fast Food Nation: The Dark Side of the All-American Meal.* Perennial, 2002.

Shapiro, F. *Eye Movement Desensitization and Reprocessing: Basic Principles, Protocols and Procedures.* The Guilford Press, 2001.

Silberman, C. E. *Crisis in the Classroom: The Remaking of American Education.* Vintage Books, 1970.

Simmons, R. *Odd Girl Out: The Hidden Culture of Aggression in Girls.* Harcourt Books, 2002.

Slaby, R.G., Roedell, W.C., Arezzo, D., Hendrix, K. *Early Violence Prevention: Tools for Teachers of Young Children.* NAEYC, 1995.

Smith, C. *The Magic Castle.* St. Martin's Paperbacks, 1998.

Smith, C. S. (2006, May 10). Romanian Orphans Face Widespread Abuse, Group Says. *New York Times.*

Soltis, J. (2003). The Signal Functions of Early Infant Crying. *BBS Online.* Retrieved on April 19, 2007 from http://www.bbsonline.org/Preprints/Soltis-11072002/Referees/#IVgevolution

Stahl, S. M. *Psychopharmacology of Antidepressants*. Martin Dunitz, 1997.

Stone, J.G. *A Guide to Discipline*. NAEYC, 1997.

Strand, W. R. Urinary Infection in Children: Pathogenesis, Bacterial Virulence, and Host Resistance. In Gonzales, E. T., Bauer, S. B. (Eds.). *Pediatric Urology Practice* (pp. 433-436). Lippincott Williams & Wilkins, 1999.

Straus, M. A. *Beating the Devil Out of Them: Corporal Punishment in American Families*. Lexington Books, 1994.

Straus, M. A., Sugarman, D.B., Giles-Sims, J. (1997). Spanking By Parents and Subsequent Antisocial Behavior of Children. *Archives Pediatric Adolescent Medicine, 151*, 761-767.

*The Sudbury Valley School Experience*. Sudbury Valley School Press, 1992.

Sweet, W., Sweet, B. *Living Joyfully with Children*. Acropolis Books, 1997.

Teacher In Urination Flap Jailed. (2000, February 11). *The New York Times on the Web*. Retrieved March 18, 2000 from http://www.nytimes.com/aponline/a/AP-BRF-Teacher-Urination.html

Teicher, M.H. (2002). Scars that Won't Heal: The Neurobiology of Child Abuse. *Scientific American, 286*, 68-75.

*The Temiars*. (n.d.). Retrieved on April 19, 2007 from http://www.temiar.com/temiar.html

Theodore, W. *Wayne: An Abused Child's Story of Courage, Survival, and Hope*. Harbor Press, 2003.

Tips to Grow By: Urinary Tract Infections. (2002, February). *Children's Hospital Medical Center of Akron.*

Urinary Frequency, Urgency and Urge Incontinence (Overactive Bladder). (1999). *Florida Urological Associates p.a.* Retrieved on April 12, 2003 from http://www.urologyweb.com/Production/Urology_Primer/Pediatric/Urinary%20frequency.htm

Urinary Incontinence in Children. (2000, December). *National Kidney and Urologic Diseases Information Clearinghouse*. Retrieved on January 4, 2002 from http://kidney.niddk.nih.gov/kudiseases/pubs/uichildren/

Urinary Incontinence in Children. (2001, March 21). *KeepKidsHealthy.com*. Retrieved on March 13, 2003 from http://www.keepkidshealthy.com/welcome/conditions/urinary_incontinence.html

UTI After. (2003). *American Foundation for Urologic Disease*. Retrieved on March 5, 2003 from http://www.afud.org/conditions/utiafter.html

Varon, L. *Adopting On Your Own: The Complete Guide to Adopting as a Single Parent.* Farrar, Straus and Giroux, 2000.

Verrier, N. N. *The Primal Wound: Understanding the Adopted Child.* Gateway Press, Inc., 1993.

Voiding Problems in Children. (n.d.). *The Detroit Medical Center Department of Urology.* Retrieved on March 13, 2003 from http://www.med.wayne.edu/urology/DISEASES/voidingproblems.html

Waller, M., Meisel, J. (1998, October 24). Boy Facing Spanking Kills Himself. *Arkansas Democrat-Gazette.*

Wan, Greenfield. (1997, October). Enuresis and Voiding Abnormalities. *Pediatric Bulletin*, 1117-1129. Retrieved on March 13, 2003 from http://home.coqui.net/myrna/enu.htm

Weiten, W._*Psychology Themes and Variations.* Brooks/Cole Publishing Company, 1997.

Wendorf, K. *Kindred/Byronchild Magazine.* Byron Publications, 2002-2008.

*The White Paper on Coercion in Treatment.* (2007, April 21). Association for Treatment and Training in the Attachment of Children. Retrieved on October 11, 2007 from *http://www.attach.org/WhitePaper.pdf*

Winn, M. *The Plug-In Drug: Television, Computers, and Family Life.* Penguin Books, 1977-2002.

Yekuana Orientation. (2007). *World Culture Encyclopedia: South America.* Retrieved on April 19, 2007 from www.everyculture.com/South-America/Yekuana-Orientation.html

Your Guide to Urinary Tract Infections. (2007). *WebMD.* Retrieved on December 13, 2007 from http://women.webmd.com/your-guide-urinary-tract-infections?page=3

Zinn, H. *A People's History of the United States 1492- Present.* Perennial Classics, 2003.

## About the Author

Laurie A. Couture is a licensed mental health counselor, parenting educator, writer, public speaker and children's rights activist. She is the founder of ChildAdvocate.org and is a Board member of Parents and Teachers Against Violence in Education (PTAVE). She is a contributor to *Life Learning*, *Kindred* and several other publications and websites. She is a mentor and has worked in the fields of social work and early childhood education. Ms. Couture is also a human rights and environmental activist as well as an artist and photographer. She is the author of the comic series, *The Hypocrisy Chronicles*. Ms. Couture's writing and advocacy on behalf of children have reached an international audience. She unschools her son, Brycen, who is a singer and the creator of Feendz homemade stuffed toys. She and her son live in beautiful New England.

LaVergne, TN USA
21 April 2010
180027LV00010B/45/P